AF321631

SIGNS OF CONTINUITY

Signs of Continuity

The Function of Miracles in Jesus and Paul

GREG RHODEA

EISENBRAUNS | University Park, Pennsylvania

Library of Congress Cataloging-in-Publication Data

Names: Rhodea, Greg, 1983– author.
Title: Signs of continuity : the function of miracles in Jesus and Paul / Greg Rhodea.
Other titles: Bulletin for biblical research supplements.
Description: University Park, Pennsylvania : Eisenbrauns, [2019] | Series: Bulletin for biblical research supplement series | Includes bibliographical references and index.
Summary: "Explores the debate over whether Paul was a faithful follower of Jesus or a corruptor of Jesus's message. Focuses on an element of similarity between the two men: the place of miracles in their ministries"—Provided by publisher.
Identifiers: LCCN 2018060801 | ISBN 9781575069784 (cloth : alk. paper)
Subjects: LCSH: Miracles—Biblical teaching. | Jesus Christ—Miracles. | Paul, the Apostle, Saint—Miracles. | Bible. New Testament—Theology. | Bible. New Testament—Criticism, interpretation, etc.
Classification: LCC BS2545.M5 R46 2019 | DDC 225.6—dc23
LC record available at https://lccn.loc.gov/2018060801

Published by The Pennsylvania State University Press,
University Park, PA 16802-1003

Eisenbrauns is an imprint of The Pennsylvania State University Press.

The Pennsylvania State University Press is a member of the Association of University Presses.

It is the policy of The Pennsylvania State University Press to use acid-free paper. Publications on uncoated stock satisfy the minimum requirements of American National Standard for Information Sciences—Permanence of Paper for Printed Library Material, ANSI Z39.48-1992.

To my father, Paul Rhodea,
whose support enabled my studies at every stage

CONTENTS

Many thanks are due. First of all, I am indebted to Jay E. Smith, whose support for my interest in the Jesus-Paul debate began in our Pauline Theology Seminar in my very first semester of doctoral work. Despite being on sabbatical in Germany for nearly the entire writing phase of my dissertation, he took the time to go over many of my submissions multiple times. Thanks are also due to Darrell L. Bock, who was a consistent voice of input throughout all my time at Dallas Theological Seminary. I am additionally indebted to Gerry Schoberg, who not only provided valuable input on my dissertation but whose own book on the Jesus-Paul debate came along at just the right time to help my research coalesce.

I am beyond grateful to my parents, Paul and Susan Rhodea, whose support— financial and otherwise—allowed my years of study to be not only efficient but worry-free. Thank you for everything!

As a book like this is really the culmination of an entire course of study, I also wish to extend my gratefulness to my friend and co-laborer in the Dallas Theological Seminary doctoral program, Kevin Patton. I will remember with fondness our year of studying together in the Fireside Room! I am also grateful to Daniel B. Wallace, who was instrumental in my decision to enter doctoral studies and whose support was a tremendous encouragement. Thanks as well to Richard A. Taylor, the director of the Ph.D. program at Dallas Theological Seminary, for his leadership and encouragement along the way. Thanks are also due to our longsuffering research librarian, Debbie Hunn, who helped me track down a number of sources and alleviated a variety of problems along the way. Tina Karnes (the NT department administrative assistant) and Linda Wallace (the Ph.D. program administrative assistant) both helped me innumerable times over the years. Thanks for your cheerful service!

As part of the process of turning a dissertation into a published book, I would also like to thank Richard S. Hess and Craig L. Blomberg for their assistance in the process and for their helpful editorial suggestions. Thanks are also due to the good folks at Grace Bible Chapel, in Grand Rapids, Minnesota, for letting me spend some time working on revisions to this book as part of my duties. I would also like to thank the staff of the Grand Rapids Area Library in Grand Rapids, Minnesota, who helped me get access to certain books for my revisions that would have been impossible otherwise.

Closest to home, I am grateful to my wife, Kailoni, for her years of love and support. Her positive attitude throughout ups and downs has been priceless. Finally, to my children, Chavalah, Josiah, Christopher, Anastasia, Aletheia, and Timothy—thanks for making coming home fun and for filling my carrel in the library with so many delightful drawings.

1 En.	1 Enoch (Ethiopic Apocalypse)
2 Bar.	2 Baruch (Syriac Apocalypse)
2 En.	2 Enoch (Slavonic Apocalypse)
AB	Anchor Bible
ABRL	Anchor Bible Reference Library
Acts Thom.	Acts of Thomas
Ag. Ap.	*Against Apion*
AGJU	Arbeiten zur Geschichte des antiken Judentums und des Urchristentums
Alex.	*Alexander*
ANRW	Hildegard Temporini and Wolfgang Haase, editors. *Aufstieg und Niedergang der römischen Welt: Geschichte und Kultur Roms im Spiegel der neueren Forschung.* Part 2: *Principat.* Berlin: de Gruyter, 1972–
Ant.	*Jewish Antiquities*
Apoc. Mos.	Apocalypse of Moses
Apol.	*Apologia (Pro se de magia)*
ArBib	Aramaic Bible
ATDan	Acta Theologica Danica
B. Qam.	Baba Qamma
Bar	Baruch
Barn.	Barnabas
BBR	*Bulletin for Biblical Research*
BDAG	Frederick W. Danker, Walter Bauer, William F. Arndt, and F. Wilbur Gingrich. *Greek-English Lexicon of the New Testament and Other Early Christian Literature.* 3rd ed. Chicago: University of Chicago Press, 2000
BECNT	Baker Exegetical Commentary on the New Testament
Bek.	Bekorot
Bell. civ.	*Bella civilia*
Ber.	Berakot
BHT	Beiträge zur historischen Theologie
Bib	*Biblica*
BibSem	Biblical Seminar
BNTC	Black's New Testament Commentaries
BSac	*Bibliotheca Sacra*
BTB	*Biblical Theology Bulletin*
BZNW	Beihefte zur Zeitschrift für die neutestamentliche Wissenschaft
CBQ	*Catholic Biblical Quarterly*
Cels.	*Against Celsus*
ConBNT	Coniectanea Biblica: New Testament
ConcC	Concordia Commentary
Det.	*Quod deterius potiori insidari soleat*

Did.	Didache
Diog. L.	Diogenes Laertius, *Lives of Eminent Philosophers*
DJG	Joel B. Green, Jeannine K. Brown, and Nicholas Perrin, editors. *Dictionary of Jesus and the Gospels*. 2nd ed. Downers Grove, IL: InterVarsity, 2013
DPL	Gerald F. Hawthorne and Ralph P. Martin, editors. *Dictionary of Paul and His Letters*. Downers Grove, IL: InterVarsity Press, 1993
DSD	*Dead Sea Discoveries*
ECL	Early Christianity and Its Literature
Ep.	Pliny the Younger, *Epistulae*
ESV	English Standard Version
ETL	*Ephemerides Theologicae Lovanienses*
EuroJTh	*European Journal of Theology*
Gig.	*De gigantibus*
Gos. Thom.	Gospel of Thomas
GRBS	*Greek, Roman, and Byzantine Studies*
Ḥag.	Ḥagigah
HBT	*Horizons in Biblical Theology*
Hist. eccl.	*Historia ecclesiastica*
Hist.	*Historiae*
HNTC	Harper's New Testament Commentaries
Hom. 1 Cor.	*Homiliae in epistulam i ad Corinthios*
HTR	*Harvard Theological Review*
ICC	International Critical Commentary
Il.	*Iliad*
IRT	Issues in Religion and Theology
J.W.	*Jewish War*
JBL	*Journal of Biblical Literature*
JETS	*Journal of the Evangelical Theological Society*
JJS	*Journal of Jewish Studies*
Jos. Asen.	Joseph and Aseneth
JSNT	*Journal for the Study of the New Testament*
JSNTSup	Journal for the Study of the New Testament Supplement
JSOTSup	Journal for the Study of the Old Testament Supplement
JSP	*Journal for the Study of the Pseudepigrapha*
JTS	*Journal of Theological Studies*
Jub.	Jubilees
LAB	Liber antiquitatum biblicarum (Pseudo-Philo)
LCL	Loeb Classical Library
LNTS	Library of New Testament Studies
Mos.	*De vita Mosis*
NAC	New American Commentary
NCB	New Century Bible
Neot	*Neotestamentica*
NIB	Leander E. Keck, editor. *New Interpreter's Bible*. 12 vols. Nashville: Abingdon, 1994–2004
NICNT	New International Commentary on the New Testament

NIGTC	New International Greek Testament Commentary
NovT	*Novum Testamentum*
NovTSup	Supplements to Novum Testamentum
NRSV	New Revised Standard Version
NTL	New Testament Library
NTOA	Novum Testamentum et Orbis Antiquus
NTS	*New Testament Studies*
NTTS	New Testament Tools and Studies
OTP	James H. Charlesworth, editor. *Old Testament Pseudepigrapha*. 2 vols. New York: Doubleday, 1983, 1985
Peregr.	*De morte Peregrini*
Pesaḥ.	Pesaḥim
Philops.	*Philopseudes*
Pss. Sol.	Psalms of Solomon
Pyth.	*Pythionikai*
Resp.	*Respublica*
Sac. Tales	Aristides, *The Sacred Tales*
Sanh.	Sanhedrin
SBLDS	Society of Biblical Literature Dissertation Series
SBLTT	Society of Biblical Literature Texts and Translations
SBT	Studies in Biblical Theology
SCHNT	Studia ad Corpus Hellenisticum Novi Testamenti
Sib. Or.	Sibylline Oracles
Sir	Sirach
SJT	*Scottish Journal of Theology*
SNTSMS	Society for New Testament Studies Monograph Series
Spec.	*De specialibus legibus*
ST	*Studia Theologica*
STI	Studies in Theological Interpretation
SymS	Symposium Series
T. Ab.	Testament of Abraham
T. Benj.	Testament of Benjamin
T. Job	Testament of Job
T. Jud.	Testament of Judah
T. Levi	Testament of Levi
T. Sim.	Testament of Simeon
T. Zeb.	Testament of Zebulun
Taʿan.	Taʿanit
TDNT	Gerhard Kittel and Gerhard Friedrich, editors. *Theological Dictionary of the New Testament*. Translated by Geoffrey W. Bromiley. 10 vols. Grand Rapids: Eerdmans, 1964–76
TDOT	G. Johannes Botterweck and Helmer Ringgren, editors. *Theological Dictionary of the Old Testament*. Translated by John T. Willis et al. 8 vols. Grand Rapids: Eerdmans, 1974–2006
Tob	Tobit
Treat. Shem	Treatise of Shem
TS	*Theological Studies*

TUGAL	Texte und Untersuchungen zur Geschichte der altchristlichen Literatur
TynBul	*Tyndale Bulletin*
TZ	*Theologische Zeitschrift*
Var. hist.	*Varia historia*
Vesp.	*Vespasianus*
Virt.	*De virtutibus*
Vit. Apoll.	*Vita Apollonii*
WBC	Word Biblical Commentary
Wis	Wisdom of Solomon
WMANT	Wissenschaftliche Monographien zum Alten und Neuen Testament
WTJ	*Westminster Theological Journal*
WUNT	Wissenschaftliche Untersuchungen zum Neuen Testament
ZTK	*Zeitschrift für Theologie und Kirche*

CHAPTER 1

Introduction

The relationship between Jesus and Paul is a critical issue in New Testament scholarship and Christianity in general.[1] Several reasons account for this: (1) Paul's writings comprise a significant part of the New Testament itself; (2) Pauline theology has played a large role in the theology of Christianity; and (3) there are serious arguments that can be made against continuity between Paul and Jesus, arguments that may be taken to support Wrede's famous statements that Paul was "the second founder of Christianity," one who "exercised beyond all doubt the stronger—not the better—influence."[2]

Assessing this issue is a broad task, and various angles can be explored with reference to both theological continuity and historical connection. Some issues are close to the surface and have thus received much attention (e.g., Jesus's message of the kingdom and its scarcity in Paul). Some issues are less prominent and yet may prove significant if enough lines of evidence can be found.

In 1989, Christian Wolff wrote an article that focused on practical similarities in how Jesus and Paul conducted their day-to-day ministries. He noted that both led lives of deprivation, renounced marriage, engaged in humble service, and suffered persecution.[3] While these similarities do not prove Paul's dependence on Jesus, they are suggestive for one who urged the imitation of Christ (e.g., 1 Cor 11:1). In addition to the four connections adduced by Wolff, another similarity between the ministries of Jesus and Paul exists—the place of miraculous phenomena. Both Jesus and Paul are presented as miracle workers in the New Testament, and in both cases strong arguments for the historicity of that portrait can be made.[4]

This deserves an exploration within the Jesus-Paul debate. The working of miracles is widely acknowledged as being close to the center of Jesus's activity, and this is increasingly being recognized for Paul as well. Significantly, since Acts presents a portrait of Paul as a miracle worker who is somewhat parallel to Jesus, we have already in the first century an interpretation of Paul that sees continuity

---

1. Indicative of currency on even the popular level are: Wenham, *Did St. Paul Get Jesus Right?*; Tabor, *Paul and Jesus*.

2. Wrede, *Paul*, 179–80, emphasis removed.

3. Wolff, "Humility and Self-Denial in Jesus' Life," 145–60.

4. Historicity at least in the sense that Jesus and Paul and their contemporaries would have *interpreted* them as miracle workers.

with Jesus in miracle working.[5] While miracles are but one piece of the Jesus-Paul debate, any similarities in such a practical aspect of ministry may prove illuminating. This is especially so if we can draw patterns of similarity in how both Jesus and Paul *interpreted* the significance of their miracles.

Thesis

Similarities in the sign function of miracles performed by Jesus and Paul strengthen the historical and theological continuity between both figures and suggest that Paul deliberately imitated Jesus in the performance of miracles.

Method of Study

This study particularly builds on three studies within the Jesus-Paul debate. The first, as mentioned above, is Wolff's article on parallels between the ministries of Jesus and Paul. In addition to the similarities Wolff notes, this study will add miracle working as another parallel. As Wedderburn writes of Wolff's essay, such a similar pattern of lifestyle suggests some cause and effect.[6]

The second foundational study is Twelftree's *Paul and the Miraculous* (2013), which fills a longtime gap in Pauline studies.[7] Twelftree argues that the experience of the miraculous was indeed central to Paul, and Twelftree takes what we might call a "maximalist" view of references to miracles in passages such as 1 Cor 2:4 and 1 Thess 1:5, passages where disputes exist as to whether Paul is alluding to miracles. Twelftree finally argues, however, that there is some final discontinuity between both figures in that Paul did not actively perform miracles, but God caused them to happen while Paul was preaching—and Twelftree sets this against the portrait we find in Acts, where Paul is presented much more as a miracle worker.[8] I will adopt many of Twelftree's arguments about the importance of miracles to Paul, as well as Twelftree's treatment of several Pauline passages. Finally, however, I will challenge his view of major discontinuous elements between Jesus and Paul as miracle workers.

The third foundational work for this study is Schoberg's *Perspectives of Jesus in the Writings of Paul* (2013), which argues for continuity in terms of a "common mindset," "core commitment," or "family resemblance," in which Jesus and Paul persevered despite opposition.[9] Helpful in terms of methodology, Schoberg

---

5. E.g., Acts 2:22; cf. 14:3.
6. Wedderburn, "Paul and the Story of Jesus," 180–81.
7. Twelftree, *Paul and the Miraculous*.
8. Ibid., 326.
9. Schoberg, *Perspectives of Jesus in the Writings of Paul*, 14, 16.

argues that, in order to move the debate forward, three elements must be borne in mind: (1) consideration must be given to the results of the Third Quest of the Historical Jesus and the New Perspective on Paul; (2) focus must lie on issues of key importance to both Jesus and Paul; and (3) particularly debated issues (such as the significance of Jesus's death and his identity) must be avoided so as not to prejudice certain ranks of scholars.[10] The three shared commitments that Schoberg develops are: (1) the welcome of outsiders, (2) the need to share in Jesus's death, and (3) the presence of a theology of new creation. Schoberg further writes that, in order to demonstrate each of these shared commitments, three requirements must be met: (1) the historicity and importance of each element must be established; (2) a "family resemblance" must be demonstrated between Jesus and Paul; and (3) an argument must be made for why Paul is most likely dependent on Jesus for the similarity.[11]

This study will build on the results of Schoberg's work by considering three sign functions that the miracles of Jesus and Paul seem to share, which correspond in varying degrees to Schoberg's three core commitments. Considering the place of *miracles* fulfils Schoberg's first three requirements for how to advance the discussion, because: (1) Third Quest results and New Perspective considerations will be included; (2) miracles were indeed significant to Jesus and Paul (as I will argue); and (3) the issue of miracles crosses no major fault lines of debate (at least healings and exorcisms, which most scholars accept in the case of Jesus). This study will also try to emulate Schoberg's three requirements for each sign function. In my chapters on proposed sign functions (chs. 2, 3, and 4), authenticity and importance will be addressed, and I will argue for a family resemblance. In ch. 5, I will go back and present reasons Paul is likely depending on Jesus.

If this approach is successful, the working of miracles in the ministries of Jesus and Paul will be seen *minimally* to form its own pattern of similarity, as well as strengthening the shared commitments argued by Schoberg by extending them to a practical aspect of the ministries of Jesus and Paul. My approach will also *maximally* suggest that Paul's practice was done in imitation of Jesus. If one is not convinced by the evidence enough to accept this latter suggestion, the former, more modest, results remain valuable.

According to this methodology, then, in chs. 2, 3, and 4, we will consider the place of miracles in the ministries of Jesus and Paul, as well as three proposed sign functions. On the Jesus side, we will focus on material that can be corroborated using typical Third Quest criteria, while remaining mindful of recent critiques of the traditional "criteria" approach.[12] We will begin by examining each sign function

---

10. Ibid., 11–13.

11. Ibid., 16–17. See also Drane, "Patterns of Evangelization in Paul and Jesus," 291.

12. E.g., Theissen and Winter, *The Quest for the Plausible Jesus*; Allison, *Constructing Jesus*; Keith and Le Donne, eds., *Jesus, Criteria, and the Demise of Authenticity*. For a discussion of our use of the criteria, including some interaction with these volumes, see ch. 2.

on the Jesus side, since we have more material concerning miracles in the traditions flowing from Jesus than we do in the case of Paul. On the Pauline side, I will restrict us to his seven undisputed letters.[13] For this reason, evidence from Acts or from Paul's disputed letters will be mostly left aside, though they may give important secondary attestation at points. Throughout chs. 2, 3, and 4, I will also bring in some Hellenistic and Jewish backgrounds whenever helpful.[14]

Chapter 5 will consider three central issues. First, I will address whether Paul likely knows about Jesus's miracles. Second, I will discuss the arguments of Twelftree's *Paul and the Miraculous* where he argues for some final discontinuity between Jesus and Paul on the subject of miracles. Third, I will discuss each of the sign functions and present possible arguments that Paul was *dependent* on Jesus for miracle working. This, of course, is the most difficult part of the whole enterprise.

Definitions

We will be using a handful of key terms throughout the study, and it is worthwhile to clarify that usage here briefly. Particularly, I need to address the terms *miracle*, *sign function*, and *initial realization*. Other terms could merit discussion, of course. For example, medical anthropology has carefully differentiated *disease* from *illness* and *curing* from *healing*, and this has been applied to New Testament studies in intriguing ways.[15] Yet because this study does not depend on such precision, we will use these latter terms interchangeably.

Miracle

Most obviously, we have the thorny problem of defining a miracle.[16] This can be framed in a variety of ways, but three main issues concern us. First, we want to avoid reading modern conceptions of violations of "natural law" into an ancient understanding of miracle.[17] This is because what we might understand by the

---

13. Romans, 1 and 2 Corinthians, Galatians, Philippians, 1 Thessalonians, and Philemon.

14. We will save consideration of discontinuity until ch. 5.

15. E.g., Pilch, *Healing in the New Testament*, 24–25, passim.

16. For useful discussions, see Twelftree, *Jesus the Miracle Worker*, 24–27; Eve, *Jewish Context of Jesus' Miracles*, 1–3; Twelftree, *Paul and the Miraculous*, 20–26; Meier, *Mentor, Message, and Miracles*, 512–15.

17. Note, for example, the (somewhat idiosyncratic) reservations of Horsley, *Jesus and Magic*, 3–32. For us, it is enough to focus on how such events were *viewed*. Chilton ("An Exorcism of History," 233) writes: "The historical question centers fundamentally on what people perceived, and how they acted on their perception; the question of how ancient experience relates to modern experience is a distinct, interpretive matter." Eve (*Healer from Nazareth*, xvi) explains some problems with bringing in the concept of natural law to a definition: "This is problematic in itself since it is unclear in such a definition whether 'laws of nature' means how nature actually behaves, or how it ought to behave

concept of natural law might be rather different from how ancients would have thought about the same issue. This is not to say, however, that the ancients did not have a sense of what was "normal" and what was not. Remus has delineated from ancient sources what he calls "canons of the ordinary," against which the unusual stood out.[18]

Second, a miracle should also not be defined *only* as something surprising or anomalous. The reason for this is that such a definition would leave out a religious significance, which is certainly involved in approaching miraculous phenomena as the biblical authors would consider it.[19]

Third, there is also the question how to distinguish (if at all) the concept of "miracle" from "magic." Though this issue is not precisely necessary for our discussion, I favor the view that the distinction between "magic" and "miracle" is primarily social and perspectival, whereby "magic" is a pejorative term for phenomena wrought by an individual of whom the evaluator does not approve.[20] Yet there may be some value in the view of Meier, who argues for a sliding scale of distinction, with ideal types of magic and miracle on opposite ends.[21] Perhaps a blending of the two methods is best, with the distinction between magic and miracle being *primarily* perspectival but at times with aspects of differing practices.

In light of all this, for a working definition of a miracle, we will follow Eve: "A strikingly surprising event, beyond normal human capacity, believed to be a significant act of God."[22] This definition helpfully includes the issue of unusual

---

according to the best scientific theories currently available. The latter of these is probably the more useful way of taking it, since we may not in fact know how nature actually behaves under all circumstances, and on the former way of taking it a breach of the laws of nature would have to mean an occasion when nature does not actually behave as it actually behaves, which is simply incoherent."

18. See Remus, *Pagan-Christian Conflict*, 3–26; cf. Theissen, *Miracle Stories*, 276–77, 284.

19. Eve (*Healer from Nazareth*, xvi) writes: "If the Tower of London were suddenly to turn into a block of green cheese or the Pentagon to launch itself into orbit for no apparent reason, we might well conclude that the laws of nature . . . had been breached, but if such events lacked any apparent significance they would be just bizarre events, not miracles. This type of event is thus better given some name other than 'miracle.'"

20. Twelftree ("Jesus and Magic in Luke–Acts," 47) says that "the new orthodoxy" in defining magic is that it is "a socially constructed label identifying opponents and their ideas and activities," though he demurs somewhat. Witmer (*Galilean Exorcist*, 31) writes: "'Magician,' 'magic' and 'demon-possessed' are normally attributed to those persons and activities not sanctioned by the central religious structures of a society, while 'miracle,' 'miraculous' and 'sanctioned by God' are associated with those who are considered legitimate by these same standards. . . . Whether a person was labeled a magician or miracle worker, then, depended in the ancient world on whether his or her action was considered legitimate or illegitimate vis-à-vis the accepted norms of the society or the particular religious perspective of the writer." See further: Aune, "Magic in Early Christianity," 1507–57; Sanders, *Historical Figure*, 135–43; Meier, *A Marginal Jew*, 2:537–52; Theissen and Merz, *The Historical Jesus*, 305–7; Eve, *Jewish Context*, 361–68; Dawson, *Healing, Weakness and Power*, 10–14; Eve, *Healer from Nazareth*, 21–25; Horsley, *Jesus and Magic*, 37–100.

21. Meier, *A Marginal Jew*, 2:537–52.

22. Ibid., 2:xvii. For similar definitions, see Swinburne, *Concept of Miracle*, 1, but cf. p. 11; Keener, *Miracles*, 1:110. The definition of Meier (*A Marginal Jew*, 2:512) is similar but longer—and is both more

phenomena, along with a perceived divine agency and its corresponding religious significance.[23] This definition seems fair to the kind of miraculous happenings we are considering in this study.

Sign Function

Also important to our study is the term *sign function*. Here we are attempting to convey the *symbolism, significance,* or *implications* a miracle might hold for ancient viewers.[24] How would witnesses perceive miracles when seen (or heard about second hand)? How would the miracle worker perceive miracles? What would the miracles be understood to mean or imply? Of course, miracles may have been performed for their own sake, or perhaps out of compassion. But as Eve writes, most of the time compassion alone is insufficient to explain Jesus's miracles.[25] Beyond this, numerous scholars have identified various *symbolic meanings, significances,* or *implications* to Jesus's miracles, and we will interact with several of these suggestions over the course of the study. My use of sign function attempts to convey this aspect of miracles.

Initial Realizations

Although I am primarily using the term *sign function* to describe the implications or symbolic significances of miracles, I wish to clarify that this does not restrict a miracle to being *only* a symbol. Rather, a miraculous healing or exorcism also, by definition, *accomplishes* something—at least in the experience of the recipient. Thus, in ch. 2, I will speak of miracles as not only *accompanying* the messages of

---

and less helpful for that reason: "A miracle is (1) an unusual, startling, or extraordinary event that is in principle perceivable by any interested and fair-minded observer, (2) an event that finds no reasonable explanation in human abilities or in other known forces that operate in our world of time and space, and (3) an event that is the result of a special act of God, doing what no human power can do."

23. It also, at least probably from the point of view of the early Christians, rules out what might be considered "magic," since the Christians behind our sources likely would not view what they would call magic to be "significant acts of God." Others might consider the same phenomena more favorably, but again this would be more a sociological or theological judgment.

24. Bock and Simpson (*Jesus According to Scripture,* 179) describe what they call "a fundamental characteristic of Jesus' miracles": "They are more than simply events of power and authentication. These miracles picture some type of significant 'deeper' reality to which Jesus' power relates. This claim neither interprets these miracles as allegories nor views them as mere literary depictions of this reality. The miracles are portrayed as real events, but as events with illustrative teaching power." Keener (*Miracles,* 1:28) writes: "Jesus presumably intended his miracles as prophetic symbolic actions, hence with some metaphoric significance from the start." Of course, miracles could be open to interpretation, as the Beelzebub controversy demonstrates so clearly (Mark 3:22–27 parr.). One person's miracle worker is another person's charlatan magician! Cf. Harvey, *Jesus and the Constraints,* 113–14; Sanders, *Historical Figure,* 162–68.

25. Eve, *Healer from Nazareth,* 139.

Jesus and Paul but also in some sense "realizing" the gracious inclusion of outsiders that both men proclaimed, at least initially or partially. Near-synonyms for what I am trying to convey here include: *actualizing, manifesting, making operative,* or *fulfilling*—with the important qualification that this action still has an eschatological "not-yet" aspect to it.

Scholars have used a variety of expressions for what I am attempting to convey.[26] Closest to my usage is Meier, who nicely brings together both *sign function* and *initial realization* when he describes Jesus's miracles as they stand in the Gospels as "*symbols* and *partial concrete realizations* of the kingdom of God."[27]

This is precisely what I am aiming to convey. While my term *sign function* clearly focuses on symbolism and implication, the miracles of Jesus and Paul also directly affected the lives of individuals and brought more fully into the recipients' personal experience the gracious inclusion about which they would have heard from Jesus and Paul. In other words—these perceived miracles involved symbolism, but they also entailed more in the lives of recipients than mere symbols—they were God's gracious inclusion *experienced*.

Literature Review

The sea of literature relevant to the subjects of this study is indeed vast, but I will attempt to highlight and discuss the most important sources. I will divide the literature up into four natural categories: (1) the Jesus-Paul debate, (2) Jesus and the miraculous, (3) Paul and the miraculous, and (4) the Jesus-Paul debate and the miraculous.

---

26. Speaking of Jesus's miracles, Wright (*Jesus and the Victory of God*, 196) says: "They were signs which were intended as, and would have been perceived as, the physical inauguration of the kingdom of Israel's god, the putting into action of the welcome and the warning which were the central message of the kingdom and its redefinition. They were an integral part of the entire ministry, part of the same seamless robe as the parables, and on a level with Jesus' other characteristic actions." Twelftree (*Jesus the Exorcist*, 170) writes: "They do not illustrate, extend, or even confirm Jesus' preaching. In the casting out of demons, the mission of Jesus itself is taking place, being actualized or fulfilled." Twelftree (*Paul and the Miraculous*, 217–18, emphasis added) also writes this elsewhere: "As the miracles of Moses were the means of salvation for those involved, and also the miracles of Jesus were *the realization of salvation* for the supplicant, so Paul saw the apostolic miracles, including of his ministry, having the same function: *miracles were realized soteriology.*" Kim ("Jesus, Sayings of," 486) frames it within the Jesus-Paul debate like this: "As Jesus actualized through miracles the salvation of the kingdom he preached, so also Paul, his apostle, has actualized through miracles the salvation of the gospel he has preached." For this latter quotation, we would only want to make sure the forward-looking eschatological "not-yet" element be preserved in this understanding of actualization.

27. Meier, *A Marginal Jew*, 2:548, emphasis added. Earlier, he calls them "signs and realizations of the gracious power of the God of Israel" (2:545) and says that they "not only supported but also dramatized and actuated his eschatological message" (2:970). These terms and concepts are all broadly synonymous with what I am trying to convey.

The Jesus-Paul Debate

Within New Testament studies, the debate over the continuity between Jesus and Paul has been discussed for more than a century and a half.[28] A few high-water marks, however, can be identified within the early and middle stages. F. C. Baur stands toward the head of the debate with his famous division of the early church into opposing Paulinist and Petrine factions.[29] But the subject of the continuity and discontinuity between Jesus and Paul was launched into the worldwide consciousness by Wrede's *Paul*, a book the impact of which was all out of proportion to its size and that ended with the famous assessment that Paul was the second founder of Christianity.[30] Bultmann was the dominating figure of the mid-twentieth century, and his judgment was that, while there were significant theological similarities between Jesus and Paul (e.g., on eschatology and the Law), Paul himself cared nothing for the personality, practice, and teaching of the *historical* Jesus—nothing mattered save the *fact* of Jesus's coming, death, and resurrection.[31] From this framing of the issue comes the helpful point that theological continuity and a real historical connection between Jesus and Paul are two separate issues and must not be confused.[32] Of course, more conservative voices gave rejoinders to these claims along the way.[33]

In recent years, there has arisen a variety of approaches to evaluate the Jesus-Paul issue.[34] One approach focuses on exploring the citations and allusions Paul makes in connection to the Jesus tradition. This is one of the most obvious methods of exploring the situation and has been vigorously pursued.[35] It is somewhat

28. For summaries of the history of the debate, see Furnish, "The Jesus-Paul Debate," 17–50; John Barclay, "Jesus and Paul," 492–503; Simmons, *A Theology of Inclusion*, 8–33; Holzbrecher, *Paulus und der historische Jesus*, 7–121.

29. Baur, *Church History*, 1:44–152.

30. Wrede, *Paul*, 180–81. A position still argued today. See, e.g., Lüdemann, *Paul*.

31. E.g., Bultmann, *Theology of the New Testament*, 293–94; Bultmann, "Significance of the Historical Jesus," 239–46.

32. Barclay, "Jesus and Paul," 495–96. Cf. Kümmel, "Jesus und Paulus," 171.

33. E.g., in response to Baur: Matheson, "Historical Christ," 1:43–62, 125–38, 193–208, 264–75, 352–71, 431–43; 2:27–47, 137–54, 287–301, 357–71; to Wrede: (arguing for a moderate position) Weiss, *Paul and Jesus*; and to Bultmann: Bruce, *Paul and Jesus*.

34. On ten hinge points of the debate, see Allison, "Pauline Epistles," 1.

35. The maximalist position is famously represented by Resch, *Paulinismus und die Logia Jesu*. More restrained, and thus more convincing, versions of the maximalist position are: Wenham, *Paul: Follower of Jesu*; Kim, "Jesus, Sayings of," 474–92. Additional recent studies arguing for some significant allusions to the Jesus traditions in Paul are: Dungan, *Sayings of Jesus*; Fjärstedt, *Synoptic Tradition*; Thompson, *Clothed with Christ*; Wolfe, "Uses of Jesus"; Yeung, *Faith in Jesus and Paul*; Blomberg, "Quotations, Allusions, and Echoes," 129–43. Some scholars who reject that Paul was at many of these points influenced by Jesus include Neirynck, "Paul and the Sayings of Jesus," 265–321; Walter, "Paul and the Early Christian Jesus-Tradition," 51–80, though he still thinks there is continuity between them in message, just that it was more indirect (see pp. 79–80); Tuckett, "Paul, Tradition and Freedom," 307–25. A middle position, between the maximalists and those who reject much

hindered, of course, because Paul does not make many explicit references to Jesus's teaching and life and because there is room for debate in the identification of allusions.[36]

Another approach is to investigate shared theological themes or emphases. This approach has received fresh impetus in recent years because of the more positive results of the Third Quest, as well as new examinations of Paul initiated by the New Perspective.[37] A diverse collection of works has argued for various points of similarity.[38] Three are particularly important for this study and will now be discussed.[39]

Simmons argues for theological continuity between Jesus and Paul on the basis of their shared message of gracious inclusion.[40] This is seen in Jesus's acceptance of outcasts and sinners in table fellowship and Paul's ministry to Gentiles without demands of Jewish practice. Simmons sees a historical connection between Jesus and Paul by arguing that the traditions of Jesus were mediated to Paul via the Hellenistic Christian community that Paul joined after conversion. Simmons

---

direct influence, is represented by: Hunter, *Paul and His Predecessors*, 45–51, 126–28; Allison, "Pauline Epistles," 1–32; Dunn, "Jesus Tradition in Paul," 1:169–89; Furnish, *Jesus According to Paul*, 40–65; Tàrrech, "The Use of the Story," 1–14. Relevant studies also include: Hollander, "The Words of Jesus," 340–57; Wong, "De-radicalization of Jesus' Ethical Sayings," 245–63; Wong, "Deradicalization of Jesus' Ethical Sayings," 181–94; Stettler, "'Command of the Lord,'" 42–51; Walt, "A Non-Canonical Jesus in Paul?" 55–74; Pokorný, "Words of Jesus in Paul," 4:3437–67; Labahn, "The Non-Synoptic Jesus," 3:1933–96.

36. For the most helpful discussions of identifying allusions, see Thompson, *Clothed with Christ*, 28–36; Blomberg, "Quotations, Allusions," 129–43.

37. See, e.g., Bockmuehl, *Seeing the Word*, 42–43; cf. Holzbrecher, *Paulus und der historische Jesus*, 89–93, 113–21.

38. For example, Wedderburn ("Similarity and Continuity," 117–43) has argued that Jesus and Paul shared an openness to outsiders, and that this perspective came to Paul via the channel of Hellenistic Christians. Dunn (*Jesus, Paul, and the Law*, especially pp. 10–36) has explored continuity between Jesus and Paul with reference to the Old Testament law. Patterson ("Paul and the Jesus Tradition," 23–41) argued for similarity for Jesus and Paul as social radicals; Witherington (*Jesus, Paul and the End of the World*) focused on eschatological views. Drane ("Patterns of Evangelization," 281–96) has argued that both Jesus and Paul share a common style of evangelism. Wenham (*Follower of Jesus*) has argued for many lines of theological continuity. Bauckham ("Kingdom and Church," 1–26) has argued for similarity in how Jesus and Paul understood the kingdom. Freyne ("The Jesus-Paul Debate Revisited," 143–63) has argued that both figures worked toward the eschatological restoration of Israel, understood geographically. Bartchy ("Who Should Be Called Father?" 135–47) has argued that Paul and Jesus rejected the prevailing patriarchal system in favor of a new kind of kinship. Barclay ("'Offensive and Uncanny,'" 1–17) has noted how both understood God's grace as good news to outsiders and as challenge to insiders. Longenecker ("Good News to the Poor," 37–65) has argued that concern for the poor was emphasized by both Jesus and Paul. Addressing "practice of life," Rescio and Walt ("'There Is Nothing Unclean,'" 53–82, especially p. 55) have focused on similarities in how Jesus and Paul approached purity in contexts of itinerant ministry.

39. We already discussed Schoberg's *Perspectives of Jesus in the Writings of Paul* and will not take it up again here.

40. Simmons, *Theology of Inclusion*. He interacts with those who have addressed the same issue. See, e.g., Hengel, *Between Jesus and Paul*, 1–29; Räisänen, "The 'Hellenists,'" 149–202; Wedderburn, "Similarity and Continuity," 117–43.

argues that these Hellenistic Christians were the first to waive the circumcision requirement for Gentiles.[41] Because he understands these Hellenists to have done this in imitation of Jesus's example, here we have a historical and theological link between Jesus and Paul.

Thompson considers allusions to Jesus tradition in Paul and focuses on Romans 12:1–15:13.[42] He argues for allusions and echoes of the Jesus tradition throughout this section of Romans, and he argues that it indicates Paul was indeed influenced by traditions about Jesus. Thompson also includes an important discussion about why we have so little Jesus tradition in Paul's letters, and he argues that the pattern in Paul actually matches the pattern we see in all other early Christian epistolary literature.[43] Paul is not so unusual in this regard as it first appears.

In a study refreshing for its willingness to think outside the box of recent interpreters, Porter argues that Paul actually met Jesus in person during Jesus's earthly ministry.[44] Porter argues this both on the basis of the general probabilities of both figures meeting, given their presence at the same time in the same region and city, and on the basis of three main New Testament passages: the Acts account of Paul's conversion (Acts 9, 22, and 26), 1 Cor 9:1, and 2 Cor 5:16. Following this is a discussion on how this increases the level of continuity we should see between Jesus and Paul.[45] While some of Porter's arguments do not convince, their collective weight should be felt, and he is to be commended for bringing back to New Testament studies as a strong possibility (or probability) the suggestion that Paul actually encountered Jesus in person.

Jesus and the Miraculous

While often downplayed during early investigations into the historical Jesus, the miracle tradition has in recent years risen to a place of prominence.[46] During the First Quest, the miracles were at times understood as fabrications, explained away rationally, or understood as having been permeated with myth.[47] Within the so-

---

41. E.g., Simmons, *Theology of Inclusion*, 100–102.

42. Thompson, *Clothed with Christ*.

43. Ibid., 37–76. Arguments bolstered now by Lee, *Paul, Scribe of Old and New*.

44. Porter, *When Paul Met Jesus*.

45. Ibid., 12–28, 73–121, 122–77.

46. For a six-stage history of research, see Theissen and Merz, *Historical Jesus*, 285–91; for a special focus on recent years, see Twelftree, "The History of Miracles," 191–208; for a summary of the current consensus on the importance of the miracle tradition, see Roskovec, "Miracle Worker," 875–78. For other helpful summaries, see Porterfield, *Healing in the History of Christianity*, 21–41; cf. Evans, *Life of Jesus Research*, 210–19.

47. For a charge of fabrication, see Reimarus, *Reimarus: Fragments*, 229–35; cf. Schweitzer, *Quest for the Historical Jesus*, 19. On the rationalistic interpretations culminating in the work of Heinrich E. G. Paulus, see ibid., 27–55; cf. pp. 56–64. For the mythological understanding, see Strauss, *Life of Jesus*, 413–534; cf. Schweitzer, *Quest for the Historical Jesus*, 49–52, 78–80. See also Evans, "Life-of-Jesus

called no-quest period, Bultmann and Dibelius saw many of the miracle stories
(or at least elements of them) as foreign intrusions.[48] In part because the Second
Quest focused so much attention on the saying tradition, the miracles of Jesus
were generally not given much attention.[49] Crossan saw Jesus's "magic" (along with
meal habits) as important in enacting the (sapiential) kingdom, though Crossan
held that the cures affected only the social effects of the condition.[50]

By contrast to much of the Second Quest, the Third Quest brought an increased
emphasis on Jesus's actions.[51] Smith argued for Jesus as a magician, and Vermes
placed Jesus among wonder-working Jewish holy men—and despite problems
with both arguments, Smith and Vermes rightly emphasized Jesus's miracles.[52]
Harvey argued that Jesus should not be viewed among Jewish charismatics, that
his miracles were not performed to gather a crowd or give unassailable authority, and that the pattern of Jesus's miracles is essentially unprecedented in the
background material.[53] Though Sanders argues that Jesus's miracles were important in understanding the attention he received, Sanders views the miracles as
unhelpful for defining Jesus's person since they were so open to interpretation.[54]

Research," 3–36. I retain the conventional terminology of the quests despite problems. See Brown,
"Quest of the Historical Jesus," 718–56; cf. Craffert, *Galilean Shaman*, 41–42.

48. Bultmann, *Synoptic Tradition*, 209–44; cf. Bultmann, "Problem of Miracle," 63–75. Dibelius,
From Tradition to Gospel, 70–103. While Dibelius (*Jesus*, 76–88) suggests that many of the "tales" were
intrusions, he accepts that Jesus was involved with perceived extraordinary healings and that these
deeds were important alongside Jesus's kingdom-proclamation.

49. See Roskovec, "Miracle Worker," 878 n. 14. Twelftree ("History of Miracles," 192) points
out by way of example that Bornkamm hardly mentions the *deeds* of Jesus (see Bornkamm, *Jesus
of Nazareth*, 169–78). Funk and The Jesus Seminar (*Acts of Jesus*, 530–32) accept that Jesus was an
exorcist and healer, though none of the exorcisms warranted red or pink, and only six of the healings
were considered pink; they also reject the nature miracles. For himself, Funk (*Honest to Jesus*, 253)
writes: "Jesus was originally probably only a minor miracle worker." Of course, depending on one's
definitions and emphases, the Jesus Seminar could also be considered part of the Third Quest.

50. Crossan, *The Historical Jesus*, 303–53; John Dominic Crossan, *Jesus*, 82. I put Crossan in the
Second Quest since conceptually he seems to belong here. Though he includes Jewish contexts, the
resulting figure seems more Hellenistic than Jewish. Again, others might categorize him as being part
of the Third Quest.

51. A point that naturally leads to an emphasis on Jesus's miracles. Sanders (*Jesus and Judaism*,
157–73) and Ben F. Meyer (*The Aims of Jesus*, 154–58) acknowledge this and devote some attention
to miracles, though relatively small sections. Sanders (*Historical Figure*, 132–68) does devote more
space to the subject later.

52. Despite problems (approaching parallelomania), Morton Smith (*Jesus the Magician*, e.g.,
pp. 10–20) rightly argued for the central importance of the miracle tradition. He also helpfully
emphasized potential background sources and highlighted the charge of magic from opponents. For
a critique of Smith, see Twelftree, *Jesus the Exorcist*, 190–207; cf. Horsley, *Jesus and Magic*, 37–100.
For Vermes's opinion, see Geza Vermes, *Jesus the Jew*, 58–82. For critiques, see Meier, *A Marginal Jew*,
2:581–88; Twelftree, "History of Miracles," 194–95.

53. Harvey, *Constraints of History*, 98–119.

54. Sanders, *Jesus and Judaism*, 157–73. Sanders (*Historical Figure*, 164) also writes that because
many did not respond to Jesus favorably, either the miracles have been exaggerated or miracles generally did not make people commit themselves to Jesus.

Wright spends even less space proportionally on Jesus's miracles, but he argues that they were important aspects of Jesus's ministry that served as signs of the coming kingdom and the reintroduction of outcasts into Israel.[55] Borg follows Vermes in several respects and stresses Jesus's experience with the Spirit, along with his healings and exorcisms. Among "Jewish charismatic healers," Jesus was "the most extraordinary figure," who left a legacy of "charismatic holy men" such as Paul and Peter.[56] Allison has recognized the place of miracles in authenticating millenarian movements generally, and for Jesus.[57] Dunn sees both the authenticity of the miracle traditions and the significance of the eschatological interpretation that Jesus put on them.[58] Theissen divides up the miracle stories according to formal features and argues that Jesus had a unique eschatological understanding of his healings and exorcisms, as well as that the way the saying tradition matches the miracle-story tradition shows that Jesus was a healer and exorcist—despite Theissen's view that the miracle stories were transmitted for a time outside the circle of Jesus's followers.[59]

For comprehensive treatments of the historical Jesus that include prolonged focus on the miracle tradition, pride of place goes to Meier, whose second volume of *A Marginal Jew* takes up the subject. Throughout this study, Meier finds the arguments for the historicity of Jesus's healings and exorcisms as strong as any other aspect of the tradition. As mentioned above, Meier also highlights how Jesus's miracles reinforced and realized his eschatological preaching.[60]

Some studies have focused on Jesus's exorcisms. Noteworthy contributions have been made by Twelftree, who focuses on Jesus's exorcisms (and healing) and argues that the connection Jesus makes between his exorcisms and eschatology is unprecedented.[61] Some scholars treat exorcisms against a social, political, and anthropological backdrop where spirit-possession is seen to arise especially among distressed people groups.[62] The most sustained recent contribution is from Witmer, who helpfully addresses relevant backgrounds and passages.[63]

Similar in its anthropological backgrounds, but wider in its scope, is Craffert's study, which argues that Jesus fits the social type of a shaman.[64] One of his pro-

---

55. Wright, *Victory of God*, 186–96.

56. Borg, *Jesus*, 71.

57. Allison, *Jesus of Nazareth*, 91, 205.

58. Dunn, *Jesus Remembered*, 667–96. Of course Dunn (*Jesus and the Spirit*, 41–92) has also emphasized Jesus's experience of the Spirit more generally.

59. Theissen and Merz, *Historical Jesus*, 285, 301–2, 309; Theissen, *Miracle Stories*, 277–80.

60. Meier, *A Marginal Jew*, 2:509–1038, 970; 2:545, 548, 970.

61. Twelftree, *Jesus the Exorcist*, 170–71; cf. Twelftree, *Miracle Worker*, 281–92, 346–59; Twelftree, *In the Name of Jesus*, 25–173.

62. Crossan belongs here, e.g., *Revolutionary Biography*, 84–93.

63. Witmer, *Galilean Exorcist*.

64. Craffert, *Galilean Shaman*, 213–422. Davies (*Jesus the Healer*, 100–104) presents a similar study, though he prefers the model of a medium.

posals is that there may be no need to slice up the Gospel traditions into earlier and later aspects since most of what is said of Jesus in the Gospels could easily be attributed to a shaman-like figure during his lifetime.[65] This is a helpful reminder.

Horsley has recently argued that using the terms *miracle* and *magic* with reference to Jesus is actually modernizing Jesus—because what scholars call "magic" is only a composite generalization of different ritual practices, and because the healings and exorcisms of Jesus generally have no reference to divine agency.[66] While his points on terminology are well made, and he has effectively countered the arguments of Smith and Crossan concerning Jesus and magic, Horsley's opposition to the term *miracle* on the basis of a supposed lack of God's involvement in the accounts is idiosyncratic and unhelpful. For example, Horsley comments that the healing in Mark 1:40–45 does not fit the modern definition of a miracle because "the episode suggests no supernatural agency."[67] Yet for a prophetic figure to enact a healing certainly *implies* divine agency. Horsley's treatment almost seems to fall into the category of the word-concept fallacy, and one wonders if Horsley's intent is to help focus strictly on a naturalistic social understanding of the healings. As Theissen argues, the Christians were aware of the surprising nature of miracles.[68]

Some studies have focused specifically on the "signs" (σημεῖα) theme within the Gospel of John. Dealing with the use of this term on the rhetorical level, Salier's study first deals with background material and shows that the term had uses in both religious and persuasive contexts.[69] He then argues that these signs are key to the Gospel of John's presentation of Jesus and are portrayed in order to lead readers to faith in Jesus as the divine messiah.[70] Considering the issue of signs in John on a source-critical level instead, Fortna has famously argued for an independent signs source from which the Gospel of John was (in part) constructed.[71]

Part of the increased focus on the miracles of Jesus in recent years comes from how the rationalistic impulses of the enlightenment have given way to the view that in order to understand Jesus we must view him as his contemporaries would have seen him.[72] It is possible to accept that miracles "really happened" in the eyes

65. See, e.g., Craffert, *Galilean Shaman*, 420–22.

66. Horsley, *Jesus and Magic*, 163–67.

67. Ibid., 121.

68. Theissen, *Miracle Stories*, 276–77, 284. Cf. Remus, *Pagan-Christian Conflict*, 3–26. Though Wright (*Resurrection of the Son of God*, 10) is speaking of Jesus's resurrection, his point is also helpful more broadly: "The discovery that dead people stayed dead was not first made by the philosophers of the Enlightenment."

69. Salier, *Rhetorical Impact*, 18–45.

70. E.g., "They are an essential part of the Gospel's presentation and the cumulative weight of their presentation is intended to prompt a response of faith in Jesus by the reader" (ibid., 172). See also Udo Schnelle, "Signs in the Gospel of John," 231–43.

71. Fortna, *Gospel of Signs*. For later reflection and development, see Fortna, "Gospel of John," 149–58.

72. For example, Evans ("Eclipse of Mythology," 17) writes: "The scientific or metaphysical problem of how to define a miracle is just that—a scientific and metaphysical problem. It is not an item

of Jesus and his contemporaries, at least healings and exorcisms, while withholding judgment on whether any violation of the natural order occurred.[73] Postmodern shifts, along with growing insights that reality is more complicated than previously thought, have also helped.[74] Added to this is the view that one's perception of reality is to a degree socially constructed, and there is plenty of evidence that healings and exorcisms commonly occur in various cultures and settings.[75]

Of course, a variety of backgrounds have also been brought to bear on Jesus's miracles. These help us understand how Jesus and his contemporaries would have understood the miracles, as well as how Jesus was in both continuity and discontinuity with these traditions.[76] A few works in particular stand out.

Keener's two-volume work on miracles focuses on witnesses who claim to have seen the miraculous, both ancient and modern, with a view to arguing that the carte blanche dismissal of miracles by much of Western academia is inconsistent and approaches ethnocentrism.[77] The book's scope is far-reaching, and it includes a good discussion of philosophical issues concerning miracles. If one is philosophically and theologically inclined to see the actual working of God in the miracle reports Keener recounts, the book is also enormously stimulating in regard to personal faith. Yet the most useful section for us is his survey of ancient-backgrounds material on miracles.[78]

Kahl's study examines 150 or so ancient miracle stories and divides the actors by using the labels "bearer of numinous power" (e.g., Yahweh, Jesus, Asclepius, Apollonius), "petitioner of numinous power" (e.g., Moses, Elijah, Ḥanina, Paul), and "mediator of numinous power" (e.g., Tobit, Vespasian, Alexander [and sometimes Moses and Abraham]).[79] His findings conclude that Jesus is presented as an "immanent bearer of numinous power," who can best be compared to Apollonius,

---

that should bring historical inquiry to a standstill. The historian need not know just exactly how Jesus healed someone or just exactly what happened when a person was exorcized of a 'demon.' What the historian needs to know is whether Jesus did those sorts of things and, if he did, what they meant to his contemporaries."

73. One might demur from accepting a "miracle" because of either philosophical positions that hold miracles to be impossible, or because of a methodological naturalism that rules miracles out in order to engage better with a wider audience. For an elucidating discussion of this latter approach, see Webb, "Historical Jesus Enterprise," 41–54.

74. See Roskovec, "Miracle Worker," 876–78.

75. See, e.g., Theissen and Merz, *Historical Jesus*, 311–13.

76. E.g., on the Jewish side: Eve, *Jewish Context*, passim; Koskenniemi, *Old Testament Miracle-Workers*, passim. On the Hellenistic side: Cotter, *Miracles in Greco-Roman Antiquity*, passim; Blackburn, *Theios Anēr and the Markan Miracle Traditions*, 13–96. More generally: Kee, *Medicine, Miracle and Magic*, passim; Kahl, *New Testament Miracle Stories*, 56–62; Meier, *A Marginal Jew*, 2:576–601; Keener, *Miracles*, 1:35–82; Twelftree, *Paul and the Miraculous*, 31–105.

77. Keener, *Miracles*, 2:762.

78. Ibid., 1:35–82.

79. Kahl, *Miracle Stories*, 76.

because Apollonius is the only other figure presented as an immanent bearer of numinous power who has more than one miracle story told about him.[80]

Eric Eve has written two works that are particularly relevant. His published dissertation examines the Jewish backgrounds on the issue of miracle workers and argues that Jesus was distinctive, both in terms of his status as a bearer of numinous power and by virtue of the authority with which he performed miracles.[81] The most likely category into which Jesus would fit would be that of a prophet.[82] Eve's later book considers the miracles of Jesus more broadly.[83] What is particularly valuable about this latter study is how it combines a discussion of Jewish backgrounds, Greco-Roman backgrounds, the Gospel traditions themselves, and social-scientific perspectives on the miracle tradition. Eve argues vigorously against a purely sapiential understanding of Jesus but also discusses the ways in which an eschatological message of the kingdom would ring against the social setting of Galilee.

At the conclusion of his own literature survey, Eve offers the following points of general agreement among scholars concerning the miracles of Jesus, and his summary still seems fair despite being more than a decade old: (1) Jesus performed exorcisms and healings that impressed those around him; (2) this miracle-working ministry is close to the center of Jesus's work; (3) a minority of conservatives aside, the so-called nature miracles are the creation of the church; (4) eschatology is the proper background for Jesus's miracles; (5) Jesus should be understood not primarily as a magician but as a prophet, and probably an eschatological prophet; and (6) Jesus's miracles were unique in a variety of suggested respects (e.g., healings with eschatological significance).[84]

Paul and the Miraculous

The best discussion of the history of research on Paul's relation to the miraculous is given by Twelftree, and his discussion demonstrates how this aspect of Paul's experience has been largely overlooked.[85] He says one reason for this is that the majority of scholars have focused more on Paul as a thinker or theologian.[86] Beyond this, the general inattention paid to the "historical Paul" in terms of miracles comes not

80. Ibid., 236.

81. Eve, *Jewish Context*, 384–86.

82. Ibid.

83. Eve, *Healer from Nazareth*.

84. Eve, *Jewish Context*, 16–18.

85. Twelftree, *Paul and the Miraculous*, 3–17. For a summary of recent research into Paul generally, see Fisk, "Paul: Life and Letters," 283–325; Dunn, "Paul's Theology," 326–48.

86. Twelftree, *Paul and the Miraculous*, 4. Similarly, Ashton (*Religion of Paul*, 168–69; cf. pp. 238–44) says the general neglect is because of too much skepticism among historians and a distaste among theologians for depending on observable signs.

only from the relative silence in the epistles but also because it is possible to argue that Paul downplayed or resisted the practice of miracle working.[87] Of course, Paul's experience with the miraculous has not been completely ignored. Some studies are particularly important.

Jervell has written two important articles on the question of Paul and miracles. His first article focuses on the interplay of Paul as a miracle worker along with Paul's suffering and weakness, arguing that Paul's opponents in 2 Corinthians had a problem not with Paul's lack of charismatic phenomena but with Paul's illness.[88] Jervell's second article argues that there is indeed some similarity between the Paul of Acts and the Paul of the epistles on the subject of miracles. Because of the occasional nature of Paul's epistles, the important place that miracles held in Paul's ministry and proclamation is somewhat obscured, and Jervell argues that miracles are almost more central to Paul's ministry than Acts would suggest.[89] These are helpful counterpoints to the more usual perspectives on miracles in Paul.

Similar to Jervell in many ways is an article by Kollmann.[90] He too compares the image of Paul as a miracle worker in the epistles and in Acts, and he argues for some significant continuity between both portraits. This is the case, in Kollmann's view, despite the fact that miracles appear less important to Paul in the epistles than they do in Acts.[91]

Fee's *Empowering Presence*, while focused more broadly on Paul's pneumatology, is naturally an important source on the miraculous in Paul. Fee treats the pertinent passages, connects the miraculous with the work of the Spirit, and concludes that the performing of miracles was important to Paul.[92] Both the book's scope and detail make it a key resource for our purposes.

Schreiber's study compares the reports of Paul's miracles in Acts with Paul's discussion in the undisputed epistles. He argues that, of the accounts in Acts, only 14:8–10 and 16:16–18 are historical.[93] In Paul's letters, Gal 3:5, 1 Cor 2:4, and 1 Thess 1:5 do not represent miracles of Paul. Schreiber agrees that in Rom 15:19 (and 2 Cor 12:12) Paul refers to his miracles, yet Schreiber still argues that Paul downplayed miracles and did not consider them central to his ministry.[94]

Alkier's study considers the issue of the *reality* of Pauline miracles with reference to the communication theory of semiotics.[95] It discusses essentially all the

---

87. E.g., Robinson, "Kerygma and History," 59–65, though cf. pp. 50–51; Koester, "One Jesus," 189–91; Kuhn, "Der irdische Jesus bei Paulus," 317–20; Georgi, *Opponents of Paul*, 271–83; cf. pp. 170–74; Koester, "*GNOMAI DIAPHOROI*," 150–53.

88. Jervell, "Der schwache Charismatiker," 185–98.

89. Jervell, "Signs of an Apostle," 91.

90. Kollmann, "Paulus als Wundertäter," 76–96.

91. E.g., ibid., 95–96.

92. Fee, *God's Empowering Presence*, 849.

93. Schreiber, *Paulus als Wundertäter*, 143, 287.

94. See ibid., 207–8, 234, 274–82.

95. Alkier, *Wunder und Wirklichkeit*.

relevant Pauline passages in 1 Thessalonians, Galatians, 1 and 2 Corinthians, and Romans. Because even the resurrection itself counts as a miracle, the theme can be seen as central for Paul: "Pauline theology can be understood as a theology of miracles."[96]

In his series of published lectures, Ashton argues that Paul should be viewed through the lens of shamanism.[97] By so doing he emphasizes the role of the miraculous in Paul's religion and life experience—in the end doing for Paul, as Twelftree suggests, what Morton Smith did for Jesus.[98] Ashton touches on many of the key passages concerning miracles in Paul and emphasizes that it was Paul's miracle working that would have earned him a successful hearing.[99]

González has a helpful article on healing in Paul.[100] He explores various reasons for the apparent differences between the Paul of Acts and the Paul of the epistles and concludes that there is no reason to pit either portrait against the other. His treatment includes an important discussion on the relative silence in Paul's letters on the subject of healing.[101]

The Jesus-Paul Debate and the Miraculous

Within the Jesus-Paul debate, the issue of miracles has not received much attention. Sometimes the only comment is that Paul's letters do not refer to the miracles of Jesus—just one part of the Gospel traditions that Paul does not discuss (and perhaps does not know).[102] On the other hand, some scholars hold that Paul knew of Jesus's miracles, and some argue that he alludes to them at points.[103] In the

---

96. Ibid., 14 (my translation).

97. Ashton, *Religion of Paul*.

98. Twelftree, *Paul and the Miraculous*, 15.

99. Ashton, *Religion of Paul*, 163–70.

100. Eliezer González, "Healing in the Pauline Epistles," 557–75.

101. Ibid., 575, 567–75.

102. E.g., Lloyd, "Historic Christ," 279; Lucas, *Fifth Gospel*, 205, 212; Furnish, "The Jesus-Paul Debate," 43; Bruce, *Paul and Jesus*, 20; Bent Noack, "Teste Paulo," 11, 15; Simmons, *Theology of Inclusion*, 6; Fisk, "Life and Letters," 310; Walter, "Paul and the Early Christian," 61. Bultmann (*Theology of the New Testament*, 1:35, 294) argues that miracles did not become part of the kerygma and that the life of the historical Jesus meant nothing to Paul. Schweitzer (*Mysticism of Paul*, 73) says that, compared to Jesus's work on the cross, the miracles are so insignificant that Paul does not mention them. Strauss (*Life of Jesus*, 415) actually argued in the other direction and said the minimal references in the epistles cast doubt on the historicity of the miracle traditions in the Gospels. Note the brief comments by Holzbrecher, *Paulus und der historische Jesus*, 144–45.

103. E.g., Matheson, "Historical Christ," 1:274; Wenham, "Story of Jesus," 305–9; Evans, "Eclipse of Mythology," 21; Schlatter, *Theology of the Apostles*, 191; Twelftree, *Miracle Worker*, 255–56; Barnett, *Paul*, 21; Pokorný, "Words of Jesus," 3459. Dawson (*Healing, Weakness*, 207) says it is a "near-certainty" that Paul knew of Jesus's miracles, though Paul was more concerned with Jesus's suffering. Eddy and Boyd (*Jesus Legend*, 209–10) write that the similarities between Jesus's and Paul's healing ministries are not coincidence. Twelftree's earlier work (*Name of Jesus*, 60–77) makes a case for Paul's knowledge of Jesus's miracles and argues that exorcism and miracles were indeed significant for Paul. While not

middle are those who view such knowledge and allusions as uncertain but possible.[104] Some studies are particularly important.

Dawson focuses on the perspectives of healing held by Mark, Luke, and Paul, treating each writer individually before comparing their views.[105] Her section on Paul is naturally the most important for our purposes. While she writes that it is likely Paul knew of Jesus's miracles, she argues that Paul did not highly value miraculous healing and instead focused on showing compassion within the midst of suffering and hardship—suffering that Paul felt especially keenly because of his own unhealed illness.[106]

Wenham's *Paul: Follower of Jesus or Founder of Christianity?* is a comprehensive argument for the close relation between Jesus and Paul. Almost every conceivable point of connection is explored, including a section on miracles, where Wenham argues that it is probable that Paul knew about Jesus's miracles and worked at some level in imitation of them.[107] Both Jesus and Paul have a ministry of "'word' and 'deed'" but in some sense recognize as problematic the need for "signs" in order to believe.[108]

Yeung's study is written within the context of the Jesus-Paul debate and examines the significance of faith for both figures, specifically in relation to miracles.[109] She has detailed sections on methodology and backgrounds and argues for both historical and theological continuity between Jesus and Paul. She identifies faith in Jesus's ministry as believing in Jesus's person as one sent from God with the power to heal. In Paul, this has transitioned to faith in the resurrection as the ultimate miracle.[110] In terms of backgrounds, she shows that in Jewish thinking the concepts of healing and salvation went hand-in-hand and argues for a connection between Jesus's healing and the restoration of the impure and alienated into the people of God.[111]

Nielsen's study, while not specifically within the Jesus-Paul debate, usefully considers the understanding of healing in the early church with a particular focus on proclamation.[112] Nielsen addresses Jesus's healings, Jesus's understanding of

---

addressing the Jesus-Paul debate, Smith (*Jesus the Magician*, e.g., pp. 35, 110) notes similarities between Jesus and Paul using his model of magicians. Similarly, Ashton (*Religion of Paul*, 72) argues that both Jesus and Paul should be considered "shamans."

104. Theissen and Merz (*Historical Jesus*, 299) note that the miracles of Jesus can be known from Paul's letters only indirectly and suggest some reasons for this. Eve (*Healer from Nazareth*, 82–84) treats a knowledge of the miracle tradition as possible.

105. Dawson, *Healing, Weakness*.

106. Ibid., 207.

107. Wenham, *Follower of Jesus*, 351–53.

108. Ibid., 353.

109. Yeung, *Faith in Jesus and Paul*.

110. Ibid., 282, 294.

111. Ibid., 194.

112. Nielsen, *Heilung und Verkündigung*.

those healings, and their connection with proclamation in Jesus, for both the historical Jesus and the Gospel writers. The author has a section on Paul's miracles, where he discusses all the key texts and argues that, as for Jesus, miracles for Paul were connected with the proclamation of the gospel and eschatological realities.[113]

Conclusion to Literature Review

As can be seen from this review, the Jesus-Paul debate has been addressed from a variety of helpful angles over the years, and the miracles of Jesus especially have been studied thoroughly. While the miracles of Paul have received relatively less attention, there is still a good foundation on which to build. It will be our task now to draw together what is helpful from all this work and apply it to our question of the presence and significance of miracles within the ministries of Jesus and Paul.

---

113. Ibid., 210.

CHAPTER 2

Signs of Gracious Inclusion

This chapter will argue that, for Jesus and Paul, miracles both *accompanied* their message of gracious inclusion and in some sense *realized* the gracious inclusion of God that both figures proclaimed. After treating Jesus and Paul, we will compare both figures and look for any family resemblance.

The Miracles of Jesus as Accompanying His Message

Before we can discuss the significance of Jesus's miracles, we must first consider the historicity of Jesus as a miracle worker. We will then consider how Jesus's miracles accompanied his message.

The Historicity of Jesus as a Miracle Worker

The majority of scholars studying the historical Jesus agree that Jesus performed what were considered healings and exorcisms.[1] This view is held even by those who might not accept the supernatural on philosophical grounds or who view the miraculous as something historical methods cannot assess. Rather, what is accepted is that Jesus's contemporaries *believed* he performed healings and exorcisms. For example, Ehrman writes that, regardless of one's philosophical view, what cannot be denied is that Jesus had a reputation for performing miracles.[2]

---

1. For a summary of this consensus, see Keener, *Miracles*, 1:22–27. Specifically, Eve, *The Jewish Context of Jesus' Miracles*, 16–18; Dunn, *Jesus Remembered*, 670–71. Theissen and Merz (*The Historical Jesus*, 281) summarize: "Just as the kingdom of God stands at the centre of Jesus' preaching, so healings and exorcisms form the centre of his activity." Nielsen (*Heilung und Verkündigung*, 16, cf. pp. 8–20) says of the tradition, "Dennoch muß es als unwahrscheinlich bezeichnet werden, daß in der kurzen Zeit, um die es hier geht, eine so umfassende Überlieferung über die Heilungstätigkeit Jesu hätte entstehen können, wenn nicht das Heilen ein Teil der Tätigkeit gewesen ist, die der irdische Jesus ausgeübt hat." See also Smith, *Jesus the Magician*, 14; Borg, *Jesus: A New Vision*, 65–67; Crossan, *The Historical Jesus*, 303–10, 332; Sanders, *Historical Figure of Jesus*, 144–54; Twelftree, *Jesus the Exorcist*, 136–42; Vermes, *Religion of Jesus*, 206; Keener, *Historical Jesus*, 241–42. Even Bultmann (*Jesus and the Word*, 172–74) accepted Jesus as an exorcist and healer. A minority would downplay miracles, however (e.g., Funk, *Honest to Jesus*, 253).

2. Ehrman, *Jesus: Apocalyptic Prophet*, 199. As Chilton ("An Exorcism of History," 233) writes, "The historical question centers fundamentally on what people perceived, and how they acted on their perception; the question of how ancient experience relates to modern experience is a distinct, interpretive matter."

Because the same consensus does not extend to the so-called nature miracles, we will focus only on exorcisms and healings in this study.[3]

The chief reason healings and exorcisms are regarded so highly in terms of historicity is their pervasive place in the tradition, with Dunn calling their presence in the tradition one of the most secure aspects we have of the historical Jesus.[4] As Meier indicates, using what we might call the "traditional" criterion, that Jesus was a miracle worker, is *multiply attested* in all the Gospel *sources*, in summaries of each Evangelist, and in Josephus; it is also *multiply attested* in *forms*.[5] This leads to a strong argument from the *criterion of coherence*—all the evidence "fits" the picture of Jesus as someone who performed works that were viewed as miraculous.[6] The criteria of *discontinuity, embarrassment,* and *rejection/execution* also play a supporting role in fleshing out this portrait of Jesus.[7] It can even be said that Jesus attracted so much attention due to healings and exorcisms.[8] Meier's oft-quoted summary is worth another hearing: "Put dramatically but with not too much exaggeration: if the miracle tradition from Jesus' public ministry were to be rejected *in toto* as unhistorical, so should every other Gospel tradition about him."[9]

The preceding paragraph uses what might be considered the "traditional" criteria of historical-Jesus study, framed essentially for us by Meier.[10] Yet because of the variety of ongoing discussions concerning which criteria are most helpful—and indeed even whether the whole concept of criteria is useful—it is worthwhile to consider briefly some issues raised by the usage of these criteria generally.[11]

---

3. For some of the unique challenges presented by the so-called nature miracles, see Meier, *Mentor, Message*, 874–80; Eve, *Healer from Nazareth*, 145–60. Cf. Keener, *Miracles*, 1:536–99.

4. Dunn, *Jesus Remembered*, 670.

5. Meier, *A Marginal Jew*, 2:619. Gospel sources, e.g.: Mark 4:35–5:43; Q 7:1–10; M 17:27; L 5:1–11; John 2:1–11. Summaries, e.g.: Matt 19:2; Mark 3:7–12; Luke 8:2–3; John 6:2: Josephus, *Ant.* 18.63–64. Forms beyond summaries, e.g.: miracle stories (Mark 1:23–28); sayings (Luke 13:32); parables (Mark 3:27); pronouncement stories (Mark 2:1–12). Gospel of Thomas records Jesus's command for his disciples to perform miracles of healing (14:4), plausibly implying that Jesus too had the power to heal (cf. 31:2; 35; 44; 48). On the likely authenticity of Josephus calling Jesus a παραδόξων ἔργων ποιητής, see Whealey, *Josephus on Jesus*, passim; Whealey, "*Testimonium Flavianum*," 573–90; Vermes, "Jesus Notice," 1–10; Meier, *Roots of the Problem*, 56–69; Paget, "Some Observations on Josephus," 539–624. For later accusations of magic, see Origen, *Cels.*1.28, 68; b. Sanh. 43a.

6. Meier, *A Marginal Jew*, 2:622–23. Cf. Theissen and Merz, *Historical Jesus*, 298–301.

7. Meier, *A Marginal Jew*, 2:623–28. Miracle workers were not so pervasive that such a portrait need be fabricated if untrue; passages such as Mark 3:22 show, embarrassingly, that some attributed Jesus's power to demons; miracles probably contributed to both his fame and opposition, leading to his death. For more relevant criteria, see Evans, "Life-of-Jesus Research," 21–33.

8. E.g., Allison, *Jesus of Nazareth*, 49; Sanders, *Historical Figure*, 154.

9. Meier, *A Marginal Jew*, 2:630. Even those who see problems with the criteria (e.g., Keith and Le Donne, eds., *Jesus, Criteria, and the Demise of Authenticity*) should acknowledge the pervasive evidence for Jesus as a miracle worker. One who does is Allison (*Constructing Jesus*, 17–20), who advises looking to the big picture of Jesus's life and uses the evidence for Jesus as an exorcist for an example.

10. For discussion of his choices in using various criteria, see Meier, *Roots of the Problem*, 167–95.

11. E.g., Porter, *Criteria for Authenticity*, 17–123; Theissen and Winter, *Quest for the Plausible Jesus*; Keith and Le Donne, *Demise of Authenticity*, passim; Allison, *Constructing Jesus*, 10 n. 52.

A key criterion for authenticating miracles in the Jesus tradition is the criterion of *multiple attestation*, because the single most-convincing evidence for Jesus's being regarded as a miracle worker is the sheer number of miracle reports about him and how these reports are scattered across so many streams of tradition.[12] Yet this criterion has come under fire from some quarters. For example, Goodacre argues that this criterion is flawed because of the uncertainties regarding Q, the relationship between Mark and Q, the independence of Thomas, and a contradiction with the *criterion of embarrassment*.[13]

Yet while uncertainties about source criticism and synoptic relationships are of course just this—uncertain—the majority view on synoptic relationships remains. And as long as we are not seeking absolute certainty in the application of criteria (impossible to obtain in any case), the broader spread of a feature across traditions is still—all things being equal—stronger in terms of historical plausibility. Goodacre himself notes the general preferability of a tradition that is widespread across early sources.[14]

More interesting is his argument that the *criterion of multiple attestation* stands in contradiction to the *criterion of embarrassment*. His point is that, if the Christians held something to be embarrassing, it is strange that they would repeat it additional times. Thus, perhaps these events are not as embarrassing as we might assume. An example here is the case of Jesus's baptism by John, which is generally treated as an embarrassing feature that the Christians would not invent but also an event that is multiply attested.[15] This is an interesting point, but it is not one that should make us mechanically dismiss either criterion out of hand. For example, an event from Jesus's life could indeed have been considered embarrassing in some respects, but the event could have been of such importance for other reasons that it still ended up being broadly remembered.[16] Again, Jesus's baptism by John comes

12. Meier (*A Marginal Jew*, 2:967) puts it like this: "As we saw in our global survey of Gospel miracles, the single most important criterion for judging that the historical Jesus was viewed as a miracle worker by his contemporaries was the criterion of the multiple attestation of sources."

13. Mark Goodacre, "Criticizing the Criterion," 154.

14. "When historians say that they prefer traditions that are attested in a variety of different sources, they are stating the obvious. As a general principle, no one seriously prefers ill-attested late traditions to well-attested early ones. When historical-Jesus scholars appeal to the criterion of multiple attestation, they are, on one level, behaving as one would expect sane historians to behave. They are drawing attention to the best evidence, looking for multiple, early, independent attestation of traditions about Jesus with a view to setting up the bedrock for a strong reconstruction. In principle, the criterion of multiple attestation is simply a statement of sound historical method. On the face of it, there ought not to be any controversy here" (ibid., 152).

15. Ibid., 166.

16. Goodacre (ibid., 166–67) acknowledges this but says the objection is based on a conservative old-fashioned view of the Gospel writers as "archivists rather than authors" and that the objection is countered by the clear examples of Gospel authors omitting features of the tradition. These points are also fair, but still, there could be plenty of reasons a feature of the tradition could be both embarrassing at some level and still important enough to retain. These tensions are not sufficient to lessen the weight of multiple attestation completely.

readily to mind in this regard. So while Goodacre's arguments are important to consider, it seems best to take them as chastening a blunt, mechanical application of the *criterion of multiple attestation* rather than banishing it completely. The line of thought associated with the use of this criterion still has its value.

Among the traditional criteria, the most blatantly problematic is double dissimilarity, where one seeks aspects of Jesus that are unique against both the backdrop of Judaism and the later Christian movement. As is often discussed, a rigorous application of this criterion ends up giving us a portrait of Jesus utterly disconnected from both (1) the Jewish world and Scriptures, both influences with which a Jewish prophet of restoration would naturally orient themself; and (2) the Christian movement, which saw itself as a direct outgrowth of the ministry of Jesus.[17]

A variety of scholars have suggested refinements of this criterion to make it more helpful. Theissen and Winter use the concept of plausibility—in contrast to dissimilarity—and speak of "contextual plausibility" in terms of Jewish backgrounds and "plausibility of historical effects" in terms of the later Christian movement.[18] Within "contextual plausibility" are the subcategories "contextual appropriateness" and "contextual distinctiveness," which essentially are concerned with continuity and discontinuity.[19] Within "plausibility of effects" are the subcategories "source coherence" and "resistance to tendencies of the tradition," which, again, we might classify as essentially continuity and discontinuity.[20] Wright similarly argues for a double dissimilarity and double similarity.[21] Somewhat distinct is Holmén's continuum approach, which explicitly looks for Jesus's effect on early Christianity.[22] In another approach, Allison writes that, after we can establish a general pattern in the traditions about Jesus, we must consider that pattern against both Judaism and the later Christian phenomena.[23] Yet Allison eventually abandons

17. Probably the best treatment of this criterion across the history of Jesus studies is Theissen and Winter, *Plausible Jesus*, 27–171. Particularly fascinating is their appendix, which compiles definitions and discussions of this criterion from Martin Luther on down through the centuries (pp. 261–316).

18. Ibid., 172. They also write: "What we know of Jesus as a whole must allow him to be recognized within his contemporary Jewish context and must be compatible with the Christian (canonical and noncanonical) history of his effects" (p. 212, emphasis removed).

19. Ibid., 211. The first subcategory means that what Jesus did must make sense within the Judaism of that day, and the second subcategory means that what Jesus did must make him able to be identified as an individual within the Judaism of that day.

20. "Those elements within the Jesus tradition that contrast with the interests of the early Christian sources, but are handed on in their tradition, can claim varying degrees of historical plausibility" (ibid., emphasis removed).

21. Wright, *Jesus and the Victory of God*, 131–33.

22. Holmén, "Continuum Approach," 1–16; cf. Holmén, ed., *Jesus in Continuum*.

23. "Above all, I believe that once recurrent attestation highlights a theme or motif, we should seek to interpret that theme or motif in the light of early Judaism, and in such a way that helps us make sense of what we otherwise know about Christian origins. If we can credibly do all that, we are likely getting a glimpse of Jesus" (Allison, *Constructing Jesus*, 21).

the traditional criteria completely and employs what we might call a "big picture" approach that finds in the most general impressions the safest repository of human memory.[24]

All of these suggestions are helpful, and each alternative approach helps us view the material from a different angle.[25] And yet the classic criterion of dissimilarity can still serve a purpose—as long as we recognize it to be a significantly "higher bar" of evidence and recognize that it works well positively but not negatively.

In light of all this, I will continue to use the "traditional" criteria of authenticity in these discussions—but with: (1) an awareness of the benefits brought to bear by some of these recent nuances, especially refinements to the criterion of dissimilarity; (2) the wisdom of Allison's approach in which broad patterns found within the tradition are brought to bear; (3) a reminder that the criteria must not be applied mechanically, and (4) the realization that the application of criteria will never get us "assured results" that will bring complete certainty—least of all across the entire field in a kind of united opinion. But the value of the criteria remains—they are not perfect tools, but they are useful tools nonetheless. In my judgment, an example of an effective recent work that essentially makes use of the traditional criteria is Bock and Webb's *Key Events in the Life of the Historical Jesus* (2009).[26]

---

24. Ibid., 10 n. 52. He helpfully illustrates his approach like this: "Modern medical experiments supply an analogy to my approach. Even a perfectly devised double-blind, randomized trial counts for little if taken by itself. What matters is replication. And for highly controverted issues, what finally matters is meta-analysis, the evaluation of a large, bundled number of individual studies, including those with possible design flaws. The tendency of the whole is what instills conviction, not any one trial or single piece of evidence. Why should it be any different with research about Jesus? We should, at least initially, be looking at macrosamples. We are rightly more confident about the generalities than about the particulars. We are more sure that Jesus was a healer than that any account of him healing reflects a historical event, more sure that he was a prophet than that any one prophetic oracle goes back to him. When the evangelists generalize, in their editorial comments, that Jesus went about teaching and casting out demons, these are, notwithstanding the redactional agendas, the most reliable statements of all" (ibid., 19). Scot McKnight favorably discusses Allison's views and says: "If what the memory remembers is the 'gist,' then the overall trends of the Gospels are more or less what Jesus did and what he said" ("Why the Authentic Jesus Is of No Use," 183). The portrait of Jesus as a miracle worker certainly falls into this category of something widespread in the Gospels.

25. These alternative approaches also are especially useful for our specific interest, namely, the influence of Jesus on Paul in terms of miracle working. Here is an area in which a continuity or continuum approach will be critical. Specifically in terms of Jesus, because miracle working is present in early Christianity, we do not automatically then have a reason to discount the presence of miracle working among the Jesus traditions. The emphasis on miraculous phenomena in early Christianity is plausibly an effect of the historical Jesus on the early church. Yet at the same time we must also wrestle with miracle working present in antecedent Judaism, since the influence on Paul could come from this part of the continuum instead of purely from Jesus.

26. Bock and Webb, eds, *Key Events in the Life.* In his chapter on method, Webb ("Historical Jesus Enterprise," 72) helpfully points out that the application of the traditional criteria is more an art than a science. In terms of some dependence on the traditional criteria within the context of the Third Quest, I would also judge Gerry Schoberg (*Perspectives of Jesus*) to be successful—which is of course one reason this study is explicitly modeled on his method.

The Miracles of Jesus as Accompanying His Message

Looking very broadly, the remembered works of Jesus in the tradition are chiefly two—teaching/preaching and healing/exorcising.[27] Setting aside the passion narratives, infancy narratives, and material about John the Baptist, the bulk of the Gospels consists either of the teaching or miracles of Jesus. All three Synoptic Gospels balance their presentation of Jesus in terms of word and deed, teaching and miracle.[28] John maintains a similar balance, emphasizing the signs that Jesus performed and using them as occasions for instruction (e.g., 6:1–71), but also presenting large blocks of teaching material (e.g., 3:1–15; 7:1–52; 14:1–17:26). Q favors sayings, to be sure, but it also mentions a number of miracles, concerning both Jesus (Q [Luke parr.] 7:1, 3, 6b–9, 10 [?]; 7:18–19, 22–23; 10:13; 11:14–15, 17–20) and the disciples on mission (10:9).[29] Even Josephus calls Jesus a wise man and teacher alongside a worker of remarkable deeds (*Ant.* 18.63).[30] In the end, we cannot excise either Jesus's teaching or healing from his ministry without doing violence to the sources.

Beyond the implicit linking of message and miracle, we have explicit connections drawn between Jesus's ministry of proclamation and miracles. As Twelftree summarizes, Jesus connects his exorcisms with the coming of the kingdom (Luke 11:20 par.), which is generally regarded as his central message. Jesus also connects them with the overthrow of Satan's kingdom (e.g., Mark 3:27 par.), associates miracles with his call to repent (Luke 10:13–15 par.), and sees his uniting of word and deed as indicative of eschatological realities (Luke 7:22 par.). Some miracle narratives are also interwoven with Jesus's teaching, such as the paralytic and friends (Mark 2:1–12 parr.) and the man with the withered hand (Mark 3:1 6 parr.).[31]

While I will take up the significance of these connections later, for now this interconnectedness between miracle and message supports the general picture of Jesus as both a teacher and miracle worker. The evidence for this image is strong. There should be no serious question that Jesus was a teacher who combined his message with what were at least viewed by his contemporaries as miraculous healings and exorcisms.

27. The image of Jesus as a teacher/preacher is also pervasive. See Dunn, *Jesus Remembered*, 696–704.

28. See Twelftree, *Jesus the Miracle Worker*, 95–96, 140, 178. This is not to say the balance is the same among them. Matthew focuses on Jesus as a teacher and downplays somewhat the miracles as compared to Mark. For example, Matthew begins Jesus's ministry with a large block of teaching (5:1–7:29), while Mark has a series of healing narratives (1:21–2:12). Yet Matthew has begun with a summary of Jesus's miracles (4:23–25) and follows up the Sermon on the Mount with healing narratives (8:1–17), and Mark highlights the teaching of Jesus in his opening section (e.g., 1:14–15, 21–22, 38–39; 2:2).

29. Robinson, Hoffmann, and Kloppenborg, eds., *The Critical Edition of Q*.

30. I discuss sources on the authenticity of this in n. 5 above.

31. Twelftree, *Jesus the Exorcist*, 168.

The Miracles of Jesus as Initial Realizations of Gracious Inclusion

Can we go beyond identifying Jesus's miracles as something merely accompanying his ministry? Meier suggests that Jesus's miracles are described as both "signs and realizations of the gracious power of the God of Israel."[32] In this section, we will consider the latter, namely, how Jesus's miracles, in some sense, bring about the aspect of *gracious offer* in Jesus's message of the kingdom.

In ch. 3, we will consider how miracles might serve as authentication, so that is not our interest here. Rather, our concern is the *experiential* aspect of miracles, whereby the recipient of a miracle is affected personally by a positive change that corresponds to the message of God's gracious salvation. This realization is only *initial*, however, because for both Jesus and Paul, as we will discuss in ch. 4, miracles were only *partial* realizations of an eschatological fulfillment in which final consummation was still future. So my attempt in this chapter is to highlight how miracles for both Jesus and Paul allowed God's gracious inclusion to be *experienced* in the personal lives of the recipients. While this inclusion is directly connected to the theme of eschatological fulfillment, we will focus primarily in this chapter on the theme of inclusion and focus on eschatological fulfillment more generally in ch. 4. We will first consider here the nature of Jesus's gracious message of the kingdom, as seen especially in his message of inclusion toward outsiders. We will then consider miracles as they relate to the same theme of gracious inclusion.

Jesus's Gracious Inclusion Seen in the Acceptance of Outsiders

It is generally agreed that the central message of Jesus was the announcement of the kingdom of God within the context of a mission of restoration to Israel.[33] But Jesus did not merely proclaim the kingdom—he also offered it to his hearers in ways that were startlingly gracious.

Traces of this can be seen all over the tradition. The description of God's restoring mercy in Isa 61:1 is alluded to by Jesus (Luke 7:22 par.; 6:20–21 par.) and is said to be cited by him (Luke 4:16–21).[34] Jesus offered forgiveness of sins, and in ways that aroused opposition (Luke 7:36–50; Mark 2:1–12 parr.). The kingdom is offered to the poor, humble, and downtrodden (Luke 6:20 par.; 4:18; 7:22 par.;

---

32. Meier, *A Marginal Jew*, 2:545. Keener (*Miracles*, 1:28) writes similarly: "Jesus presumably intended his miracles as prophetic symbolic actions, hence with some metaphoric significance from the start." On symbolism in Jesus's healings, see Baum: "Die Heilungswunder dienten nicht nur der Legitimation des messianischen und göttlichen Anspruchs Jesu. Sie waren zugleich Teil seiner Botschaft" (Baum, "Die Heilungswunder Jesu," 13). Cf. Richardson, *The Miracle-Stories*, 50–80. On how compassion is insufficient to explain Jesus's miracles, see Eve, *Healer from Nazareth*, 139.

33. E.g., Dunn, *Jesus Remembered*, 506–16.

34. Ibid., 516–17.

Matt 21:31–32). Disciples are called to be radically merciful as God is merciful (Luke 6:27–36 par.; 11:4 par.; Mark 11:25; Matt 18:21–35; Luke 7:40–47). Many parables reflect a gracious and merciful view of God and his interactions with humans (e.g., Luke 7:41–42; 14:16–24; 15:1–32; 18:9–14; Matt 18:23–35; 20:1–16).

Now it is true that Jesus's message was also one of radical discipleship and rigorous obedience (e.g., Matt 5:20; 5:29–30 par.; Luke 14:26–27 par.). Repentance is probably implied in Jesus's message (Mark 2:17 parr.), even where it is not made explicit (as in Luke 5:32).[35] What is remarkable about Jesus's proclamation is how he combines *both* God's gracious forgiveness *and* a requirement of righteousness with a "characteristically radical intensity" (e.g., Mark 9:47 par.; 5:20; Luke 9:62).[36]

Nowhere is the gracious nature of Jesus's message better seen than in his association with elements of society outside the norms of Israelite religion and purity, a pattern cutting across all the traditions and that Borg calls "the politics of compassion."[37] Jesus's easygoing manner of association brought opposition (Luke 7:34 par.).[38] He is remembered as having favorably treated tax collectors (Luke 18:13; 19:7; Matt 21:31–32), disreputable women (Luke 7:36–50 parr.; 8:2), Samaritans (Luke 10:29–37; 17:11–19; John 4:9), and on occasion, Gentiles (Mark 7:24–30 par.; Luke 7:1–10 par.; Mark 5:1–20 parr.). He described himself as a doctor helping the sick (Mark 2:17 parr.) and urged inviting the poor and the disabled to banquets instead of those able to reciprocate (Luke 14:12–14). He put forward surprising models for would-be kingdom participants, such as children (Matt 18:1–5 parr.).[39] Even if one were to dispute some of these specifics, the broad contours of the evidence remain.[40] Jesus's understanding of God as gracious and open, even to the most unworthy, and as understanding that God's graciousness provided the grounds for response and change is multiply attested.[41]

Probably the most noteworthy indicator of Jesus's inclusion of outsiders is his table fellowship with tax collectors and sinners. This prominence has resulted from the fact that the theme has typically been regarded as bedrock in terms of

35. Contra Sanders (*Jesus and Judaism*, 206–8), who argues that Jesus could only cause offense to the authorities if he was accepting sinners without requiring repentance. On repentance in Jesus's ministry generally, see Dunn, *Jesus Remembered*, 498–500. Powell ("Table Fellowship," 930) suggests most tax collectors and prostitutes would be slaves unable to change their lifestyle.

36. Bauckham, "Kingdom and Church," 10 (though he supplies wrong verse references).

37. Borg (*A New Vision*, 131–42) focuses on table fellowship with outcasts, women, the poor, peace, and a spiritualization of righteousness.

38. On the authenticity of this passage and Mark 2:17 par., see Evans, "'Who Touched Me?'" 353–56.

39. Green (*The Gospel of Luke*, 391) calls this "a pronouncement that undermines everything that the Roman world would have taken for granted regarding questions of status and social relations."

40. For example, as Eve (*Healer from Nazareth*, 119) puts it: "It may be that the memory of the sort of things Jesus did is more reliable than the accounts of individual incidents."

41. Bock and Simpson, *Jesus the God-Man*, 91–92.

historicity.[42] First, it is multiply attested (Mark: 2:13–17; [6:30–44]; Q 7:31–35; [13:28–29]; M [21:31b–32]; L 7:36–50; 19:1–10; [10:38–42]; [11:37–54]; [14:1–24]; [15:1–2]).[43] Second, it is also supported by the criterion of embarrassment, in that Christians probably would not invent accusations of Jesus's being a glutton, drunkard, and a friend of the disreputable (e.g., Luke 7:34 par.). Third, support comes from an appropriate criterion of *double-similarity* and *dissimilarity*, in that there is both similarity and dissimilarity with earlier Jewish practices and later Christian practices.[44] On the Christian side, while Christians went on to feature meals as an important part of community life (e.g., Acts 2:42), which at times concerned issues of inclusion (e.g., Acts 10:1–11:18), they focused largely on the Lord's Supper (e.g., 1 Cor 11:20–34) and actually developed the practice of excluding people from these meals (Did. 9:5; 10:6; 14:2).[45] On the Jewish side, while special meals feature prominently, the background material tends to focus on isolation in the context of meals, namely, that purity ought to be maintained while/by eating with the proper people.[46] As Chilton writes, "Meals within Judaism were regular expressions of social solidarity, and of common identity as the people of God."[47]

What exactly is being envisioned by the terms *tax collector* and *sinner*? "Tax collectors" (τελῶναι), or perhaps more properly "toll collectors," were, in Jesus's Galilee, those who contracted to collect indirect taxes.[48] The practice of earning their living by collecting more than required meant they were often considered dishonest and thus outside the bounds of propriety in terms of Jewish religion.[49] This negative association can be seen in the Gospel traditions (e.g., Mark 2:15 parr.;

---

42. Powell ("Table Fellowship," 928) writes: "This is a feature of Jesus' biography that is regarded as historical fact by virtually all scholars, regardless of the level of confidence that they typically place in the historical accuracy of biblical material." E.g., Wright, *Victory of God*, 149, 264; Dunn, *Jesus Remembered*, 526–34; Blomberg, "Authenticity and Significance," 215–50; Borg, *A New Vision*, 131–33; Simmons, *A Theology of Inclusion*, 34–87. Walker ("Jesus and the Tax Collectors," 221–38) and Horsley (*Jesus and the Spiral of Violence*, 212–23) dispute the authenticity of aspects of this material. For responses, see Simmons, *Theology of Inclusion*, 46–66; Schoberg, *Perspectives of Jesus*, 28–37. Dunn (*Jesus Remembered*, 533 n. 216) writes that "Horsley's attempt to rebut the evidence on this point is disappointingly tendentious."

43. Blomberg, "Table Fellowship," 227–43. Brackets mark passages that are suggestive concerning the theme instead of explicit.

44. On this criterion, see, e.g., ibid., 218.

45. Ibid., 218–19. Cf. Sanders, *Jesus and Judaism*, 174–211.

46. On these backgrounds, see Blomberg, "Table Fellowship," 219–27. E.g., Tob 4:17; 1QS 5.13–14: "He should not go into the waters to share in the pure food of the men of holiness, for one is not cleansed unless one turns away from one's wickedness" (Martínez and Tigchelaar, eds., *The Dead Sea Scrolls Study Edition*, 1:81).

47. Chilton, "Ideological Diets," 75.

48. Donahue, "Tax Collectors and Sinners," 48–49; cf. Schoberg, *Perspectives of Jesus*, 48. In Galilee, they would have worked for Antipas, not Rome directly, which would mean that they might not have been considered quislings per se.

49. Blomberg, "Table Fellowship," 227–28. Cf. Simmons, *Theology of Inclusion*, 52–53. For later rabbinic comments, see b. Bek. 31a; t. Demai 3:4.

Luke 3:12; 18:11; 19:8; Matt 21:31), even from Jesus in surprisingly negative ways (Matt 5:46; 18:17), given his goodwill elsewhere.

"Sinners" should probably be understood as referring to lawbreakers and the truly morally reprobate.[50] We can see this in how "sinners" are associated with unrighteousness (e.g., Mark 2:17 parr.), with gluttons and drunkards (e.g., Luke 7:34 par.), and with tax collectors (Luke 7:34 par.), which are spoken of in the same category as prostitutes (e.g., Matt 21:31–32). Yet it is important to note that the term *sinners* could also be a factional term whereby one group would decry a group differing in religious interpretation.[51] For our purposes, the results are similar either way. The "sinners" were outsiders, either through actual disregard of the Law and morality or through a perceived lack of living up to the expectations of some other religious element.[52]

What then was the significance of Jesus's fellowship with sinners and tax collectors? It demonstrated God extending grace toward the unrighteous and outsiders.[53] Blomberg describes it like this: "One could speak of these meals as enacted prophecy or symbolic of the arrived kingdom's surprising inclusions."[54]

Jesus's Gracious Inclusion Initially Realized by Miracles of Healing

How might Jesus's healings and exorcisms enact just such a gracious inclusion? We will consider several ways this might be the case.

The Miracles and a Reintegration of Outsiders into Israel
Some have argued that Jesus's miracles symbolized or actualized a person's restoration to God's people.[55] Kee writes that the miracles redefined faithful Israel in a manner that challenged the conventional norms.[56] Wright explains:

---

50. See, e.g., Sanders, *Jesus and Judaism*, 209–10; Simmons, *Theology of Inclusion*, 85; Keener, *Historical Jesus*, 212.

51. Dunn, *Jesus Remembered*, 528–32. E.g., 1QS 5.7–13. Cf. Neale, *None but the Sinners*, 95–97.

52. Against Smith and Corley, see Schoberg, *Perspectives of Jesus*, 56–62; cf. Smith, *From Symposium to Eucharist*, 232–41; Corley, *Private Women, Public Meals*, 89–93. Cf. Blomberg, "Table Fellowship," 215–50.

53. Simmons, *Theology of Inclusion*, 45, 85–87.

54. Blomberg, "Table Fellowship," 244.

55. Or restoration to God. See Baum, "Die Heilungswunder Jesu," 10.

56. The miracles "implied a redefinition of who the truly faithful community members were" and "did so in such a way as to challenge the guidelines of community definition that prevailed in Judaism in this period" (Kee, *Medicine, Miracle and Magic*, 73). Cf. Remus, *Jesus as Healer*, 32–33; Kvalbein, "The Wonders of the End-Time," 109–10; Eve, *Healer from Nazareth*, 139–40; Crossan, *Jesus: A Revolutionary Biography*, 82–83; Craffert, *Life of a Galilean Shaman*, 291; Baum, "Die Heilungswunder Jesu," 10–11; Yeung, *Faith in Jesus and Paul*, 194. Mack (*A Myth of Innocence*, 238–39) notes that, for Mark, Jesus's miracles cleansed people "by inducting them into the congregation of 'Israel.'" Mark's perspective is potentially very important. This is because, as Eve (see *Healer from Nazareth*, 119) writes, since Mark's theological view might reflect how other people would have viewed Jesus's miracles, Mark's view too

For a first-century Jew, most if not all of the works of healing, which form the bulk of Jesus' mighty works, could be seen as the restoration to membership in Israel of those who, through sickness or whatever, had been excluded as ritually unclean. The healings thus function in exact parallel with the welcome of sinners, and this, we may be quite sure, was what Jesus himself intended.[57]

Support for Wright's point comes from 1Q28a 2.3–11:

No man, defiled by any of the impurities of a man, shall enter the assembly of these; and no-one who is defiled by these should be established in his office amongst the congregation: everyone who is defiled in his flesh, paralyzed in his feet or in his hands, lame, blind, deaf, dumb or defiled in his flesh with a blemish visible to the eyes, or the tottering old man who cannot keep upright in the midst of the assembly; these shall not en[ter] to take their place [a]mong the congregation of the men of renown, for the angels of holiness are among their [congre]gation. And if [one of] these has something to say to the holy council, they shall question [him] in private, but the man shall [n]ot enter in the midst of [the congregation,] because [h]e is defiled.[58]

As Wright notes, while it is not clear how broad this understanding would have been in Jesus's day, this passage shows that at least in Qumran someone suffering from one of these ailments could not be a full member of the community. Jesus's work of healing would thus bring peace to the individual and would bring his or her restoration to Israel.[59] Numerous individuals that Jesus healed fall within these prohibited classes or similar categories: the blind (Matt 9:27–31; 12:22; Mark 8:22; 10:46–52 parr.; Matt 21:14), the deaf and mute (Matt 9:32–33; Luke 11:14 par.; Mark 7:32), lepers (Mark 1:40–45 parr.; Luke 17:11–14), the woman with an issue of blood (Mark 5:24–34 parr.), a woman bound by Satan (Luke 13:10–13), the dead (Mark 5:21–24, 35–43 parr.; Luke 7:11–17), Gentiles (Luke 7:1–10 par.; Mark 7:24–30 par.), and a Samaritan (Luke 17:11–19).[60] To one healed would come not

---

might serve as evidence of how Jesus's actions would be viewed. Stuhlmacher ("Jesus of Nazareth," 293; cf. p. 283) calls both Jesus's table fellowship and healings "messianic symbolic actions." Crossan (*The Historical Jesus*, 303–53) famously pairs Jesus's meals and "magic" as forms of commensality.

57. Wright, *Victory of God*, 191.

58. García Martínez and Tigchelaar, eds., *The Dead Sea Scrolls Study Edition*, 1:103.

59. "This means that Jesus' healing miracles must be seen clearly as bestowing the gift of *shalom*, wholeness, to those who lacked it, bringing not only physical health but renewed membership in the people of Yhwh" (Wright, *Victory of God*, 192).

60. Ibid. Bock and Simpson (*According to Scripture*, 419) note that Matt 21:14 has Jesus healing the blind and lame in the temple, where some would deny them entry (2 Sam 5:8 [LXX]; m. Ḥag. 1.1). Yeung (*Faith in Jesus and Paul*, 192) writes that the leper of Luke 17:16 had two cases of defilement, both as a leper and as a Samaritan. Horsley (*Jesus and Magic*, 131–32, 142) notes that, at least for the evangelist, the healing of a twelve-year-old girl and twelve years of bleeding (Mark 5:21–43

only a restoration to health and communal society but in a religious sense a reintegration into the people of God.[61] This goes hand-in-hand with Jesus's practice of table fellowship.[62]

This line of thought raises several questions, however. First, what kind of exclusion are we envisioning here for the sick and disabled? Were they excluded only from social or religious life (temple worship) on account of purity concerns? Might they also be considered eschatologically excluded? Second, what kind of reintegration to Israel did a healing performed by Jesus entail? Was such a return to the community merely a suggestive symbol or an offer of *potential inclusion* in the kingdom Jesus proclaimed? Or did such a miraculous restoration symbolize the person's *actual inclusion* in that kingdom? Going further, might a healing be seen to *effect* or *bring about* such an inclusion? Third, in what sense would a faithful and obedient Jew, who was maimed, not be a member of the people of God?

These are difficult questions to answer with precision. As mentioned above, some of the exclusions reversed by a healing had to do with issues of purity, which do not concern sin per se and thus might have no bearing on one's eschatological standing.[63] On the other hand, as we will see below, there were strong Jewish links between sickness and sinfulness—so the reversal of some maladies might imply forgiveness and either a gaining of, or testimony to, an eschatological right-standing with God.[64]

It is probably safest to see the situation as varying from case to case and running along a continuum of meaning. *At the very least,* a healing and its accompanying

---

parr.) seems symbolic for Israel's restoration. Both the significance of the number 12, along with the double reference to this detail, point in this direction.

61. Wright, *Victory of God*, 192. Along these lines, Fitzmyer (*The Gospel According to Luke*, 1:747 n. 48) writes that in Jesus's reply to the woman with the flow of blood (Luke 8:48), "an affectionate term is used to reassure her that she is now to be recognized as part of Israel." Evans ("'Who Touched Me?'" 368) likewise comments: "What is interesting in Jesus' pronouncement is the association of salvation (understood not only as deliverance from disease but as restoration to the community) and cleansing from a condition of perpetual uncleanness." Kee (*Medicine, Miracle*, 78) writes that "Jesus is depicted as performing healings and exorcisms in such a way as to open up participation in the group of his followers in circumstances which directly violated the Jewish (and especially Pharisaic) rules of separation."

62. Those who note the parallel between healing and table fellowship include: Evans, "'Who Touched Me?'" 375; Crossan, *The Historical Jesus*, 332; Bauckham, "Kingdom and Church," 7; and seemingly Rescio and Walt, "There Is Nothing Unclean," 69. One possible direct connection is Simon the Leper (Mark 14:3 par.). Since a leper could not have typically received guests, Simon must have been healed, possibly by Jesus (so Evans, *Mark 8:27–16:20*, 359; Bauckham, *Jesus and the Eyewitnesses*, 53). Another possibility is the feeding of the five thousand, since Matthew, Luke, and John say Jesus had healed the people (Matt 14:14 // Luke 9:11, John 6:2), and Mark may imply it (6:13, 31–34).

63. Though the relationship between impurity and sin is debated by scholars, and it is possible to see similarity or overlap between the defilement of impurity and the defilement of sin. See Klawans, *Impurity and Sin in Ancient Judaism*, passim; Kazen, *Jesus and Purity Halakhah*, 200–339. For example, impurity and sinfulness are essentially combined at Qumran, e.g., 1QH 19.10–11 (ibid., 208). On purity generally, see deSilva, *Honor, Patronage, Kinship and Purity*, 241–315.

64. E.g., perhaps, Mark 2:1–12 par.; Luke 13:11–16.

social-cultic reintegration would demonstrate the graciousness of Jesus's kingdom offer and be an experiential sign of God's favor—to which the recipient could either respond or fail to respond.[65] *Going further*, a healing could at times be seen as more than an offer, and particularly to one who had come to Jesus in faith, could be seen to symbolize or to effect a forgiveness of sins and kingdom inclusion.[66] We will accordingly use the concepts "reintegration" or "restoration" in Jesus's healings broadly, allowing a variety of nuances in differing instances.

As for a maimed-yet-pious Jew, we do see a tradition of righteous sufferers, as in the case of Job, which shows that the righteous could indeed suffer sickness. Yet the case of Job also illustrates the perception that such a disability could have within the community—his friends assume something is amiss spiritually (e.g., Job 4:7–8; 22:4–5). So in fact, a disabled person could conceivably be an actual member of the people of God, in that he was truly faithful and pious, yet his position could still *look* religiously and socially ambiguous, since the masses might judge him to be a sinner. So how should we think of Kee's and Wright's statements above about healing bringing restoration or reintegration into the people of God? We should probably qualify these statements by understanding the restoration as most basically *perceptual*—in that the one healed would be delivered from a somewhat ambiguous spiritual situation in the eyes of the community. Perhaps the individual was pious originally, perhaps not. In either case, a healing would bring social-cultic reintegration and remove the possible stigma of sin associated with illness or disability.

Kee notes, returning to the main lines of my argument, that if Jesus had merely performed these miracles in a way as that challenged the Jewish ways of thinking about inclusion and definition of the covenant people, he probably would have evoked some resistance but could have been dismissed as an outsider himself. Yet what raised the stakes for Jesus was that he claimed to perform these miracles in continuity with the Old Testament Scriptures, as in his reply to John's messengers (Luke 7:22 par.).[67]

This response to John's messengers deserves attention, since it holds the possibility of giving us an understanding into Jesus's view of his own miracles. Good arguments can be made for the reliability of the tradition. These include:

---

65. Twelftree (*Miracle Worker*, 272) summarizes Wright in a way that is similar to what we suggest: "These healings would have been seen as part of a total ministry of welcome that went with the inauguration of the kingdom" (cf. Wright, *Victory of God*, 190–91). These cases would be parallel with Jesus's table fellowship, which, while a sign of gracious inclusion, might not mean Jesus would finally accept everyone who ate with him (e.g., perhaps, Luke 13:26; 14:1). It would also be parallel with the nine lepers of Luke 17:11–19, who do not return with gratefulness. On this passage, see Meier, *A Marginal Jew*, 2:703.

66. E.g., perhaps Mark 2:1–12 par.; 10:46–52 par. That faith was usually a prerequisite to Jesus's healings and not a consequence of a healing (e.g., Mark 5:34 par.) might support this stronger sense.

67. Kee, *Medicine, Miracle*, 79. Wedderburn ("Paul and Jesus," 140) similarly points out that one offensive aspect of Jesus's table fellowship was how he claimed to act by God's authority.

(1) Christians would not likely invent a story that shows John the Baptist doubting that Jesus is the Messiah; (2) Jesus's response is not explicit in terms of high Christology; and (3) no favorable reply is included from John the Baptist.[68] The Jesus Seminar's claim that, because Old Testament citations are involved this must be a later Christian apologetic is faulty because it forces Jesus, a Jewish prophet of restoration, to be disconnected from the Jewish Scriptures, which anticipated just such a restoration.[69] Would not a Jewish prophet of restoration understand his purposes in light of Old Testament predictions, both broadly and specifically?

Accordingly, Jesus's answer to John's question is given in terms of Old Testament expectation. Jesus's response primarily invokes Isa 35:5–6 (the blind, lame, and deaf) and 61:1 (the poor), though Isa 29:18–19; 42:7, 18; and 26:19 (the dead) may be involved.[70] If Jesus was performing the deeds expected in the time of fulfillment, then indeed Jesus was the expected one—though Jesus had come with less judgment than John had expected (cf. Luke 3:9 par.).[71] Rather, Jesus's gracious proclamation meant that the blessing of God was available for all, even the lowly.[72]

What healing expectation did Isaiah envision? It is possible that the anticipated healings were figurative for a restoration needed by national Israel.[73] If so, this would not lessen my point. As Jesus applied prophecies of figurative national restoration in literal ways to individuals, they would experience restoration to God's people in a tangibly gracious way. Yet we are probably wrong to force an either/or choice between literal healing and a figurative restoration, since the symbolism could certainly work in both directions.[74]

So we see from this passage that in Jesus's thinking, his proclamation of good news apparently went hand in hand with the miracles he performed, miracles embodying and partially realizing the grace of God associated with eschatological fulfillment. This resulted in a variety of outsiders experiencing blessings that

68. See, e.g., Dunn, *Jesus Remembered*, 447–50; Meier, *A Marginal Jew*, 2:130–37; Twelftree, *Miracle Worker*, 271. Hägerland, *Jesus and the Forgiveness of Sins*, 194–96. Contra Sanders, *Jesus and Judaism*, 136–40, 172; Funk and Hoover, *The Five Gospels*, 177–78, 302.

69. See ibid. Schoberg (*Perspectives of Jesus*, 267) calls this "a classic example of an invalid use of the criterion of dissimilarity."

70. Pao and Schnabel, "Luke," 299 (though they wrongly cite Isa 35:3–4). That these expectations were current can be seen from 4Q521 2 II.

71. Bock and Simpson (*According to Scripture*, 261) write: "In effect, Jesus is answering positively by describing his activity as evidence that the expected era is present, as the language of Scripture shows." Cf. Hägerland, *Jesus and the Forgiveness of Sins*, 199; Hieke, "Q 7,22," 175–87.

72. As Evans ("'Who Touched Me?'" 375) writes, this "envisioned the extension of blessing and restoration to all Israel, including the poor and the outcast."

73. As argued by Kvalbein, "Wonders of the End-Time," 87–110.

74. As Rodríguez ("Re-framing End-Time Wonders," 236–37) argues: "Jews could express their hope in the restoration of Yhwh's faithful in terms of miraculous healings, and/or the presence of miraculous healings could herald the restoration of Yhwh's faithful." In our case, we would only need to add that Jesus's understanding of the "faithful" could be surprisingly broad.

conveyed God's welcome and helped remove their ambiguous position as members of the community of God's faithful people.

The Miracles and Links between Sin and Sickness

Another fruitful line of investigation to see how the miracles of Jesus might realize the gracious inclusion he proclaimed is, as mentioned above, to consider how sin was connected to illness in Jesus's day. This explains why some of our evidence deals with issues of sin alongside sickness, and even how the same phrase, "your faith has saved you," can be used for both physical restoration and, at times, spiritual restoration.

First, as Yeung writes, according to the Hebrew emphasis someone could not be sick in body without also being sick in the soul—a holistic state of wellness would only be possible when one was right with God.[75] This means that a person with a right standing with God should be healthy in body. Hogan argues that Exodus contains the most significant Old Testament passage about sickness, which advances just such a view:[76]

> There the Lord made for them a statute and a rule, and there he tested them, saying "If you will diligently listen to the voice of the Lord your God, and do that which is right in his eyes, and give ear to his commandments and keep all his statutes, I will put none of the diseases on you that I put on the Egyptians, for I am the Lord, your healer." (15:25b–26, ESV)

It is true, Job's story is somewhat a counterpoint in acknowledging that the righteous sometimes suffer and not all illness comes from sin.[77] But this is no real overthrow of the principle, since in the end Job is finally restored, complete with a double portion.[78]

In keeping with Exod 15:26, elsewhere in the Old Testament, the concepts of sin, sickness, forgiveness, healing, and salvation are intertwined, with various kinds of literal, associative, and metaphorical overlap. So in Num 21:4–9, God heals those who have been bitten by poisonous snakes, a healing that functions as the external mark of his forgiveness.[79] In the Prophets, healing (רָפָא) often occurs in contexts of undoing the consequences of God's judgment (e.g., Isa 19:22; 30:26), and Israel is often described as sick and injured (e.g., Isa 1:5–6; Hos 5:13). The concepts

---

75. Yeung, *Faith in Jesus and Paul*, 99. So also Hogan, *Healing in the Second*, 3.

76. Ibid., 4.

77. Ibid., 25. E.g., Job 9:15–21; 42:10. Though sometimes virtue is rewarded with healing only in the messianic age (ibid., 307, cf. 75–76, 89–91), e.g., 1 En. 96:1; Jub. 23:29–30; cf. Isa 65–66.

78. Because a double payment was required for wrongdoing (Exod 22:7, 9), this might be a hint from the author that God had indeed wronged Job (ibid., 21–22).

79. Yeung, *Faith in Jesus and Paul*, 118.

of injury, sin, healing, and restoration are especially clear in Jeremiah (e.g., 3:22 [cf. Hos 14:5]; 6:7, 14; 8:11, 21–22; 15:18; 30:12–13, 17; 46:11; 51:8–9). "Incurable" (לְאֵין מַרְפֵּא) is used to describe both literal sicknesses (2 Chr 21:18; cf. Deut 28:27, 35) and apostasy (2 Chr 36:16; cf. Jer 8:15; 14:19; 19:11; Prov 6:15; 29:1).[80] While 2 Sam 5:8 says that "the blind and the lame shall not come into the house," in the Targum it is rephrased as "the sinners and the guilty will not enter the house."[81]

At the end of his study of illness and healing in the Second Temple period, Hogan summarizes by saying illnesses were connected to a variety of influences in addition to a person's relationship with God (Exod 15:26). These include: (1) God for his own purposes, (2) intermediaries of God, (3) evil spirits, (4) astral bodies, and (5) sin.[82] The most common source for illness, however, was sin.[83] Hogan likewise writes that means of healing were several: (1) faith and/or prayer, (2) virtuous living or repentance, (3) exorcism or apotropaic measures, (4) physicians and folk remedies, and (5) magical or quasi-magical remedies.[84] Yet behind all these, God was seen as the ultimate source.[85]

It is thus no surprise to see an alignment between the concepts of healing and salvation in Jewish thinking.[86] Jeremiah uses both terms (רָפָא and יָשַׁע) in synonymous parallelism (17:14), conceptually God's eschatological salvation is described as healing in Isa 30:26 and 33:24, and in Isa 53:3–5 healing is pictured as going hand-in-hand with forgiveness.[87] Physical healing also accords with salvation and forgiveness in other texts.[88] Yeung summarizes:

> As God is the ultimate author of sickness, illness is perceived as an unfavourable plight from which man needs to be saved by God. In the case of the sinner, this is accomplished through the gracious forgiveness of God. In the case of the innocent sufferer, he is saved by the Lord who hears his prayers and intervenes to deliver him from evil forces. In this sense, healing and salvation refer to the same incident.

80. Brown, "רָפָה," *TDOT* 13:598.

81. Evans, "'Who Touched Me?'" 371; Staalduine-Sulman, *The Targum of Samuel*, 510.

82. Hogan, *Healing in the Second*, 312, 302–5. His examples include: (1) Tob 11:14–15 (1:3 tells the reader the blindness is not from sin); (2) 2 Macc 3:25–29; (3) Josephus, *Ant.* 8.46–49; (4) Treat. Shem 2:7; and (5) Sir 38:9–15.

83. Ibid., 304. Cf. Hägerland, *Jesus and the Forgiveness of Sins*, 180.

84. Hogan, *Healing in the Second*, 306–10. His examples include: (1) Aristides, *Sacr.* 70–71; (2) T. Zeb. 5:1–5; (3) Josephus, *Ant.* 8.46–49; (4) Sir 38:1–15; and (5) T. Job 46–47.

85. Hogan (ibid., 312) concludes: "The difference between what brings illness and what brings healing is this: the causes of illness are not necessarily related to sin, though they frequently are. The means of healing, however, are closely related to their source. Those means are sometimes unusual but their source is, nonetheless, the same, the One God of Israel."

86. The phrase Yeung (*Faith in Jesus and Paul*, 116–31) uses is "the inseparability of healing and salvation." See also on this Thompson, "Signs and Faith in the Fourth Gospel," 100.

87. Yeung, *Faith in Jesus and Paul*, 118–19.

88. E.g., 4QProNab; 2 Macc 3:24–40; 1 En. 96:1, 3; Wis 16:5–14; Aristides, *Sacr.* 70–71. For a discussion of these texts and more, see ibid., 120–30.

Healing emphasizes the recovery experienced by the sick person while salvation stresses the mighty act of God in delivering him from the state of illness into the state of well-being.[89]

The significance for this study is that, in Jewish thinking, sickness was often associated with sin, and healing was usually associated with God. This means there would be a natural association between physical healings and a gracious restorative act of God in Jesus's ministry.[90]

Thus, sickness and healing are sometimes connected with sin and forgiveness in the Gospels.[91] In the healing of the paralytic, there is an association between Jesus's power to forgive and Jesus's power to heal (Mark 2:1–12 parr.).[92] The perspectives of the populace on this connection are made explicit in John 9:1–2, though Jesus rejects this thinking in that case.[93] By contrast, John 5:14 would seem to support a connection in Jesus's mind between sin and sickness.[94] Additionally, Evans notes that, while the blind and lame are often not treated negatively in the Gospel tradition (most likely under the influence of passages such as Isa 35:5–6; Jer 31:8), connotations of prejudice can be detected by how they are said to be going into the kingdom ahead of the healthy (Luke 14:15–24; 16:19–31). This is presented as a surprise and a reversal of what would have been expected.[95] There is one final point to note. We have in the Gospel traditions a significant threefold connection between healing, the term *salvation*, and faith in Jesus's ability to heal (e.g., Mark 5:25–34 parr.; 10:46–52 parr.; Luke 17:11–19).[96] This further highlights how the miracles of Jesus helped initially realize the gracious inclusion he proclaimed.

89. Ibid., 131.

90. For example, Crossan (*The Historical Jesus*, 324) says when Jesus "with a magical touch cured people of their sicknesses," he "implicitly declared their sins forgiven or nonexistent."

91. Yet, similar to the perspectives above, Jesus does not always connect sickness to sin (e.g., Luke 13:16).

92. For supporting texts with connections between repentance, healing, and forgiveness of sins, see Hogan, *Healing in the Second*, 249 n. 32. For discussion of the historicity of Mark 2:1–5, 11–12 and general related themes, see Hägerland, *Jesus and the Forgiveness of Sins*, 179–249. While John Christopher Thomas (*The Devil, Disease and Deliverance*, 146) is correct that there is no explicit connection between sin and sickness here, it is implied because healing and forgiveness are parallel.

93. See Hägerland, *Jesus and the Forgiveness of Sins*, 182–83. Yet, on how Luke 13:1–5 and John 9:1–7 do not show Jesus rejecting a general correlation between sin and sickness, see ibid., 181–83. For arguments that Jesus in John 9:1–2 actually does not reject a link between sickness and sin, see Thompson, "Signs and Faith," 104.

94. See Hägerland, *Jesus and the Forgiveness of Sins*, 184.

95. Thus, as Evans ("'Who Touched Me?'" 371) writes: "Implicit is the assumption that the sick and impoverished represent the nonelect." This assumption also seems to be operative in Luke 13:1–5 (Craffert, *Galilean Shaman*, 289).

96. See Yeung, *Faith in Jesus and Paul*, 53–195; cf. Hägerland, *Jesus and the Forgiveness of Sins*, 201.

Conclusion on Jesus

We have seen it is reasonable to believe that Jesus's miracles realized the gracious inclusion he proclaimed—that inclusion itself being an aspect of eschatological fulfillment. First, we saw that Jesus's gracious message was exemplified by his table fellowship with tax collectors and sinners. Second, we saw that the miracles of Jesus had a similar function of demonstrating and realizing gracious inclusion in the kingdom. This realization can be seen in how many of those healed would have been considered religious and social "outsiders" (in various senses), as well as in how sickness carried connotations of sinfulness in both Hebrew thinking and the Gospel traditions. As a recipient experienced a healing, he or she personally experienced the kind of gracious inclusion that was the hallmark of Jesus's ministry. It was still only an *initial* realization, because a miracle did not mean automatic spiritual restoration or participation in the kingdom—but it was nonetheless significant. Wright is again helpful: "The effect of these cures, therefore, was not merely to bring physical healing; not merely to give humans, within a far less individualistic society than our modern western one, a renewed sense of community membership; but to reconstitute those healed as members of the people of Israel's god."[97]

The Miracles of Paul as Accompanying His Message

We now turn to Paul. This section will discuss the historicity of Paul as a miracle worker before arguing that miracles accompanied Paul's message in a significant way. While references to miracles within Paul's undisputed letters are not numerous, they are sufficient to demonstrate the importance of this aspect of ministry.

The Historicity of Paul as a Miracle Worker

While the historical evidence for Jesus as a miracle worker is strong, in some ways, the evidence for Paul is even stronger. This assessment comes via criteria that we may frame similarly to the traditional criteria of historical-Jesus study.

First, we have what we might dub a *criterion of a known first-person claim*. In two undisputed letters, we have from Paul the claim to have been the channel of miraculous deeds. Moving chronologically, we first have the concluding section of Paul's "fool's speech" in 2 Cor 12. Paul writes that he is not inferior to the super-apostles, and then explains why: τὰ μὲν σημεῖα τοῦ ἀποστόλου κατειργάσθη

---

97. Wright, *Victory of God*, 192. Yet, again, we need to qualify this statement in that the restoration would be most basically *perceptual*.

ἐν ὑμῖν ἐν πάσῃ ὑπομονῇ, σημείοις τε καὶ τέρασιν καὶ δυνάμεσιν (12:12). Here, the "signs" of an apostle (potentially more broad than miracles) are said to have been accompanied by "signs" (specifically miraculous), wonders, and miracles.[98] Paul writes of these miracles in a threefold description that views them from different angles: as authentication (σημείοις), as creating amazement (τέρασιν), and as showcasing spiritual power (δυνάμεσιν).[99] While Paul leaves ambiguous the nature of these miraculous deeds—a point we will discuss below—he does not shrink, when pressed, from claiming their presence in his ministry. As Thrall argues, Paul's point is clearly that he worked miracles among the Corinthians, and these miracles should serve as signs of authentication for his apostolic ministry.[100] The same can be said about Rom 15:18–19, which we shall discuss below.

While there are other more ambiguous passages where Paul might allude to miracles performed through him, 2 Cor 12:12 and Rom 15:18–19 should be considered clear.[101] Here we have letters whose authenticity almost no one doubts, where Paul claims the experience of miracles in his ministry. The significance of this is notable. One only needs to imagine how important we would deem a letter that had unquestioningly been written by Jesus, in which he discusses his miracles!

It would also be rare in what has come down to us from the ancient world. If one surveys the miracle stories relevant to our period, it is difficult to find cases where (1) the author of a document claims to have performed a miracle personally, and (2) the authorship of the document is considered authentic.[102] For that matter, it is difficult to find first-person accounts of even *witnessing* a miracle worker where, again, authorship is considered secure.[103]

---

98. See BDAG 920, 999, 263. The datives are likely datives of means (so Harris, *Second Epistle*, 876). This implies that, for Paul, miracles did not constitute *all* the signs of an apostle. As Twelftree (*Paul and the Miraculous*, 217) shows, Paul also stresses other aspects of apostleship: seeing the Lord (1 Cor 9:1; 15:8–9), enduring hardship (2 Cor 11:23–27), and churches resulting from his apostolic efforts (1 Cor 9:2; 2 Cor 3:2; 1 Thess 2:19–20).

99. Harris, *Second Epistle to the Corinthians*, 875.

100. Thrall, *Second Epistle to the Corinthians*, 2:839. It is thus difficult to understand the claim made by Betz (*Der Apostel Paulus*, 71): "Ein klares Zeugnis dafür, daß Paulus Wunder getan hat, liegt daher nicht vor." Even if the slogan "signs of an apostle" is that of the opponents, Paul adopts it and claims he is not deficient. Goulder (*Competing Mission*, 251) suggests miracles are not in view but that Paul reinterprets the terms to refer to suffering; he also says, "Healings and other signs are not performed 'in all endurance'" (so also Schmithals, *Office of Apostle*, 36–37). One wonders why that cannot be the case, but more importantly, ἐν πάσῃ ὑπομονῇ likely modifies the working of τὰ σημεῖα τοῦ ἀποστόλου, which is probably a broader category than just miracles. Interestingly, Schreiber (*Paulus als Wundertäter*, 219–21) suggests ἐν πάσῃ ὑπομονῇ is a reminder of present hardships despite inaugurated eschatology.

101. 1 Thess 1:5; Gal 3:5; 1 Cor 2:4; 4:20; and 5:3–5 are open to question.

102. Empedocles might be a possibility. See *Diog. L.* 8.58–59, 62.9, 62; Inwood, *Poem of Empedocles*, 211, 219. But the interpretation of Empedocles's words is open to question, and authorship would probably be judged not as secure as Paul's letters. See Blackburn, Theios Anēr, 51–52.

103. Near misses include: (1) Josephus's description of Eleazar's exorcism before Vespasian (*Ant.* 8.46–48); (2) inscriptions from Asclepius shrines such as Epidaurus; (3) supposed records of Damis in Philostratus's *Vit. Apoll.*; and (4) Aristides's *Sac. Tales*. These unfortunately fall short because:

This does not "prove" Paul performed genuine miracles, of course. People lie, distort, or show themselves deceived all the time. Yet the quality of witness is important in evaluating any claim, miraculous or otherwise, and firsthand testimony is preferable whenever possible. Dunn highlights Paul's first-person witness: "That miracles took place within Paul's ministry and the Pauline churches, just as in Jesus' ministry and that of the early Palestinian communities, there can be no doubt. We have the first hand testimony of Paul himself, the only assuredly eyewitness accounts we possess."[104]

To this we may perhaps add a *criterion of easy falsification*. This is similar to the criterion of embarrassment and concerns accounts that would be so easy to disprove if untrue that the authenticity of the accounts is strengthened. 2 Cor 12:12 is again the prime example. When Paul writes that the signs of an apostle were done among the Corinthians, and that this consisted in part of miraculous deeds, he was writing in a defensive mode. The very presence of 12:11–12 suggests his apostolicity was being challenged (in part) by accusations that he lacked such flashy miraculous signs (at least by degree?)—but he gives no ground to his opponents on the issue (cf., by contrast, 11:6).[105] He assumes his claim to have performed miracles among them cannot be denied.[106] Naturally, it would be hazardous to appeal to such knowledge if the miracles had not occurred.[107] Here is strong evidence that

---

(1) whether Josephus actually witnessed the exorcism is unclear because of the ambiguous meaning of the word ἱστόρησα (Duling, "Eleazar Miracle," 21); (2) inscriptions of healing at Epidaurus are a bit secondhand, since they were apparently inscribed (and reinscribed) by the priests of the temple and were based on various votive offerings combined with oral tradition (see LiDonnici, *Epidaurian Miracle Inscriptions*, 40–49); (3) *Sac. Tales*, while fascinating and fairly certain first-person accounts, do not present a miracle-working human. The god acts directly and usually through the actions of Aristides (e.g., 4.30). It is also sometimes hard to differentiate between the miraculous and the medicinal (Kee, *Miracle in the Early Christian World*, 94). This is similar to the rest of our Asclepius accounts; and (4) the biography by Philostratus is of dubious reliability, since he writes so late, and the supposed firsthand account of Damis is likely fabricated (see Jones, introduction to *Philostratus*, 5–6). Kee (*Miracle in the Early Christian World*, 256) writes, "The material allegedly drawn from Damis is so full of historical anachronisms and gross geographical errors that one could not have confidence in Damis as a reporter if there actually were a diary." Returning to Empedocles, we do have claims to have witnessed wonders, but still not exactly firsthand. Rather, we have a fragment in Diogenes Laertius from Satyrus's *Lives*, where Satyrus reports that one Gorgias of Leontini claimed to have seen Empedocles practice magic (γοητεύοντι); see *Diog. Laert.* 8.58–59; Blackburn, *Theios Anēr*, 51–52. Interestingly, several "we passages" in Acts suggest that the author is an eyewitness to miracles wrought by Paul (Acts 16:16–18; 20:7–15; 28:1–9), but of course the authorship of Acts is disputed.

104. Dunn, *Jesus and the Spirit*, 210.

105. Furnish, *2 Corinthians*, 555.

106. Jervell ("Signs of an Apostle," 78) writes, "It is certain that despite the opinion of his opponents, Paul actually claims the signs of an apostle; it is certain also that he maintains these signs have been universally and publicly known; and finally, that these signs are not at all less extraordinary than those of other apostles."

107. Matera (*2 Corinthians*, 289) states: "It is difficult to imagine Paul making such a statement about himself if God had not effected miraculous signs through him, since the Corinthians had firsthand knowledge of his ministry among them." Gal 3:5 offers a similar appeal to the presence of miracles in the experience of Paul's recipients. Keener (*Miracles*, 1:30) writes: "That Paul appeals to his

Paul and his audience would agree on some kind of miraculous phenomena as having occurred in Paul's ministry to them.

We can also talk about a *criterion of multiple attestation* for Paul as a miracle worker. Acts records Paul performing miracles, both in actual narrative mode (seven accounts: 13:4–12; 14:8–10; 16:16–18; 19:13–20; 20:7–12; 28:1–6; 28:7–8) and in summary sections (14:3; 15:12; 19:11–12; 28:9), using even the same terminology (σημεῖα καὶ τέρατα [14:3; 15:12]; δυνάμεις [19:11]). Interestingly, three of these miracles occur within the "we passages," a fact that presents the author as an eyewitness (Acts 16:16–18; 20:7–15; 28:1–9).[108] If all we had were Acts, it might be possible to dismiss these descriptions as legendary accretions, but we have Paul claiming the same phenomena in his own undisputed letters. In fact, since Acts does not record Paul performing miracles in Corinth, we might judge that Acts embellishes less than some suspect.[109]

The Miracles of Paul as Accompanying His Message

In 2 Cor 12:12, Paul claims to have performed or experienced miracles as part of his ministry among the Corinthians. What can we say about the extent of this phenomenon?

Here the most important passage is Rom 15:18–19, where Paul describes his ministry in programmatic terms to a church he has never visited: οὐ γὰρ τολμήσω τι λαλεῖν ὧν οὐ κατειργάσατο Χριστὸς δι᾿ ἐμοῦ εἰς ὑπακοὴν ἐθνῶν, λόγῳ καὶ ἔργῳ, ἐν δυνάμει σημείων καὶ τεράτων, ἐν δυνάμει πνεύματος [θεοῦ]. Paul claims the acts of speaking and doing that Christ accomplished through his ministry were performed "by the power of signs and wonders."[110] We have the same three words for miracles

___

audiences' eyewitness knowledge that miracles occurred through his ministry (2 Cor 12:12; cf. Gal 3:5) argues against deliberate fabrication on his part; he genuinely believed that miracles were occurring through his ministry, and that his audiences in locations like Corinth would have agreed with him." On Rom 15:18–19a, Cranfield (*Epistle to the Romans*, 2:759) writes that Paul's claim to have performed miracles "is difficult to brush aside." He quotes Lagrange (*Saint Paul*, 352), who says of Rom 15:18–19 and 2 Cor 12:12, "Il faut beaucoup d'audace pour le taxer d'illusion ou de mensonge." Barnett (*Second Epistle*, 580 n. 16) writes: "Here is clear evidence that God used Paul as an instrument of miraculous works. To make this statement in an almost gratuitous manner to readers who were, to say the least, unsympathetic is strong reason for believing that such miracles did occur. No one knew better than Paul that to make claims that were untrue would be a sure way to discredit him as a charlatan."

108. On using the first person, see Keener, *Acts*, 3:2363–74.

109. See Matera, *2 Corinthians*, 289. Rom 15:18–19 suggests miraculous phenomena occurred everywhere Paul ministered. Keener (*Miracles*, 1:96; cf. 1:30) writes: "Paul's letters indicate that he anticipated signs even more widely than Luke claims them for him." On how Acts actually downplays Paul as a miracle worker, see Jervell, "Signs of an Apostle," 79–87.

110. Taking ἐν as instrumental. Goulder (*Competing Mission*, 252–53) argues that the two negatives mean Paul was listing what in fact *he did not do*, thus denying miracles. Goulder says Barrett (*Epistle to the Romans*, 1991], 253) is an exception to the verse's usual mistranslation, but while Barrett translates the two negatives, Barrett still understands a reference to Paul's miracles and thus does not support Goulder's ultimate argument. Goulder's view results in the peculiar case of Paul listing what he did

as in 2 Cor 12:12, though the usage of δύναμις might be different here in Romans because we have the singular instead of the plural as in 2 Corinthians. The idea is of God's power being manifested via signs and wonders.[111] If in 2 Cor 12:12 we get the impression that Paul only grudgingly mentioned the presence of miracles in his ministry, here his tune is quite different.[112] His emphasis is positive, on the power of God, by which such charismatic wonders formed a central activity in his churches.[113] The fact that his entire ministry is in view can be seen from the geographic references of Jerusalem to Illyricum (15:19). It appears that Paul thought that miracles took place in essentially every place he preached the gospel.[114]

Corroboration comes from 2 Cor 12:13, where right after claiming that miracles had occurred among them (12:12), Paul asks how they were worse off (ἡσσώθητε) than the rest of the churches. The implication is that miracles had accompanied Paul's work in his other churches as well, and that the Corinthians knew it.[115] For further support, we may add Gal 3:5 and 1 Cor 12:9–10, 28–30, where Paul takes it for granted that various miraculous phenomena occur among the ordinary people of his churches.[116] These texts make these phenomena in the planting of Paul's churches even less surprising.[117]

Schreiber agrees that in Rom 15:19 (and 2 Cor 12:12) Paul refers to miracles, yet Schreiber still argues that Paul downplayed miracles and did not consider them important.[118] Twelftree says this view largely comes from how Schreiber excludes the disputed passages from referring to the miraculous (1 Thess 1:5; 1 Cor 2:4; 4:20; 2 Cor 6:6–7). He goes on to argue that these passages do refer to the working of miracles, and thus he sees Paul as putting a much higher value on the miraculous.[119] Though Twelftree is probably right in seeing these disputed passages as actually referring to miracles (and we will return to some of these passages later in the study), the significance of miracles to Paul should remain even if one rejected these passages.[120] Romans 15:18–19 (along with 2 Cor 12:12) should be sufficient to carry

---

not do in a description of his ministry. Far more likely is that everything Paul describes is what Christ wrought through him. On the grammar of the sentence, see Cranfield, *Romans*, 2:758. Betz (*Der Apostel Paulus*, 71) says the verse refers not to miracles but to "das Wunder der Evangeliumsverkündigung." Yet this seems to go against Paul's cluster of words associated with miracles, especially since Paul offers no reinterpretation that would point to something that was not essentially miraculous.

111. Moo, *Epistle to the Romans*, 893 n. 54. Moo is following Godet, *Epistle to the Romans*, 2:373.

112. See Dunn, *Romans*, , 2:863; cf. Jacob Jervell, "Der schwache Charismatiker," 189; contra Schreiber, *Paulus als Wundertäter*, 279.

113. Jewett, *Romans*, 911.

114. Keener, *Miracles*, 1:30.

115. González, "Healing in the Pauline Epistles," 572–73.

116. A point Fee (*God's Empowering Presence*, 887) makes from Gal 3:5.

117. See also Ashton, *Religion of Paul*, 210.

118. Schreiber, *Paulus als Wundertäter*, 207–8, 234, 274–82.

119. Twelftree, *Paul and the Miraculous*, 11, 179–225.

120. The references to the Holy Spirit and to power are least *consistent* with the occurrence of miracles because miracles are closely related to both concepts (cf. Rom 15:19). The only exception might be 1 Cor 2:4 because of 1:22. But see ibid., 197.

the point that miracles accompanied Paul's ministry in a way that he perceived to be significant.

Beyond rejecting a reference to miracles in debatable passages, why do some scholars see Paul downplaying miracles? There is the possibility that some have minimized Paul's experience of the miraculous because they have more readily considered Paul a thinker or theologian.[121] But there is textual evidence too.

First, we have Paul's infrequent mention of miracles. Is this not evidence against Paul's giving miracles an important place in his ministry? In response, we must first remember that Paul's letters are occasional, and the proportion to which a theme appears in his letters may have more to do with the needs of his congregations than with Paul's actual emphases.[122] Related to this is the pattern of *when* Paul brings up his miracles—at times when his apostleship is under fire or in need of support.[123] This link may actually increase how important we perceive miracles to be for Paul.

A second response concerns an additional pattern in which Paul unambiguously discusses his miracles—the context of "not boasting."[124] The claim in 2 Cor 12:12 comes at the end of the "fool's speech," where Paul discusses what he would never boast of (καυχάομαι) except under duress (e.g., 2 Cor 12:5–6). The same language is used in Rom 15:17–19, where his only boast (καύχησιν) is what Christ has done through him.[125] Paul is careful to present God as the one working miracles and never claims the power himself.[126] This all suggests that, as González argues, Paul's relative silence may be because of, at least in part, a refusal to glorify himself and his own gifting.[127]

A third response, as Twelftree has argued, is that miracles are actually more widespread in Paul than has often been recognized—especially if we broaden the category of miracles to include phenomena such as tongues, prophecy, protection, and revelatory experiences.[128] We must not forget that Paul is indeed a charismatic and not (simply) a systematic thinker and theologian.[129]

Leaving aside the issue of Paul's infrequent references to miracles, a second argument against the significance of miracles in Paul could be his "theology of the

---

121. As argued by ibid., 3–27.

122. See Jervell, "Signs of an Apostle," 90; González, "Why the Silence," 573.

123. Paul faces a "different gospel" in Gal 3:5, a challenge to his apostolicity in 2 Cor 12:12, and the need to establish his authority in Rom 15:18–19 (Kelhoffer, "The Apostle Paul," 170). Cf. Schreiber, *Paulus als Wundertäter*, 271–72.

124. González, "Why the Silence," 572.

125. Something similar occurs in 1 Cor 12, where Paul resists valuing one gift over others (ibid.). Cf. 1 Cor 1:31.

126. Note the passive in 2 Cor 12:12 and how Christ works through Paul in Rom 15:18–19.

127. González, "Why the Silence," 572.

128. Twelftree, *Paul and the Miraculous*, 313.

129. See ibid., 4–5; Borg, *A New Vision*, 39–51. Cf. Dunn, *Theology of Paul*, 426–34; Ashton, *Religion of Paul*, 198–213; Lincoln, "Paul the Visionary," 204–20. Jervell ("Signs of an Apostle," 172 n. 47) points to: 1 Cor 9:1; 14:18; 15:7–8; 2 Cor 5:13; 12:2–4; Gal 1:12, 16; 2:2.

cross," which we could understand to oppose a "theology of glory" emphasizing miracles and power. Indeed, in 2 Corinthians it is Paul's weakness and suffering that gets more emphasis than miracles. We will return to this in ch. 3. For now, we can simply note that Paul might value both weakness and the divine power seen in miracles.

Third, it is possible to argue that by rejecting Jewish expectation for a "sign" (1 Cor 1:22), Paul shows resistance to an evangelistic ministry that would depend in any sense on evidential miracles. This assessment depends on the understanding of σημεῖα in that passage, as well as the exegesis of 1 Cor 2:1–5, to which we will turn in ch. 3.

Fourth, it is possible to argue that Paul's opponents in 2 Corinthians accused him of being unable to perform miracles. This may be said on the basis of 2 Cor 12:12, where Paul's words can be taken as responding to a charge that he did not perform expected miracles.[130] The main difficulty with this view, of course, is that miracles are exactly what Paul claims in 2 Cor 12:12.[131] Paul thinks he did perform miracles among the Corinthians—miracles which put him at no disadvantage compared to his opponents (cf. 12:11)—and Paul apparently expects the Corinthians to agree with him. To this we may add that nowhere is it explicitly written that Paul's opponents denied his ability to perform miracles.[132] We will return to these issues in chs. 3–5. For now, we only note that there are explanations for the accusations of Paul's opponents in 2 Corinthians apart from Paul's *inability* to perform miracles—and that even if this were the accusation, Paul answers by saying he was not deficient in that regard.

In conclusion, while holding in abeyance some of these disputed issues, at this point we draw attention to Rom 15:15–19 and 2 Cor 12:12–13, with support from Gal 3:5 and 1 Cor 12:9–10, 28–30. In Romans and 2 Corinthians, Paul includes the performance of miracles as significant parts of his ministry, both in general terms to a church he has never met (Romans) and in specific terms to eyewitnesses who are in some sense inclined against him (2 Corinthians). In 1 Cor 12 and Gal 3:5,

---

130. E.g., on 2 Cor 12:12, "The exploits in question were so little out of the ordinary that his opponents flatly denied his ability to perform miracles" (Haenchen, *Acts of the Apostles*, 113, 563). Some see "signs of an apostle" as a key phrase of the opponents (e.g., Käsemann, "Die Legitimität des Apostels," 70–72). Yet the phrase is possibly of Paul's coining as well (e.g., Harris, *Second Epistle to the Corinthians*, 874; Garland, *2 Corinthians*, 529).

131. Contra Schmithals (*Office of Apostle*, 36–37), who sees in 2 Cor 12:12 only "the wondrous effect of the Word." This is not persuasive, however, because, as Furnish (*2 Corinthians*, 556) writes, this would not be the natural way for Paul's readers to take the language (cf. Twelftree, *Paul and the Miraculous*, 209–12). Nor does this suggestion work for Rom 15:18–19, where, as Borgen ("From Paul to Luke," 176) writes, Paul's mention of miracles is unforced. I discuss Paul's terminology below.

132. As argued by González ("Why the Silence," 573) and Jervell ("Signs of an Apostle," 91): "It is notable that while Paul's opponents attack his apostleship, they apparently never accuse him of *not* performing miracles"; "We must emphasize first of all that nowhere is it stated—by Paul or his opponents—that his miracles were less extraordinary than those of the other apostles." Yet to be fair, an accusation concerning Paul's lack of miracles may indeed be implied.

Paul additionally discusses the miraculous as part of the ongoing ministry of his churches. Twelftree states our point from his assessment of Rom 15:18–19 alone: "Despite the paucity of references to miracles in his letters, in this paragraph Paul makes clear that he saw the miracles not only as the basis of his work but also as central to, and profoundly important in, the routine of his ministry."[133]

The Type of Miracles Paul Describes

Now that we have touched on the main Pauline passages, we need to consider what kind of miracles Paul has in mind. The Jesus traditions are fairly clear in describing many of Jesus's miracles as healings and exorcisms. By contrast, as Ashton notes, Paul is "notoriously coy" on the topic.[134] Because it will be important later, we will particularly consider whether healings and exorcisms are referenced among Paul's hints concerning his miracles.

Paul's relatively unambiguous terminology for the miraculous includes: σημεῖον (1 Cor 1:22; 2 Cor 12:12; Rom 15:19); τέρας (2 Cor 12:12; Rom 15:19); δυνάμεις (plural, Gal 3:5; 1 Cor 12:10, 28–29; 2 Cor 12:12; Rom 15:19); and χαρίσματα ἰαμάτων (1 Cor 12:9, 28, 30). That these terms can refer to miracles is well established.[135] That these terms cluster together in our key passages ensures that Paul intended to make reference to the miraculous (2 Cor 12:12; Rom 15:18–19; cf. 1 Cor 12:9–10, 28–30).[136]

But what phenomena does Paul have in mind? At least χαρίσματα ἰαμάτων seems to refer clearly to healings, but unfortunately for our purposes, nowhere does Paul claim this gift or describe a healing he performed.[137] We are left with δυνάμεις, σημεῖον, and τέρας.

---

133. Twelftree, *Paul and the Miraculous*, 222.

134. Ashton, *Religion of Paul*, 169.

135. See, e.g., Rengstorf, "σημεῖον κτλ.," *TDNT* 7:221–25, 240–47, 258–60; Rengstorf, "τέρας," *TDNT* 8:121–26; Grundmann, "δύναμαι κτλ.," *TDNT* 2:301–5, 310–16; Oepke, "ἰάομαι κτλ.," *TDNT* 3:194–215. Related words that may imply the presence of miracles are δύναμις (singular, e.g., 1 Thess 1:5; 1 Cor 2:4; 4:20; Rom 15:19) πνεῦμα (e.g., 1 Thess 1:5; Gal 3:5; 1 Cor 2:4; Rom 15:19) and πίστις (1 Cor 12:9; 13:2). Yet Twelftree (*Paul and the Miraculous*, 26) is probably right to expand Paul's category of miracle to include phenomena such as prophecy and visions. For helpful backgrounds on σημεῖον broadly, see Salier, *Rhetorical Impact*, 18–45.

136. Twelftree (*Paul and the Miraculous*, 211) writes, "It is hardly to be doubted that, in using the phrase 'signs and wonders and mighty works,' Paul had miracles in mind, and that his readers would have taken him to mean miracles."

137. Contrast this with his claim to tongues in 1 Cor 14:18 and, by implication, prophecy in 1 Cor 13:2; 14:3 (Dawson, *Healing, Weakness and Power*, 173). Twelftree (*Paul and the Miraculous*, 205) takes this to mean Paul "was not directly involved" in the gifts of healing or miracles. On the other hand, perhaps, Paul's response to a physical problem in 2 Cor 12:8–9 was to pray for a miracle (ibid., 161). Thomas (*Origins of Illness*, 73) notes that the impression we get is that Paul only stopped praying because he realized it was God's will for the thorn to remain. Phil 2:27 is certainly consistent with miraculous healing, and, of course, some will give weight to the testimony of Acts, which remembers Paul as being involved in miraculous healing (e.g., Acts 20:7–15; 28:1–9).

In 1 Cor 12:9–10, we have the interesting case of Paul's distinguishing χαρίσματα ἰαμάτων from ἐνεργήματα δυνάμεων. This suggests that, at least in this passage, δυνάμεις must refer to "mighty deeds" distinct from healings. The term could be general, referring to a variety of miracles that would not fall under the umbrella of healings.[138] It may, however, be more specific and refer to exorcisms—a case where the presence of divine δύναμις would indeed be highlighted.[139] We should also note that the distinction in this passage perhaps should not be pressed into a technical differentiation everywhere, since it is possible Paul might elsewhere consider miraculous healings to fall under the term δυνάμεις.[140]

As Twelftree writes, probably the most important background for Paul in using the paired terms σημεῖον and τέρας would be the LXX usage, where the words refer to the miracles connected with Moses whereby God brought Israel out of Egypt.[141] Baruch 2:11 even adds δύναμις (yielding σημείοις καὶ ἐν τέρασιν καὶ ἐν δυνάμει μεγάλη), which ends up being close to Paul's usage of the three terms in 2 Cor 12:12 (σημείοις τε καὶ τέρασιν καὶ δυνάμεσιν).[142] This LXX usage might even cast a tone of national salvation, and even restorative eschatology, over the terms as Paul uses them.[143] At first consideration, then, Paul might be envisioning miracles such as were manifested during the exodus.[144]

If all we had were Paul's letters, we would not really be able to define these miracles, be they salvific acts of God as in the exodus or perhaps merely dramatic phenomena accompanying conversion experiences. Here, being informed by broader Christian tradition is helpful. This is because we have all three key terms used in other streams of early Christianity to refer to Jesus's miracles and the apostles' miracles, which notably included healings and exorcisms.[145] In light of this association

138. So also Fee (*Empowering Presence*, 169), including exorcism (Fee, *First Epistle*, 659 n. 137).

139. Debatable is whether δυνάμεων is subjective or objective, with the latter option understanding δυνάμεων as referring to evil spirits (see Thiselton, *First Epistle*, 952–53). As Tibbs (*Religious Experience*, 206) writes, though, taking it as "power over evil spirits" is possible in either case. Many understand it as exorcism; Thomas (*Origins of Illness*, 41–42) says a majority. E.g., Dunn, *Jesus and the Spirit*, 210. Grundmann (*TDNT* 2:315) writes: "The δυνάμεις are obviously acts of power invading the kingdom of demons. In δυνάμεις demonic forces are resisted and vanquished." Twelftree (*In the Name of Jesus*, 74–76) argues that it is wiser to not be specific and that exorcism would be inappropriate in a list of gifts building up the church. He does think it likely that Paul included exorcisms in 2 Cor 12:12 (ibid., 68).

140. Fee (*Empowering Presence*, 169) writes that Paul probably would include gifts of healing under the umbrella of δυνάμεις, though they are distinguished here.

141. Twelftree, *Paul and the Miraculous*, 210. E.g., Exod 7:3, 9; 11:9, 10; Deut 4:34; 6:22; 7:19; Pss 77:43 [LXX]; 103:27 [LXX]; Wis 10:16; Jer 39:20–21 [LXX]; Bar 2:11.

142. Ibid.

143. A significance to which we will return in ch. 4.

144. I.e., plagues and authenticating signs (e.g., Exod 4). Alternatively, Paul might use these terms from the exodus to color different types of miracles with allusions to the exodus.

145. All three terms together: Acts 2:22; 6:8; 2 Thess 2:9 (negative, and arguably Pauline); Heb 2:4. Τέρατα and σημεῖα together: Acts 2:43; 4:30; 5:12; 14:3; 15:12; Mark 13:22 par. (negative); John 4:48 (negative). Σημεῖον alone: Luke 23:8; John 2:11, 18, 23; 3:2, 4:54; 6:2, 14, 26, 30; 7:31; 9:16; 10:41; 11:47; 12:18, 37; 20:30. Of course, other kinds of miracles are also said to be performed by Jesus and his

among early Christians, and of how Paul shows himself at points connected to early Christian tradition,[146] it is probable that Paul would have envisioned miracles like healings and exorcisms through his use of the terms δύναμις, σημεῖον, and τέρας.[147] Twelftree argues that, because Paul's readers most likely knew of Jesus's miracles being called "signs and wonders," this language on Paul's lips makes it likely that the readers would interpret Paul's words to include the kinds of miracles known from the Jesus traditions, namely, exorcisms and healings.[148] Very significantly, these are miracles that Acts remembers Paul as performing (e.g., 16:16–18; 28:8–9). Yet because we cannot know on the basis of Paul's letters only, this study will avoid making a case dependent on Paul's performing either healings or exorcisms specifically, and leave the Pauline category "miracle" somewhat broader.

The Miracles of Paul as Initial Realizations of Gracious Inclusion

We have seen that arguments for the historicity of Paul's miracles are strong and that Paul himself writes of miracles accompanying his ministry in significant ways. Can we go beyond this and say that Paul's miracles in some sense realized the gracious inclusion he proclaimed, as in the case of Jesus? We will first consider Paul's ministry as it was performed without mention of miracles.

Paul's Gracious Inclusion as Seen in the Acceptance of Gentiles

As Barclay writes, the problem with the topic of grace in Paul is choosing what to select and highlight among the numerous potential references.[149] Yet here we are particularly interested in Paul's focus on including outsiders, chiefly Gentiles.[150]

---

followers, including resuscitations (Mark 5:21–43 par.; Acts 20:7–12); nature miracles (Mark 6:45–52 par.); punishment miracles (Mark 11:12–14 par. [arguable]; Acts 13:4–12); and miraculous protections (Luke 4:30 [arguable]; Acts 28:3–6).

146. See Schoberg, *Perspectives of Jesus*, 123–26. E.g., 1 Cor 11:2, 23–26; 15:1–5, 16:22; Gal 4:6; Rom 8:15.

147. Some accordingly understand that Paul includes healings or exorcisms, e.g.: Remus, *Jesus as Healer*, 98; Turner, *Holy Spirit and Spiritual Gifts*, 252–53; González, "Why the Silence," 572–73; Hogan, *Healing in the Second*, 288; Stuhlmacher, *Paul's Letter to the Romans*, 238; Thrall, *Second Epistle to the Corinthians*, 2:839; Wright, "Letter to the Romans," 754; Jewett, *Romans*, 911. Kee (*Medicine, Miracle*, 1–2) says the terms of 2 Cor 12:12 "presumably include healings" and that this interpretation is assumed by the writer of Acts. Some suggest healing or exorcism as a possibility, e.g.: Furnish, *2 Corinthians*, 556; Bultmann, *Second Letter*, 270–71; Martin, *2 Corinthians*, 437; Garland, *2 Corinthians*, 529; Harris, *Second Epistle to the Corinthians*, 875. Dawson (*Healing, Weakness*, 164, 172, 207) writes that Paul's terms "*may* designate miraculous healing" and then goes on to discuss Paul as a healer.

148. Twelftree, *Paul and the Miraculous*, 212.

149. Barclay, "Offensive and Uncanny," 12. Cf. Dunn, *Theology of Paul*, 319–23.

150. Though other "outsiders" are also recipients of God's grace: the foolish, weak, and ignoble (1 Cor 1:26–29); the poor (Gal 2:10); women and slaves (Gal 3:27); and even persecutors of the church

This theme and its similarity to Jesus has been previously argued by Wedderburn, Simmons, and Schoberg.[151]

Paul's role as apostle to the Gentiles is close to the center of his self-understanding (Rom 11:13; cf. 15:16). It is this focus on Gentiles that he identifies as an integral part of his prophetic and apostolic call (Rom 1:5; Gal 1:16), whether he realized it at that instant purely as revelation or through a mixture of revelation, Christian tradition, and reflection.[152] Accordingly, outreach to Gentiles is the major focus of his evangelism (Rom 1:13; 15:15–17), an area of responsibility recognized by other apostles (Gal 2:7–9), and a source of tension with other Christians (Gal 2:11–21; 5:11–12). For some opponents, Paul's gospel seemed too easygoing on sin (Rom 6:1, 15).[153] Several times, Paul highlights the Gentiles' status as outsiders from God's people, usually in the context of its reversal (Rom 9:25, 30; 10:19; 11:17, 24, 30), a reversal that Paul labored to connect with Old Testament expectation (Rom 9:25; 15:8–12). For Paul, there is soteriological and ecclesiological equality (Gal 3:28; Rom 3:9, 29–30; 10:12)—except for, perhaps, the proud and the strong, who will miss out (1 Cor 1:26–31). As Bruce writes, "Like his Master before him, Paul was a great breaker-down of barriers."[154]

Behind this breaking down of barriers was an understanding of God as radically gracious, merciful, and compassionate. Gentiles were sinners (Gal 2:15) and disobedient (Rom 11:30; cf. 1:18–32). Thus, their inclusion was an act of God's mercy (Rom 11:30, 15:9), especially since they had not been seeking God (Rom 10:19–20; cf. 1:18–32). God saved those who were opposed to him, in the very midst of their opposition (Rom 5:6–8, 10).[155] In perhaps his most audacious framing of the point, Paul describes God as he who justifies the ungodly (Rom 4:5; cf. Exod 23:7 [LXX]; Isa 5:22–23 [LXX]).

Of course, this modeled Paul's own experience, a point to which Paul draws attention several times. Paul the persecutor and opponent (Gal 1:13–14, 23; Phil 3:6; 1 Cor 15:9) had experienced not only the grace of a right standing with God

---

(Gal 1:13; 1 Cor 15:9; Phil 3:6). On the poor, see Longenecker, "Good News to the Poor," 37–65.

151. Wedderburn, "Similarity and Continuity," 117–43; Simmons, *Theology of Inclusion*, passim; Schoberg, *Perspectives of Jesus*, 64–136.

152. Kim (*Origin of Paul's Gospel*, 56–66, 62–63) argues from Gal 1:16 that Paul received his calling to the Gentiles at conversion, though Kim acknowledges from the example of the "Hellenists" in Acts that Paul's outreach to Gentiles was not completely new. As Schoberg (*Perspectives of Jesus*, 118–35) argues, it seems more likely that Paul's understanding developed over time via both tradition and revelation.

153. Wedderburn, "Similarity and Continuity," 135. This opposition is important, because, as Schoberg (*Perspectives of Jesus*, 16) writes, one of the ways to see whether an issue is of central importance for either Jesus or Paul is to see whether they continued in the face of resistance.

154. Bruce, *Paul and Jesus*, 60.

155. As Simmons (*Theology of Inclusion*, 131) writes, "Transcending all barriers to his grace, God expressed loving solidarity with those who were inimical to his person and will."

(Phil 3:9) but the grace of apostolic service (Gal 1:15–16; 1 Cor 15:10).[156] Paul was an outsider who had been brought into God's people—except this outsider had been so far outside he had been unaware of his status. It must have been with special poignancy that Paul wrote, "while we were enemies we were reconciled to God" (Rom 5:10), for Paul had been an enemy *par excellence*.[157] Paul himself experienced the message of inclusion that he preached.

The significance of Paul's message of inclusion to outsiders has only grown because of the New Perspective on Paul. The debate has had the salutary effect of showing that the "presenting problem" Paul faced, in Galatia for example, was not Jews trying to "earn their salvation" by doing good works but rather other Jewish Christians arguing that the distinctives of the Mosaic law should be placed on Gentile Christians (e.g., Gal 3:2–5; 4:21; 5:2, 4; 6:12–13).[158] In other words, the issue was more about ecclesiology than soteriology.[159] Paul was much exercised to show that, because of Christ, both Jew and Gentile were on equal footing with God regardless of the identity markers of the Mosaic law (e.g., Gal 2:12–21). These outsiders were to be included on God's new terms, through connection with the risen Messiah, the "seed" to whom the promise had been made (Gal 3:16–29).

Paul's Gracious Inclusion Initially Realized by the Spirit and Miracles

If, as we have seen, miracles *accompanied* Paul's ministry to outsiders, how did his miracles relate? We will first consider the miracles' relationship to the Holy Spirit and how the Spirit operated for Paul as *realizing* the inclusion of outsiders into God's eschatological people, in that it involved an experiential manifestation of that inclusion. We will also consider whether there are any links in Paul between sin and sickness, as we did with Jesus.

The Spirit and Miracles

How might Paul's miracles have in some sense realized or actualized the inclusion he proclaimed to Gentiles? We are somewhat hampered in our study because Paul

---

156. See where Paul connects his ministry with God's grace: Rom 12:3; 15:15; 1 Cor 3:10; Gal 2:9; and mercy: 1 Cor 7:25; 2 Cor 4:1.

157. As Simmons (*Theology of Inclusion*, 125) writes: "His experience conveyed a God who unconditionally offered his acceptance and one who, in his love, provided the basis for reconciliation irrespective of the moral condition of the recipient."

158. Probably by arguing that the Law of Moses was always binding on God's people, and circumcision was an eternal mark of the covenant (e.g., Gen 17:2–14). E.g., "The subject of Galatians is not whether or not humans, abstractly conceived, can by good deeds earn enough merit to be declared righteous at the judgment; it is the condition on which Gentiles enter the people of God" (Sanders, *Paul, the Law*, 18).

159. Borrowing the expression of Wright (*What Saint Paul Really Said*, 119). This is not to accept all the points raised by the New Perspective on Paul. It may be that Paul gave an essentially "old perspective" answer to a "new perspective" presenting problem. To put it differently, one could plausibly see soteriological implications in an ecclesiological problem.

refers to miracles so infrequently in his letters. Yet we can gain some insight if we expand the discussion to the role of the Holy Spirit more generally, a broader category under which Paul likely understood his miracles to operate.[160]

The connection between the Holy Spirit and miracles is, of course, easy to demonstrate. In 1 Corinthians, Paul attributes gifts of healing (χαρίσματα ἰαμάτων [12:9]) and the performance of miracles (ἐνεργήματα δυνάμεων [12:19]) to the working of the Spirit (12:11), and the Spirit is referred to a total of eleven times within 12:1–13.[161] In Rom 15:19, the power of signs and wonders is parallel to the power of the Spirit (ἐν δυνάμει σημείων καὶ τεράτων, ἐν δυνάμει πνεύματος [θεοῦ]). Something similar occurs in Gal 3:5, where supplying the Spirit and working miracles are parallel (ὁ οὖν ἐπιχορηγῶν ὑμῖν τὸ πνεῦμα καὶ ἐνεργῶν δυνάμεις ἐν ὑμῖν). Only one of our key passages does not mention the Spirit (2 Cor 12:12).[162]

Unsurprisingly, there is for Paul a close association between the Spirit and power (power in the sense of enablement, not social rank). In addition to the previous passages, Jesus himself is said to have been appointed Son of God in power via the Spirit of Holiness (Rom 1:4), and Christian hope could come by the power of the Holy Spirit (Rom 15:13). As far as Paul's experience, his gospel proclamation to the Thessalonians came "in power and in the Holy Spirit" (1 Thess 1:5), and the same was true in Corinth, where Paul's spoke "in demonstration of the Spirit and of power" (1 Cor 2:4). Of course, Paul is not alone in connecting the two concepts of Spirit and power.[163]

On the basis of this evidence for a connection between the Holy Spirit and miracles, any miracles in the ministry of Paul should be understood as specific manifestations (1 Cor 12:7) and workings (1 Cor 12:11) of the Spirit. The significance of this connection for our purposes is that some of the aspects associated with the *Spirit* can thus plausibly be associated with *miracles*. This understands the concept of the Spirit being more *general*, with miracles being more a *specific* subcategory of the Spirit's working.

The Spirit and Gentile Inclusion

Two aspects of the Spirit concern us when asking how miracles might have, in some sense, realized the gracious inclusion of God that Paul proclaimed. The first

---

160. As Jervell ("Signs of an Apostle," 93) states, "For Paul . . . the theme of miracle belongs to pneumatology."

161. "Faith" here also probably has miraculous associations (e.g., Dunn, *Jesus and the Spirit*, 211; Fee, *Empowering Presence*, 168).

162. Here Paul uses an enigmatic passive (κατειργάσθη). The agent of both the "signs of an apostle" and the "signs and wonders and mighty works" goes unnamed, and possibilities include: (1) Paul; (2) either God, Christ, or the Spirit; or (3) an overlap where both Paul and the divine were somehow co-agents (cf. Rom 15:18 where *Christ* worked through *Paul's* words and deeds).

163. E.g., Mic 3:8 (cf. 1 Sam 11:6; Judg 3:10; Luke 1:17, 35; 4:14; Acts 1:8 (Twelftree, *Paul and the Miraculous*, 183). Cf. 1 Cor 5:4.

aspect has to do with the *prominence* of the Spirit in Paul's conception of salvation, and the second aspect has to do with proof of *acceptance* into God's people.

In terms of prominence, Dunn convincingly argues that the three main ways Paul describes the beginning of salvation are justification, participation with Christ, and reception of the Spirit.[164] He shows that, in terms of actual references, reception of the Spirit is the most prominent of the three, with a noticeable consistency across Paul's letters. In Galatians, the presence of the Spirit is central to Paul's argument of Gentile equality (3:5). In 1 Thessalonians, the gospel was received "with the joy of the Holy Spirit" (1:6), and the readers are warned against rejecting God, "who gives his Holy Spirit to you" (4:8). In 1 Corinthians, Paul's preaching and their conversion had been via the work of the Spirit (2:4–5; 6:11, 17; 12:13), and their worship was intensely focused on the Spirit (12–14). In 2 Corinthians, the Spirit is the seal and down payment that ensures inheritance (1:21–22; 5:5) and is central to the era of the New Covenant (3:1–18). In Romans, reception of the Spirit is the defining mark of the believer (8:9) and central to the Christian life (8:14–15). In Philippians, fellowship in connection with the Spirit is a mark of Christian life (2:1), and the Spirit is associated with the circumcision of heart that marks the people of God (3:3).[165]

This means that when we consider the Spirit, we are close to the heart of Paul's gospel. Dunn writes that the Spirit as the center of the growing life of the Christian is a key for Paul's ministry.[166] Fee concurs: "For Paul, therefore, whatever else happens at Christian conversion, it is the experience of the Spirit that is crucial."[167]

Not only is the Spirit prominent in Paul's understanding of the gospel but it also has the function of marking the *acceptance* of those who belong to God in the age of eschatological fulfillment.[168] This can be seen in Romans, where, negatively, "Anyone who does not have the Spirit of Christ does not belong to him" (Rom 8:9), and positively, "all who are led by the Spirit of God are sons of God" (Rom 8:14). The Spirit is even called "the Spirit of adoption," who enables Christians to cry out to God as father and to know they are God's children (8:15). In 1 Thessalonians, all involved could be sure God had chosen the recipients (1:4) as Gentiles (1:9) because Paul's gospel had come to them ἐν δυνάμει καὶ ἐν πνεύματι ἁγίῳ καὶ [ἐν] πληροφορίᾳ πολλῇ (1:5).

---

164. Dunn, *Theology of Paul*, 334–441. Dunn (pp. 442–59) also discusses baptism. All four aspects are of course important: "There is a danger that we subdivide into distinct and discrete elements what Paul simply saw as the same event with differing emphases in differing cases" (p. 455).

165. On all these passages, see ibid., 419–24.

166. "The centrality of the gift of the Spirit in and as the beginning of Christian discipleship is one of the foundational principles of Paul's work as evangelist, theologian, and pastor" (ibid., 419).

167. Fee, *Empowering Presence*, 855. He notes how in Gal 3:2–5; 1 Cor 6:11; 12:13 the Spirit is used as the primary way to describe conversion (p. 854). Cf. Schoberg, *Perspectives of Jesus*, 115.

168. As Fee (*Empowering Presence*, 855) puts it, for Paul, "it is the Spirit alone who identifies God's people in the present eschatological age."

Nowhere, however, is the Spirit's role in Gentile inclusion seen more clearly than in Galatians. In this letter, where Paul's Gentile converts had come under pressure to adopt the distinctives of the Mosaic law, probably with particular reference to circumcision (6:12–13; but cf. 4:10), the presence of the Spirit is a major argument to show the sufficiency of faith in Christ for Gentiles.

Within the central section of 3:1–5:12, Paul refers to the Spirit seven times.[169] At the very beginning of his argument, Paul asks whether they had received the Spirit by "works of the Law" or "hearing with faith" (3:2). The answer is obvious, and Paul describes them as "having begun by the Spirit" (3:3), which included a clear experiential factor (3:5).

In the argument from Abraham in 3:7–14, Paul speaks of the promise of blessing given to Abraham in Gen 12:3 (Gal 3:8). He goes on to say that Christ's redeeming death on the cross (3:13) took place "so that in Christ Jesus the blessing of Abraham might come to the Gentiles, so that we might receive the promised Spirit through faith" (Gal 3:14). The parallelism in this verse suggests that Paul here identifies the promised blessing of Abraham (3:8) with the reception of the Spirit.[170] Accordingly, the Spirit was to remain a central aspect of their Christian lives (Gal 5:5, 16–25; 6:8).

As in Romans, the Spirit is also associated here with sonship: "Because you are sons, God has sent the Spirit of his Son into our hearts, crying, 'Abba! Father!' So you are no longer a slave, but a son, and if a son, then an heir through God" (4:6–7). Here is a powerful statement of inclusion for those who had been Gentile outsiders. Not only were they sons of God, but because they had been born of the Spirit, they were also Abraham's children (4:29).[171]

All of this shows that, for Paul, as Simmons puts it, "the presence of the Spirit among the Galatians was the divine sign authenticating their salvation experience."[172] Yet we can probably say more. Because the coming of the Spirit was something *experienced* (e.g., Gal 3:5, 4:6; Rom 8:15–16), the Spirit was not only a *sign* of their salvation but it was also an experiential manifestation or, as we might put it, in some sense a *realization* or *actualization* of God's gracious inclusion of them as Gentile outsiders.[173]

---

169. The Spirit is mentioned nine additional times after 5:12. Divisions are, of course, debated. Dunn (*Epistle to the Galatians*, 150) and Moo (*Galatians*, 177) take 3:1–5:12 as the central argument. Betz (*Galatians*, 19–23) identifies 3:1–4:31 as the *probatio* and 5:1–6:10 as the *exhortatio*.

170. So also most, e.g., ibid., 152–53; Dunn, *Epistle to the Galatians*, 179–80; Martyn, *Galatians*, 323; de Boer, *Galatians*, 214–15; Schreiner, *Galatians*, 218–19. Moo (*Galatians*, 216) suggests because of the reference to justification in 3:8 that the blessing of Abraham is justification and that reception of the Spirit is a "related but separate" gift. The point for us is much the same—for Paul the Spirit is central to the gospel.

171. Dunn, *Theology of Paul*, 420–21. The Spirit brought soteriological egalitarianism, whether "Jews or Greeks, slaves or free" (1 Cor 12:13).

172. Simmons, *Theology of Inclusion*, 141.

173. See Dunn, *Theology of Paul*, 426–34.

Miracles and Gentile Inclusion

So far, I have argued that, for Paul, miracles were a subset of the Spirit's working, and the presence of the Spirit was a manifestation of God's gracious inclusion of Gentiles. If we put these two arguments together, we see that, for Paul, any miracles performed in his ministry might plausibly function as manifestations and initial realizations of the eschatological grace of God that Paul proclaimed. There are two passages where Paul comes very close to making this connection.

The first passage is Gal 3:5. As above, here Paul begins his argument for Gentile inclusion by focusing on the Galatians' reception of the Spirit, which had come not by works of the law but by faith (3:2). That their conversion is in view can be seen from 3:1, where Paul writes that Christ had been portrayed before them as crucified, and from 3:3, where Paul describes them as having "begun by the Spirit."[174]

In 3:5, Paul asks another question: "Does he who supplies the Spirit to you and works miracles among you do so by works of the law, or by hearing with faith?" (ὁ οὖν ἐπιχορηγῶν ὑμῖν τὸ πνεῦμα καὶ ἐνεργῶν δυνάμεις ἐν ὑμῖν, ἐξ ἔργων νόμου ἢ ἐξ ἀκοῆς πίστεως;). Here, the one who supplies the Spirit is also the one who works miracles among them. Who is the unstated agent? Some suggest Paul himself.[175] Far more likely, however, is God.[176]

What timeframe is in view? The question is complicated by an ellipsis of the finite verb in the sentence—should a present- or past-time verb be understood? Longenecker argues that, because 3:5 is a summary of 3:2–4, aorist verbs should be understood: "Did God, then, give you his Spirit and work miracles among you . . . ?"[177] Further support for action in the past might come from the repetition in 3:5 of ἐξ ἔργων νόμου and ἐξ ἀκοῆς πίστεως from 3:2. If so, the time of their conversion is likely still in view. Of course, one could supply present-tense verbs as well: "does he do so . . . ?"[178] This is probably most natural given that the participles are in the present tense.

In either case, the present tense of the participles probably emphasizes the regular experience of the Spirit and miracles among them, and thus their present experience.[179] This experience should then be understood as a continuation

---

174. Lull (*The Spirit in Galatia*, 54–59) argues for Paul's preaching as the occasion of their receiving the Spirit and its attendant manifestations.

175. E.g., Ashton, *Religion of Paul*, 202. The view of White ("Rhetoric and Reality in Galatians," 333) is of Paul "declaring himself as the benefactor (or 'broker,' perhaps) for their reception of the spirit through his own presentation of the gospel in their hearing."

176. For it is God who gives the Spirit, e.g., Gal 4:6; 1 Thess 4:8; 2 Cor 1:22; Rom 5:5; 8:15 (Betz, *Galatians*, 135). So also most.

177. Longenecker, *Galatians*, 105.

178. Betz, *Galatians*, 136.

179. Betz (ibid., 135) takes both as emphasizing the present. So also Fee, *Empowering Presence*, 387–88; Bruce, *Epistle to the Galatians*, 151.

of what they experienced at their conversion.[180] Twelftree describes it like this: "What happened in the initial coming of the Spirit was part of an ongoing experience."[181]

That Paul intends miracles by his use of δυνάμεις is not to be doubted.[182] What exactly does he envision? Possibilities include deeds of power performed by Paul during his ministry among them (cf. Rom 15:19; 2 Cor 12:12) or deeds of power performed by Galatian believers among themselves (cf. 1 Cor 12:10).[183] Alternatively, one might suggest that both are in view, with God performing miracles through Paul and, after their conversion, through the Galatians.[184] Due to Paul's vagueness, it is difficult to decide.[185] Perhaps the emphasis of the passage makes the working of miracles among the Galatians themselves more likely, though this does not exclude miracles having occurred during Paul's ministry—a fact that would enhance Paul's credibility.[186] Yet the central issue was that they had received the Spirit and that this reception had been demonstrated by some kind of miraculous phenomena.[187]

One important aspect of 3:1–5 is how Paul's questions direct the Galatians to reflect on their own experience. Betz puts it well:

> In every case the answers to the questions are self-evident and need not be recorded. Paul is not only fortunate in being able to question the eye-witnesses themselves, but he also compels them to produce the strongest of all possible defense arguments—undeniable evidence. This undeniable evidence is the gift of the Spirit, which the Galatians themselves have experienced. The gift of the Spirit was an ecstatic experience. Together with the miracles which are being performed at present among the Galatians, this constitutes evidence of supernatural origin and character which is, for ancient rhetoric, evidence of the highest order.[188]

---

180. Moo (*Galatians*, 186–87) takes the first participle as referencing the Galatians' conversion and the second as the ongoing work of the Spirit. Despite supplying aorist finite verbs, Longenecker (*Galatians*, 105) takes the same position.

181. Twelftree, *Paul and the Miraculous*, 189.

182. The pairing of δύναμις with ἐνεργέω indicates miracles, as in Mark 6:14 par.; cf. 1 Cor 12:10, 28; 2 Cor 12:12; 2 Thess 2:9; Acts 2:22 (Betz, *Galatians*, 135 n. 78).

183. De Boer, *Galatians*, 182–83. Fee (*Empowering Presence*, 389) thinks that usage elsewhere suggests "a variety of supernatural phenomena, including healings."

184. So also Bruce, *Galatians*, 151.

185. Nielsen (*Heilung und Verkündigung*, 203–4) concludes it is unclear whether Paul or the Galatians are in view.

186. Contra Twelftree, *Paul and the Miraculous*, 190–91. Schreiber (*Paulus als Wundertäter*, 269) says Paul refers to miracles here, but not his own.

187. As Schreiner (*Galatians*, 186) puts it: "The main point, in any case, is that God had given the Spirit to them, and the presence of the Spirit had been manifested among them by works of power."

188. Betz, *Galatians*, 130.

So, here in Gal 3:5 we have a clear example where Paul interprets miracles as evidence that God's gracious inclusion had been extended to the Gentiles. The very experiential nature of the Spirit's coming—including miracles—is the very basis of Paul's argument.[189] The coming of the Spirit was an initial realization of salvation, made tangible—at least in part—by miracles.[190] This meant that God had accepted them as Gentiles.[191] Though miracles performed by Paul among the Galatians might not be in view, it is likely Paul would see the same significance in miracles that God performed through *him* in ministry to the Gentiles.

Support for this can be seen in Rom 15:18–19. After discussing the "weak" and the "strong" in Rom 14, in 15:1–13 Paul wraps up his argument for unity by focusing on the inclusion of the Gentiles as the great example of Christ's acceptance. While Christ's ministry was to Israel (15:8), it was also in order that Gentiles might praise God for their merciful inclusion (15:9a), as anticipated in the Old Testament (15:9b–12). Paul's prayer is that the Romans, both Jew and Gentile, would be filled with hope via the power of the Spirit (15:13).

From the Gentiles, as examples of God's inclusive grace, Paul moves to his own unique ministry as apostle to the Gentiles (15:14–16). By God's grace (15:15), Paul is "a minister of Christ Jesus to the Gentiles in the priestly service of the gospel of God," with a specific purpose: "that the offering of the Gentiles may be acceptable, sanctified by the Holy Spirit" (15:16). In all of this, Paul pictures himself as a priest offering up the Gentiles as a sacrifice to God.[192] Because Gentiles would be unclean, however, they had to be sanctified before they could be acceptable, a preparation accomplished by the Holy Spirit.[193] As in Galatians, here we see it is the Holy Spirit who at least accompanies, and in some sense effects, the inclusion of Gentiles into God's people.

Miracles come into play in 15:17–19, where Paul continues speaking of Gentiles and the Spirit. He writes that it was Christ acting in him who accomplished his work "to bring the Gentiles to obedience." How had Christ worked through him to bring conversion to the Gentiles? It was accomplished by λόγῳ καὶ ἔργῳ, ἐν δυνάμει σημείων καὶ τεράτων, ἐν δυνάμει πνεύματος (15:19).[194] "Word and deed" probably

189. See Lemmer, "Mnemonic Reference," 383–85.

190. A two-step process is likely in play here. Miracles function as manifestations of the Spirit, with the presence of the Spirit in turn demonstrating their inclusion into the people of God.

191. As Simmons (*Theology of Inclusion*, 140) writes, "The activity of the Spirit among the Galatians meant that God had accepted them as they were."

192. Moo, *Romans*, 890. The genitive is also possibly subjective and referring to an offering the Gentiles were making, perhaps praise (cf. 15:9–11).

193. Thus, Moo (ibid., 891) writes that "it is ultimately God himself, by his Holy Spirit, who 'sanctifies' Gentiles, turning them from unclean and sinful creatures to 'holy' offerings fit for the service and praise of a holy God."

194. Curiously, Twelftree (*Paul and the Miraculous*, 219) says most translations err by translating "through word and deed"; he prefers "Christ accomplished through me … word and deed," apparently taking λόγῳ καὶ ἔργῳ as direct objects. This seems to be without justification.

refers to the two broadest categories of Paul's ministry, what he said, and what he did.[195] While some see a chiasm with the next lines, where the power of signs and wonders corresponds to "deed" and the power of the Spirit corresponds to "word," it is better to see ἐν δυνάμει σημείων καὶ τεράτων and ἐν δυνάμει πνεύματος [θεοῦ] as parallel to each other with *both* describing *both* word and deed.[196]

Here, we see Paul claiming that his ministry of proclamation and action was accomplished by means of, or accompanied by, both miracles and the power of the Holy Spirit—with both phrases closely related. He immediately says within the entire geographical regions of his activity he had "fulfilled the gospel of Christ" (πεπληρωκέναι τὸ εὐαγγέλιον τοῦ Χριστοῦ, my translation). Whatever the exact nuance of this phrase, Paul closely associates the preaching of the gospel with miracles and the Spirit's power.[197]

The significance of this for my argument is the close connection between Paul's ministry to Gentiles and the accompanying power of the Spirit—and miracles. The focus of 15:9–19 has been Paul's ministry to the Gentiles, a ministry enabled by the power of the Spirit (15:19) and the power of miracles (15:19). The result of this Spirit-empowered and miracle-empowered ministry was that the Gentiles were sanctified by the Holy Spirit (15:16). This means the concepts of the Spirit and Gentile inclusion are closely associated with miracles wrought by that Spirit.[198]

From this, it seems likely that Paul's view of the miracles God worked through *him* in the course of outreach to Gentiles would have the same significance as the miracles worked among the *converts* in Gal 3:5. Miracles in both cases would be at least *signs* of the gracious inclusion whereby God welcomed the nations into his people, and insofar as any of the miracles (healings, exorcisms, or the like) affected those to whom Paul ministered, they would also be tangible *manifestations* of that same gracious inclusion. The same would be true of any Spirit-empowered phenomena that would have fallen on the Gentiles at the time of Paul's proclamation or their conversion.[199]

In conclusion, miracles for Paul should be understood as falling within the operation of the Spirit generally. This is significant, for one of Paul's major

---

195. As Jewett (*Romans*, 910) puts it: "On the one hand to words spoken in preaching and teaching, and on the other hand to missionary actions, labors, sufferings, travels, and so on."

196. The chiastic view falters in that it limits Paul's works to signs and wonders and limits the Spirit's power to Paul's words. E.g., essentially for a chiasm: Leenhardt, *Epistle to the Romans*, 369; M. Black, *Romans*, 203. Against: Cranfield, *Romans*, 2:759; Dunn, *Romans*, 2:863; Schreiner, *Romans*, 768.

197. Twelftree (*Paul and the Miraculous*, 223) explains: "For Paul, therefore, (fulfilling or proclaiming) the gospel involves not only words or propositions, but also actions or deeds empowered by the Spirit, in particular miracles."

198. As Grant R. Osborne (*Romans*, 390) puts it, "The Spirit both undergirds everything Paul does, including his miracles, and brings the Gentiles into the sanctifying presence of God (v. 16)."

199. As is perhaps in view in passages such as Gal 3:2; 1 Thess 1:5; and 1 Cor 2:4. In all cases, the Spirit seems to be something *experienced*.

emphases concerning the Spirit was that it both marked out and, in some sense, brought about Gentile inclusion. For this reason, any miracles that occurred during Paul's own ministry or among Paul's converts would be not only evidence for but also tangible experiences of God's gracious salvation.

Links between Sin and Sickness

We turn to this theme not because of its prominence in Paul but because of its prominence in the Jesus traditions. We saw that one of the ways Jesus's miracles would, in some sense, realize or actualize God's gracious kingdom would be that healings could be connected with the forgiveness of sin. Might this be true for Paul as well? Again, we are hindered in that Paul never claims in his letters to have healed anyone. Despite the plausible suggestion that Paul intended to convey healing at points (2 Cor 12:12; Rom 15:19), we cannot be sure. Additionally, references to forgiveness in Paul are notoriously sparse. Accordingly, we will only briefly consider this point.

In terms of connecting sin and sickness, we saw that the Jewish backgrounds pointed to this sort of association. On the one hand, since Paul's ministry focused on Gentiles, this connection might be deemed less likely.[200] On the other hand, if much of Paul's success was among Gentile sympathizers to Judaism, they might indeed have been influenced by Jewish connections between sin and sickness.[201]

In his study on the origin of illness in the New Testament, Thomas highlights one passage where Paul connects sickness with sin and one passage where Paul connects some malady with Satan.[202] The former is 1 Cor 11:30, where Paul attributes sickness and death to the community's abuse of the Lord's Supper, and the latter is 2 Cor 12:7, where Paul's thorn is likely understood to be some physical ailment.[203] In both cases, God is also an agent—the former is judgment on his people, and the latter is by divine will so Paul may depend upon God's power. To these passages we should add 1 Cor 10:1–14, where Paul refers to the disobedience of the wilderness generation that led to their sickness and death (e.g., Num 25:8–9).[204]

---

200. As Remus (*Jesus as Healer*, 31) notes, the connection between sin and sickness among pagans is rare, though not unattested. The best example Remus gives is a testimony from Epidaurus where a slave is given disfiguring marks for lying. For this, see Edelstein and Edelstein, *Asclepius*, 1:231. Oepke (*TDNT* 3:196–97) writes that sickness was commonly viewed as divine punishment and gives examples of Epimenides sacrificing to an unknown god to stop a plague (*Diog. L.* 1.110) and Apollo's role in bringing pestilence (Homer, *Il.* 1.1–100). For more, see Steinleitner, *Die Beicht im Zusammenhange*, 96–99.

201. On the "God-fearers," see Trebilco, *Jewish Communities*, 145–66; McKnight, *A Light among the Gentiles*, 109–14; Keener, *Acts*, 2:1750–53, 1839, 2095.

202. On most of the passages in this paragraph and the next, see Thomas, *Origins of Illness*, 38–90.

203. Cf. Jervell, "Der schwache Charismatiker," 194. Depending on how one takes σάρξ, 1 Cor 5:5 may also constitute evidence for both categories.

204. Dawson, *Healing, Weakness*, 189.

By contrast, Paul also speaks of sickness where there seems to be no connection with sin or Satan, as in the illness of Epaphroditus (Phil 2:25–30) or his own sickness in Galatia (Gal 4:13–15). So for Paul, sickness is not always connected with sin or Satan. Yet 1 Cor 11:30 and 2 Cor 12:7 show that the connection existed for Paul in some cases.

While we might judge it likely that Paul performed healings, this does not get us very far in terms of evidence in the epistles. Presumably, a restoration of health to the sick in 1 Cor 11:30 would have been perceived as divine forgiveness. We also see Epaphroditus's restoration as God's having mercy on him (Phil 2:27), and it is possible that this involves a miraculous healing.[205] But again, there is no connection with sin in this case. We might connect healing with how Paul views gifts of healing as χαρίσματα (1 Cor 12:9), gifts connected lexically (and conceptually) with God's grace.[206] It is true that healing would thus be seen as a manifestation of God's grace, but this would be the case with all the gifts.

Probably all we can say based on the limited evidence is that any healings that might have taken place in Paul's ministry could have, *in certain circumstances*, been understood as picturing or demonstrating divine forgiveness in a tangible way. It would not be inconsistent with anything we see in Paul, though he does not emphasize the connection.

Conclusion on Paul

We have seen that miracles in Paul's ministry would probably be understood as signs and tangible manifestations of God's gracious inclusion of outsiders. This is because Paul viewed the presence of the Spirit as a powerful sign of Gentile inclusion and miracles as experiential evidence of the Spirit's presence. The evidence for this is strong. More tentatively, the point would be strengthened by associating any miraculous healings with God's forgiveness and mercy. By way of summary, Jervell writes:

> Miracles assume a quite central role in Paul's preaching, almost to greater degree than in Acts. . . . Though Paul seldom and only on occasion speaks of his miraculous activity, he still states clearly that miracles occur *wherever* he preaches the gospel. This is in itself self-evident, because miraculous deeds were a part of his

---

205. Some take it as showing Paul as not always having access to healing gifts (e.g., Moule, *Studies in Philippians*, 81). Yet, as Thomas (*Origins of Illness*, 81) writes, what Paul says does not exclude a miraculous healing, and in fact, the point is that God *did* grant recovery to Epaphroditus; also, the Synoptic Gospels use ἐλεέω to refer to Jesus's healings, and surely Paul and the other Christians *did* pray for Epaphroditus. Fee (*Paul's Letter to the Philippians*, 279) takes it as a miracle via a gift of healing.

206. On this connection see Dunn, *Theology of Paul*, 553–54, 559.

proclamation of the gospel, and for Paul, proclamation is inconceivable apart from deeds of power.[207]

Comparing Jesus and Paul

The time has come to compare these findings concerning Paul and Jesus. Here we are looking for "family resemblances," a "complicated network of similarities overlapping and criss-crossing: sometimes overall similarities, sometimes similarities of detail."[208] We are particularly interested in areas where, as Schoberg puts it, both figures might have had the same central conviction, despite perhaps communicating that conviction in different ways.[209]

First, we have just this sort of resemblance in terms of historical evidence for both figures as miracle workers. For Jesus, we have a plethora of miracle accounts, written within a generation after his death, and this element of his ministry is almost unanimously held to be authentic.[210] For Paul, we have first-person claims of performing miracles in letters where Paul's authorship is beyond doubt (Rom 15:18–19; 2 Cor 12:12).

Second, we have a clear family resemblance in how miracles accompanied their ministries. Healings and exorcisms stand alongside Jesus's teachings as his most important activities. While the evidence in Paul is more sporadic, by his own testimony miracles played a crucial role in his entire ministry (Rom 15:18–19). The ministry of both figures was one of both "word" and "deed."

Third, we can go beyond this and say that, for both figures, miracles in some sense made manifest or realized the gracious inclusion of God that they proclaimed. For Jesus, his miracles of healing paralleled his table fellowship with sinners as tangible expressions of inclusion for outsiders and forgiveness of sins. For Paul, miracles in his ministry were manifestations of the Spirit that evidenced God's acceptance of Gentile believers.

Something akin to this last family resemblance has been noted by several others. Barclay is struck by the "congruity" between Jesus's table fellowship and Paul's mission to the Gentiles.[211] Wedderburn recognizes that Jesus and Paul both prominently welcomed outsiders within the contexts of their respective ministries.[212]

---

207. Jervell, "Signs of an Apostle," 91.

208. The term and quotation is from Wittgenstein, *Philosophische Untersuchungen*, §§66–67. In relation to the Jesus-Paul debate, see: Drane, "Patterns of Evangelization," 291; Schoberg, *Perspectives of Jesus*, 16–17.

209. Ibid., 14.

210. On the uniqueness of the early witnesses, see Meier, *A Marginal Jew*, 2:624.

211. Barclay, "Offensive and Uncanny," 17, emphasis removed.

212. "Both Jesus and Paul were in their lives and ministries characterized by what might be called an openness to the outsider, and that in the name of their God" (Wedderburn, "Similarity and

Simmons makes a specific connection with Paul's understanding of the Spirit and argues that the reception of the Spirit by the Gentiles in Paul's ministry is parallel to Jesus's table fellowship with sinners—both resulted in significant breaking down of barriers.[213]

Simmons's point is well made. Yet in Jesus's ministry there is an even closer parallel to Paul's emphasis of the Spirit coming upon Gentiles—the *miracles* of Jesus. Here we have in many ways the same significance of Jesus's table fellowship with sinners. The exorcisms and healings of Jesus were signs of God's favor, meant reintegration into the community of God's people, and held implications for the forgiveness of sins. Furthermore, Jesus's healings and exorcisms would be clearly interpreted as *God's* work, since they would be regarded as beyond human power. This is precisely Paul's point in Gal 3:1–5.

The evidence we have covered in this chapter shows there is indeed a family resemblance between Jesus and Paul. Both figures proclaimed a message of God's gracious inclusion, both combined that message with miracles, and for both, those miracles signified and, in some sense, initially realized the gracious inclusion associated with the age of fulfillment. Kim makes my point like this: "As Jesus actualized through miracles the salvation of the kingdom he preached, so also Paul, his apostle, has actualized through miracles the salvation of the gospel he has preached."[214]

Continuity," 131, emphasis removed). Meyer (*Aims of Jesus*, 160) writes that Jesus's table fellowship with sinners was the "concrete presupposition" for Rom 4:5. Sanders ("Jesus and the Sinners," 30) sees similarity between Jesus's table fellowship with sinners and Paul's inclusion of Gentiles in the opposition both received. Dunn ("From Jesus' Proclamation to Paul's Gospel," 105) also writes: "As Jesus broke through the boundaries *within* Israel, Paul broke through the boundary *round* Israel."

213. "The theological significance of the reception of the Spirit by uncircumcised Gentiles is seen to be analogous with and essentially equivalent to Jesus' table-fellowship with outcasts and sinners. Just as Jesus portrayed a God who removed all barriers in order to identify with the outcasts of his day and bestow an abundance of grace and love upon the unworthy, so too the activity of the Spirit revealed a God who accepted Gentiles as they were and one who desired fellowship with them as his people. Just as Jesus' understanding of God tended to relativize the distinction between the righteous and unrighteous in Israel, the presence of the Spirit tended to break down the distinctions that existed between Jews and Gentiles" (Simmons, *Theology of Inclusion*, 141). So also Wedderburn, "Similarity and Continuity," 139.

214. Kim, "Jesus, Sayings of," 486.

CHAPTER 3

Signs of Authoritative Power with a Lifestyle of Weakness

This chapter will explore how the miracles of Jesus and Paul demonstrated their divine authority and in some sense authenticated them. We will also consider how both figures at the same time showed reservations about authenticating themselves with miracles and refused to give a "sign" when asked. Finally, we will examine how a lifestyle of what we will generalize as "weakness" accompanied their ministries of miracle-working power.

The Miracles of Jesus as (Qualified) Signs of Authoritative Power with a Lifestyle of Weakness

When we reach the question whether Jesus's miracles in some sense authenticated or legitimized him, we reach a diversity of opinion.[1] Some scholars see Jesus's miracles functioning for him as some kind of personal authentication.[2] Others disagree and argue that Jesus prominently did *not* use the performance of miracles for authentication.[3] This difference of opinion probably arises because of the strains of conflicting evidence within the Gospels. We will consider both lines of evidence

---

1. In the terms *legitimation* and *authentication*, I follow Keener (*Miracles*, 1:61), who accepts the division of Talbert (*Reading John*, 162) who divides the function of ancient miracles into "legitimization," "evangelization," and "instruction." It is true that distinctions can be made between authority and legitimacy and between authority and power. See Meeks, introduction, xix; Schütz, *Paul and the Anatomy*, 15–16; Polaski, *Paul and the Discourse of Power*, 35; Holmberg, *Paul and Power*, 125–35. Yet for our purposes we need not be so precise; I will use these terms nontechnically and combine categories somewhat with my term *authoritative power*.

2. Eve (*Healer from Nazareth*, 144; cf. p. 24) is an example: "Jesus' healings and exorcisms served . . . to authenticate Jesus' standing as an eschatological prophet." So, in differing degrees, Bock and Simpson (*Jesus According to Scripture*, 282): "Jesus claimed to have authority. The miracles served to underscore that claim"; Allison (*Jesus of Nazareth*, 205): "He undoubtedly . . . understood his ministry of exorcism and healing to vindicate his proclamation"; Vermes, *Religion of Jesus*, 73; cf. p. 70–75.

3. Harvey (*Jesus and the Constraints of History*, 112–13) is an example here: "Jesus nowhere appeals to the impression made by his own miracles as authentication for his personal authority and indeed he condemns the suggestion that signs and wonders are necessary in order to create faith." So, in differing degrees, Sanders (*Jesus and Judaism*, 172): "We cannot say that Jesus proffered his miracles to his audience as bearing this significance—even though it is reasonable that he saw them in this way—because of the tradition that he refused to give a sign"; Blackburn, "The Miracles of Jesus," 121.

and I will argue for a qualified position that tries to account for both. We will then consider the contrast with what might be called Jesus's lifestyle of weakness.

The Miracles of Jesus as Signs of Authoritative Power

Before turning to the Gospels, a brief consideration of backgrounds is helpful. Both in Judaism and in the larger Greco-Roman world, miracles could authenticate or exalt a mortal.[4]

In the Greco-Roman world, wonders could authenticate or glorify an individual to a variety of degrees—though there is actually a paucity of figures during the New Testament period.[5] A few examples will serve. Concerning pre-Christian figures, wonders were recounted of the philosopher Pythagoras.[6] Empedocles writes of his own healing abilities and promises his hearers control over nature.[7] According to some, Epimenides was given sacrifices as to a god because of his foresight.[8] In post-Christian eras, the story of a miraculous healing by Vespasian attempted to lend some badly needed credibility to his rule.[9] Philostratus served to heighten Apollonius's reputation by recording miracles, the miracles related by Lucian in *Philopseudes* were designed in the story world to enhance credibility, and Aristides's personal testimonies were doubtless intended to communicate the power of Asclepius.[10] Lucian tells us that Alexander the prophet spread stories of

---

4. As Keener (*Miracles*, 1:61–62) writes, "Ancient writers and storytellers often used miraculous works to authenticate deities or, more often, mortal individuals. Such signs demonstrated that the person indeed possessed numinous authority to justify his claims." This is not just an ancient phenomenon. See Aune, "Magic in Early Christianity," 1527; Allison, *Millenarian Prophet*, 91.

5. For numerous pre-Christian examples, see Blackburn, Theios Anēr, 13–72. Cf. Cotter, *Miracles*, passim. On the paucity of wonder-working figures in our era of interest, excluding Apollonius of Tyana, for whom evidence is late, Koskenniemi ("Apollonius of Tyana," 462; cf. pp. 463–64) writes: "An investigation of the sources and secondary literature yields a surprising result. From within the period of greatest interest, ca. 300 BCE to ca. 150 CE, there has not been a single important Gentile miracle worker identified in the literature. Arguably the rulers form a special class.... Moreover, even here the Greco-Roman tradition has clearly been overestimated." So, essentially, Twelftree, *Paul and the Miraculous*, 40–44.

6. E.g., in Iamblichus, *De vita pythagorica*, 28.134–35, a river greets Pythagoras, he is in more than one place at a time, he displays a golden thigh, and mention is made of "ten thousand other incidents more divine and wonderful" (Iamblichus, *Pythagorean Way*, 155–56). See Blackburn, Theios Anēr, 37–51.

7. Inwood, *Poem of Empedocles*, 211, 219. Fragments = *Diog. L.* 8.58–59, 62. See Blackburn, Theios Anēr, 51–52.

8. *Diog. L.* 1.114. See Blackburn, Theios Anēr, 36–37.

9. Eve, *Healer from Nazareth*, 44–46. Tacitus, *Hist.* 4.81; Cassius Dio, *Roman History* 65.8.1–2. For post-Christian examples, see Blackburn, Theios Anēr, 73–96.

10. Theissen, *Miracle Stories*, 260–61. E.g., Philostratus, *Vit. Apoll.* 3.39, 4:45, 6.43; Lucian, *Philops.* 34; Aristides, *Sac. Tales* 1.62–68, 2.18–23. Somewhat similar are inscriptions found at Asclepius sanctuaries, e.g., Stele 1.3 in Edelstein and Edelstein, *Asclepius*, 1:230.

healings abroad to increase his fame, a case which demonstrates that one person's authenticated wonder worker could be another person's charlatan.[11]

The theme of authentication-by-miracle is in some ways stronger within the Jewish world with its tradition of prophetic validation via signs.[12] Moses worked wonders to demonstrate that God had sent him.[13] When Elijah raised the widow's son, she said: "Now I know that you are a man of God, and that the word of the LORD in your mouth is truth" (1 Kgs 17:24).[14] The theme is also not absent in post-biblical tradition.[15] Particularly noteworthy are Josephus's so-called sign-prophets who led followers to the wilderness and promised signs (e.g., *Ant.* 20.97–99, 167–70; *J.W.* 2.259–63).[16] As these last examples demonstrate, in the Jewish tradition too was the realization that miracles did not necessarily separate true miracle workers from imposters.[17]

We see from this consideration of backgrounds that even if the Gospel traditions contained no explicit reference to Jesus's miracles bringing authentication, this sort of significance could still be plausibly understood as being operative in his cultural context.[18] Helpfully for our purposes, we do indeed have Gospel references to just such an authenticating function. We will begin by considering two key passages discussed more fully elsewhere in this study. Both are generally well regarded historically, and both present the miracles of Jesus as personal authentication in some sense.

---

11. *Alex.* 24. Cf. *Philops.* 16, where a fee is required for exorcism. Cf. *Alex.* 5. See, e.g., Remus, *Pagan-Christian Conflict,* 52–53, 56–57, 67–72.

12. Koskenniemi (*Old Testament Miracle-Workers,* 296) notes: "A strong biblical function of the miracle stories is that they legitimate a man as a leader sent by God." See Cotter, *Miracles in Greco-Roman Antiquity,* 36; Hooker, *Signs of a Prophet,* 5–6; Salier, *Rhetorical Impact,* 20.

13. E.g., Exod 4; 7:8–12. As Blackburn (*Theios Anēr,* 69) notes, Philo writes that Moses shared in God's mastery over the elements because of his closeness to God (*Mos.* 1.155–57): "Thus Moses' miracles bear witness to his partnership with God, though they do not constitute the grounds for it." In Josephus's retelling, Moses is convinced because of the miracles (*Ant.* 2.275), convinces his compatriots via the same signs (2.280), and attempts to persuade Pharaoh similarly (2.283–87).

14. Josephus recognizes this (*Ant.* 8.325–27). See also 1 Kgs 18:36–40. Elisha gets much the same (2 Kgs 2:8–15; 4:18–37 [cf. 1 Kgs 17:17–24]). An unnamed prophet is vindicated by a miracle (1 Kgs 13:1–10). Gideon asks for signs to convince himself (Judg 6:17–40). Samuel gives signs to authenticate his choice of Saul (1 Sam 10:1–9). Isaiah gives a sign to confirm his prophecy (2 Kgs 20:8–11; cf. 38:5–8). Ahaz is offered a sign but demurs (Isa 7:11–12).

15. See previous two footnotes; Koskenniemi, *Old Testament Miracle-Workers,* 296. Examples of Koskenniemi include: Jub. 11:9–24; LAB 27:10; Sir 44:23–45:5; Philo, *Mos.* 1.75–76; Josephus, *Ant.* 2.274.

16. Sanders (*Jesus and Judaism,* 171) writes: "These signs, like others, were intended to prove that the doer of them spoke the truth and acted with power given by God."

17. See Eve, *Healer from Nazareth,* 21–25; Salier, *Rhetorical Impact,* 22–23. E.g., Deut 13:1–5; Josephus, *Ant.* 2.284–87; 20.97–98.

18. Sanders (*Jesus and Judaism,* 172) admits this point: "It is entirely reasonable to assume that Jesus' following, and perhaps Jesus himself, saw them as evidencing his status as true spokesman for God, since that sort of inference was common in the Mediterranean."

First is Luke 7:22 (par.), which we considered in ch. 2. Here we have John the Baptist exhibiting doubt that Jesus is the promised one.[19] Jesus's response, couched in the language of scriptural fulfillment, is intended to legitimate himself as the one John should accept—if the expectations of Isaiah are being fulfilled, then Jesus must be the one John awaited.[20] Since five out of the six phenomena to which Jesus points are healings of one sort or another ("the blind receive their sight, the lame walk, lepers are cleansed, and the deaf hear, the dead are raised up, the poor have good news preached to them"), we see that Jesus's miracles here, in light of scriptural fulfillment, demonstrate his authority as the bringer of end-time blessings. This means that Jesus understood that these miracles in some sense demonstrated that he spoke for God.[21] As a result: "Blessed is the one who is not offended by me" (Luke 7:23 par.).

Similar is the second passage, Jesus's saying on his exorcizing ministry: εἰ δὲ ἐν δακτύλῳ [Matt: πνεύματι] θεοῦ [Matt: ἐγὼ] ἐκβάλλω τὰ δαιμόνια, ἄρα ἔφθασεν ἐφ' ὑμᾶς ἡ βασιλεία τοῦ θεοῦ (Luke 11:20 par.). Our main discussion of this passage will be in ch. 4. For now, we only note two points. First, this saying is generally well regarded in terms of authenticity.[22] Second, if Jesus saw his exorcisms as evidence of the presence of the kingdom, those exorcisms would thus also evidence Jesus's legitimacy and authority.[23] This is how Jesus's response answers the charge of using Satan's power, itself a challenge to Jesus's legitimacy.

We turn now to other potential evidence. Most promising is the Q saying of Jesus pronouncing woe on Galilean towns: "Woe to you, Chorazin! Woe to you, Bethsaida! For if the mighty works [αἱ δυνάμεις] done in you had been done in Tyre and Sidon, they would have repented long ago, sitting in sackcloth and ashes" (Luke 10:13; cf. Matt 11:21). Here we see that miracles should have elicited

---

19. Historicity is discussed in ch. 2.

20. Bock (*Luke*, 1:685) writes: "If Jesus does the work of the eschaton, then his ministry must be what he claims it is."

21. Sanders (*Historical Figure*, 167) is even stronger and uses the language of proof: "Jesus viewed them as proving that he was the true spokesman for God."

22. Evans, "Exorcisms and the Kingdom," 171. For example, Bultmann (*Synoptic Tradition*, 162) says it "can, in my view, claim the highest degree of authenticity which we can make for any saying of Jesus: it is full of that feeling of eschatological power which must have characterized the activity of Jesus," though this judgment is, as Meier (*Mentor, Message*, 413) writes, "strangely subjective, not to say romantic." The Jesus Seminar (Funk and Hoover, *Five Gospels*, 329) rates it pink. Beasley-Murray (*Jesus and the Kingdom of God*, 75) says it is "universally acknowledged to be authentic." For arguments in favor of authenticity, see Dunn, "Matthew 12:28/Luke 11:20," 29–49; Twelftree, *Jesus the Exorcist*, 110; Meier, *A Marginal Jew*, 2:413–23.

23. Bock (*Luke*, 2:1085) again: "The miracles of Jesus testify visibly to this authority—an authority etched by God's finger." Blackburn ("Miracles of Jesus," 121) sets Jesus's eschatological understanding of his miracles against Jesus's using them as authentication. Yet this is a false dichotomy, because both could go hand-in-hand. As Latourelle (*Miracles of Jesus*, 285) writes, "The miracles prove *directly* that the time of fulfillment has come and the kingdom is here; they prove *implicitly* that Jesus is he who is to come and establish the new kingdom."

a response, as Latourelle argues: "He explicitly invokes his miracles as proof of his mission and authority."[24]

Some, however, view this saying as a Christian creation. The Jesus Seminar sees the context in Q as the mission of the disciples, a mission that it rejects as unhistorical; they also judge it impossible for Jesus to damn a village when he taught love for enemies.[25] Sanders follows Bultmann in dismissing the passage because of a perceived anti-Jewish polemic.[26] Bultmann argues that the saying speaks of Jesus's work as completed and assumes the Christian mission to Capernaum has failed; he also thinks it unlikely that Jesus would think his work would lift Capernaum to heaven.[27]

None of this is decisive.[28] It is not necessary that a mission discourse was the saying's original location.[29] Warnings of condemnation for those who reject God's will are commonplace among Old Testament prophets and would not be out of character for one who came to reform Israel.[30] To say it another way, a Jewish prophet could certainly engage in anti-Jewish polemic.[31] Regarding Bultmann, (1) there is no reason to assume Jesus's work is over—and certainly Matthew did not take it this way since the passage is placed in the middle of a section dealing with Galilee; (2) the New Testament never refers to a later outreach to these areas; and (3) objecting to Capernaum's being lifted to heaven is "overinterpretation."[32] Dunn writes that, in spite of Bultmann's arguments, it is difficult to see the saying as just a creation of the church.[33]

There seem to be no strong reasons to reject the saying. As such, we have in Luke 10:13 (par.) further evidence for Jesus's viewing his miracles as—in some sense—authentication for his message. Not to respond to what they had seen from Jesus would bring judgment on themselves.

---

24. Ibid. Keener (*Gospel of Matthew*, 345) agrees: "One may . . . note here the evidential value of miracles." Twelftree (*Jesus the Exorcist*, 170) rejects authentication here because of Jesus's refusal to give a sign elsewhere.

25. Funk and Hoover, *The Five Gospels*, 181, 320.

26. Sanders, *Jesus and Judaism*, 110; Bultmann, *Synoptic Tradition*, 112–13.

27. Ibid.

28. Mussner (*The Miracles of Jesus*, 1968], 21) is very confident: "If there is one pre-Easter logion, then it is the lament of Jesus over these three cities of his native Galilee." He cites, for example, Chorazin's lack of mention in other traditions as displaying a lack of interest in the place.

29. So, more strongly, Nolland, *Luke*, 2:556. Luke could have positioned it here, or it may have come to him that way in Q. See Marshall, *The Gospel of Luke*, 424; Nolland, *Luke*, 2:555–56.

30. E.g., Isa 1:27–28; 13:1–22; 23:1–18; Jer 2–4; 15:6–9; 44:11–12 [MT]; Ezek 16; Amos 1:3–3:8.

31. Wright (*Jesus and the Victory of God*, 253) asks: "Was Jeremiah anti-Jewish? Was Amos? Was John the Baptist?" Fitzmyer (*Gospel According to Luke*, 2:852) writes: "If one detects in these sayings a prophetic proclamation, it does not follow that they stem only from some early Christian prophetic tradition."

32. Davies and Allison, *Matthew*, 2:270.

33. Dunn, *Jesus and the Spirit*, 70. So also: Twelftree, *Jesus the Exorcist*, 167–68; Keener, *Matthew*, 343–45; Bock, *Luke*, 2:989; and with reservations, Luz, *Matthew*, 2:151–54.

Three lines of supplemental evidence might also apply. First, in Mark 2:1–12 (parr.), we have a healing tied to a demonstration of Jesus's authority to forgive sins. As it stands in Mark, this healing is an authenticating miracle.[34] Unfortunately for our purposes, whether this saying goes back to Jesus is debated.[35] Due to the complexity of the debate, including issues involving the ever-elusive "son of man," we should probably consider this passage as only potential secondary evidence.

The second line of supplemental evidence comes more generally from the Gospel of John. In John, we have an entire theme of Jesus's miracles—specifically called "signs"—which are treated positively as revealing his glory and validating his person.[36] This can be seen in the remarkable closing statement of ch. 20: "Now Jesus did many other signs [σημεῖα] in the presence of the disciples, which are not written in this book; but these are written so that you may believe that Jesus is the Christ, the Son of God, and that by believing you may have life in his name" (20:30–31).[37] These signs are thus used as authentication for Jesus as a legitimate spokesman for God.[38]

---

34. So also Gibson, "Jesus' Refusal," 38–42. Hägerland (*Jesus and the Forgiveness of Sins*, 215–16) recognizes this but argues that its contradiction with Jesus's refusal to give a sign elsewhere counts against the historicity of Mark 2:10. Bock (*Luke*, 1:486) explains the passage's dynamic: "If the paralytic walks, the miracle talks about the Son of Man's authority to forgive sin. If the Son of Man possesses such unique authority, then who is the Son of Man other than God's unique agent of salvation?" Hooker (*Signs of a Prophet*, 34) argues that this is not an authenticating miracle but rather a *"prophetic sign."*

35. The Jesus Seminar (Funk and Hoover, *The Five Gospels*, 44–45) attributes the words to the narrator, with most seeing a reference to the apocalyptic Son of Man, which is judged inauthentic.

36. That the term σημεῖα is important in the Gospel of John can be seen in how the term is found in the key summary statements of 12:37 and 20:30 (Salier, *Rhetorical Impact*, 1 n. 1). Salier (p. 154) writes later in summary: "Σημεῖον is a term that has been chosen by the narrator for the purposes of communication with the reader. It is clear that the sign narratives have been deliberately recorded for a specific purpose within the context of the Gospel. Ultimately they point to Jesus' identity as the divine Son, sent by the Father to do his work. The signs point to Jesus' identity in the context of the legal motif that is so prominent in the Gospel and in the context of the matrix of expectations concerning the work of God with his people. They are integral to the achievement of the Gospel's purposes and are clearly intended to lead to the faith that is the overall goal of the writing of the Gospel." Kysar (*Maverick Gospel*, 10) writes, "The wonders are given a revelatory character along with the words of Jesus: they reveal the truth about the identity of the revealer." Also helpful is the study of Thompson ("Signs and Faith in the Fourth Gospel," 96), who treats signs as wholly positive in John, in that they lead people to faith by manifesting God's life-giving character, with Jesus as mediator of that life. See also Weder, "Deus Incarnatus," 333–34; Schnelle, "The Signs in the Gospel of John," 231–43.

37. For arguments that "signs" here refer to the miracles of the first half of the book, as well as to the death-and-resurrection of Jesus, see Salier, *Rhetorical Impact*, 149–54. E.g., "The Gospel's usage suggests that the denotation of σημεῖα is restricted to those occurrences that would fall under the rubric of miracle" (p. 150).

38. As Köstenberger (*Theology of John's Gospel*, 327) writes, "The signs are shown to authenticate Jesus as the true representative of God." He also notes that all the commonly agreed-on signs in John's Gospel are done in the presence of unbelievers as well as believers. As Salier (*Rhetorical Impact*, 127) puts it, "They are presented with the purpose of provoking belief."

Two potential objections might be raised against this evidence from the Gospel of John. The first objection is that John is often not considered as reliable a source about the historical Jesus as the other Gospels.[39] Yet a significant group of voices have argued in recent years that the Gospel of John plausibly contains significant testimony to the historical Jesus, and it should not be overlooked in the Quest.[40] This should especially be acceptable when used as I am using it here, to adduce further coherence with a line of evidence developed independently from other streams of tradition, such as the Synoptic Gospels and Q.[41] Certain differences and omissions between Jesus's miracles as portrayed by John and the Synoptics may also be plausibly assigned to a complementary approach taken by John, who specifically acknowledges that many other miracles (σημεῖα) were done by Jesus that John does not include.[42]

The second potential objection is that Jesus's miracles are explicitly and distinctively called "signs" (σημεῖα) in the Gospel of John, a usage that stands directly counter to the Jesus of the Synoptic Gospels.[43] Throughout the Synoptics, when

39. E.g., The Jesus Seminar (Funk and Hoover, *The Five Gospels*, 3) describes what they call the second pillar of modern biblical criticism within the context of a contrast between the Jesus of history and the Christ of faith: "The second pillar consisted of recognizing the synoptic gospels as much closer to the historical Jesus than the Fourth Gospel, which presented a 'spiritual' Jesus." They later write: "The first step is to understand the diminished role the Gospel of John plays in the search for the Jesus of history. The two pictures painted by John and the synoptic gospels cannot both be historically accurate. . . . In sum, there is virtually nothing of the synoptic sage in the Fourth Gospel. That sage has been displaced by Jesus the revealer who has been sent from God to reveal who the Father is. . . . The differences between the two portraits of Jesus show up in a dramatic way in the evaluation, by the Jesus Seminar, of the words attributed to Jesus in the Gospel of John. The Fellows of the Seminar were unable to find a single saying they could with certainty trace back to the historical Jesus" (ibid., 10).

40. E.g., Blomberg, *Historical Reliability*, 17–67; Anderson, *Fourth Gospel and the Quest*; Anderson, Just, and, Thatcher, eds., *John, Jesus, and History*. Part of this is the recognition that the Synoptics are also "theological" in nature and that elements of historicity in ways can look more promising in John. For example, Anderson (*The Fourth Gospel and the Quest*, 3) writes: "As well as being historical, Mark and the other Synoptic traditions are pervasively theological. Therefore, they cannot be relegated to the canons of factuality and bald historiography any more than John can. And, despite John's pervasive theological tone, John has more archaeological and topographical references, and more direct claims to first-hand familiarity, than all the other gospels put together. In some ways the Synoptic presentation of Jesus is preferable in terms of historicity, but in others the Johannine demonstrates a greater sense of historical realism."

41. For that matter, the possibility of a "signs source" lying behind the Gospel of John is intriguing from a historical perspective, though of course this is debated. See, e.g., Fortna, *The Gospel of Signs*; Fortna, *The Fourth Gospel and Its Predecessor*.

42. See Anderson, *The Fourth Gospel and the Quest*, 109. Anderson (p. 56) earlier imagines a parenthetical comment in John 20:30–31: "The evangelist is apparently aware of other signs reported that 'are *not in this* book . . .' (in other words, 'Yes, I *know* Mark is out there, and I *know* I'm leaving things out, so stop reminding me . . .')." Yet for some disjunctions between the Synoptic and Johannine miracles, see ibid., 147–48.

43. Thus, as Kysar (*Maverick Gospel*, 80) writes, "For one acquainted with the Synoptic Gospels, it is a startling use of the term."

Jesus uses the term *signs* with reference to miracles, he either refuses to offer a sign (e.g., Mark 8:12 parr.) or speaks of the dangers of false signs and wonders (Mark 13:22 par.). Yet we find an interesting distinction within the usage of the Gospel of John. As Köstenberger notes, σημεῖα is used almost always by the *narrator*, while *Jesus's* term is ἔργον.[44] This can plausibly be seen to be preserving a significant awareness that Jesus did not use the term *signs* to refer to his miracles. Instead, the author interprets the miracles in such a way as to classify them as "signs" but refrained from placing this language on Jesus's lips.

The third line of supplemental evidence to consider comes, once again somewhat generally, from the Synoptic Gospels. All three Evangelists broadly present Jesus's miracles alongside his teaching as acts demonstrating authority. In Mark, the first episode in Jesus's public ministry is an exorcism (1:23–27), exemplifying the authority with which he acted in contrast to the scribes (1:22, 27), a reoccurring theme in Mark.[45] Matthew and Luke retain Mark's depiction of amazement stemming from both teaching and miracles (Mark 1:22 parr.; 1:27 // Luke 4:36; 6:2 // Matt 13:54).[46] A variety of themes and stories color Jesus with patterns similar to Elijah or Elisha, both prophets accredited with miracles.[47]

In summarizing this supplemental evidence from John and the Synoptic Gospels, broadly considered, Meier is helpful. He concludes that all four Gospel writers indicate that Jesus's miracles are intended to bring people to faith in Jesus.[48] While some of these portrayals might be the interpretation of the Gospel writers themselves, we should note that their presentations could still be examples of how ancient viewers might have interpreted Jesus's miracles.[49]

44. Köstenberger, *Theology of John's Gospel*, 192 n. 42. Though cf. John 4:48; 6:26. See also, on this, Salier, *Rhetorical Impact*, 79–81.

45. Horsley, *Jesus and Magic*, 143. Cf. Dawson, *Healing, Weakness and Power*, 68–69. The first category of Koch (*Die Bedeutung der Wundererzählungen*, 42–55) for the significance of the Markan miracle stories is to demonstrate the authority of Jesus's teaching.

46. See Vermes, *Religion of Jesus*, 73. On how Matthew highlights Jesus's miracles as demonstrating authority, see Kee, *Miracle in the Early Christian World*, 187–88. Cf. Gerhardsson, *The Mighty Acts of Jesus*, 45–47.

47. Horsley, *Jesus and Magic*, 138. E.g., Luke 7:11–17; cf. 1 Kgs 17:17–24; 2 Kgs 4:8–37.

48. Meier, *A Marginal Jew*, 2:543–44. This might bring us to the place on the question where Allison's "big picture" approach to Jesus is helpful. Allison ("It Don't Come Easy," 198) writes this after a discussion about the discouraging implications of memory studies on historical-Jesus studies: "They further imply that we should, if we seek to be conscientious historians, work as much as possible from generalizations about and inferences from large quanities of data. The larger the generalization and the more data upon which it is based, the greater our confidence. The more specific the detail and the fewer the supporting data, the greater our uncertainty. So, in the matter of Jesus, we should start not with the parts but with the whole, which means with the general impressions that the tradition about him, *in toto*, tends to convey." Would not the fact that miracles helped people believe in Jesus be one of these general impressions?

49. As Eve (*Healer from Nazareth*, 119) says concerning Mark's Gospel. Cf. Wright, *Jesus and the Victory of God*, 194.

What can we say in conclusion to this section? We have several lines of evidence showing that Jesus viewed his miracles as personal authentication in some sense and that they were interpreted this way by others. First, this understanding is likely, given the background material from both the Greco-Roman and Jewish world. Second, we have two key passages, which are generally well regarded historically, where Jesus presents his miracles as showing his mission to be divinely directed (Luke 7:22 par.; 11:20 par.). Third, we have the proclamation of woes, which is likely authentic and which shows that Jesus thought his miracles should prompt repentance (Luke 10:13 par.). Finally, we have supplemental evidence in the interpretation of the author of the Gospel of John and the authors of all three Synoptics, who present Jesus's miracles as demonstrating his authority as God's spokesman—an interpretation that is (at the very least) plausibly similar to how those who witnessed Jesus's miracles might have interpreted them. Eve summarizes in a statement that can be judged somewhat minimalistic on the basis of all this evidence we have considered: "It would be fair to say, then, that the Gospels create the impression that Jesus' miracles served to enhance his prophetic authority."[50]

The Miracles of Jesus and a Resistance to Signs

We turn to an important counterpoint. There is also a significant line of evidence in the Gospels that shows Jesus *resisting* the idea of authentication via miracles. Most important are the accounts where Jesus refuses to give a sign (e.g., Mark 8:11–13 parr.).[51]

All four Gospels agree that Jesus would not offer authenticating miracles.[52] In Mark's account, the Pharisees ask for a "sign from heaven" (σημεῖον ἀπὸ τοῦ οὐρανοῦ), and Jesus refuses (8:11–12). In Luke, the same request occurs in the context of an exorcism dispute (11:15–16), and in the same literary context Jesus condemns the seeking of a "sign" (σημεῖον) and promises only "the sign of Jonah" (11:29–30).[53] Matthew has two occurrences of the request for a sign, once for just a "sign" (12:38) and once for a "sign from heaven" (16:1); in both cases, Jesus responds with condemnation and reference to the "sign of Jonah" (12:39; 16:4).

The theme is also present in John, despite how Jesus's miracles are used to show his exalted status.[54] In 2:18, Jesus is asked, "What sign do you show us for

---

50. Eve, *Healer from Nazareth*, 123. Yeung (*Faith in Jesus and Paul*, 295) writes: "Jesus' healing miracles serve *to authenticate the special identity of Jesus* with relation to God."

51. This is a common reason to reject an authenticating function for Jesus's miracles. E.g., Twelftree, *Jesus the Exorcist*, 170.

52. Hooker, *Signs of a Prophet*, 33. Roskovec ("Miracle Worker," 882 n. 27) also notes Mark 11:27–33 parr., which is conceptually similar.

53. Cf. Luke 23:8.

54. Anderson (*The Fourth Gospel and the Quest*, 93) speaks of a Jesus who "performs miraculous signs while at the same time de-emphasizing their importance." For a helpful discussion of the tension, see Kysar, *Maverick Gospel*, 81–86.

doing these things?" His answer is the temple threat (2:19–22).[55] In John 6:30–31, the crowd asks for a sign that they might believe and implicitly suggest something akin to manna (which Jesus in 6:32 calls "bread from heaven")—but Jesus does not oblige.[56] In 4:48, Jesus condemns (somewhat enigmatically) the need to see "signs and wonders," though in this case a healing leads to faith (4:53).[57] To Thomas, he gives a similar, though less severe, rebuke (20:29).

The refusal to give a sign in some form is usually considered authentic.[58] As displayed above, the theme is multiply attested (Mark, Q, John), and the criterion of embarrassment supports it.[59] It is also somewhat discontinuous with later Christianity, which featured "signs" as authentication for both Jesus and themselves (e.g., Acts 2:22; 5:12).

There are two further lines of evidence in the Gospels supporting the idea that Jesus resisted depending on miracles as authentication. First is the "miracle-secret" motif (Jesus's commands to silence concerning his miracles), which is present in all three Synoptics to varying degrees.[60] In Mark, we have four clear examples.[61]) Luke follows three of Mark's passages and adds no new examples.[62] Matthew follows two of Mark's passages and adds two more.[63] There are some challenges to the historicity of this theme, but they are not decisive.[64]) The theme is plausible within

55. On the possibilities in this exchange, see Salier, *Rhetorical Impact*, 51–52.

56. Salier (ibid., 85) writes: "Jesus doesn't answer this request, reinforcing that he performs signs entirely at his own initiative (cf. 2.18–19)."

57. Köstenberger (*Theology of John's Gospel*, 325–26) argues that John emphasizes Jesus's signs more as "prophetic-symbolic" rather than as miraculous per se and notes that "signs and wonders" occurs only in 4:48 and is treated negatively. Interestingly, Salier (*Rhetorical Impact*, 55–59) argues that in 4:48 Jesus is not speaking negatively of a connection between signs and faith but rather is giving a positive principle that signs do lead to faith. This may not finally convince, however. See also Kysar, *Maverick Gospel*, 82–83.

58. Dunn, *Jesus Remembered*, 659 n. 207. For example, Bultmann (*Synoptic Tradition*, 128) seems favorable. Also Roskovec, "Miracle Worker," 882.

59. In that a refusal could be interpreted as inability (Evans, *Jesus and His Contemporaries*, 222). See Smith, *Jesus the Magician*, 14–15. Yet it could also be argued that the tradition was invented to explain Jesus's *inability* to perform when pressed.

60. It is absent in the Gospel of John, which is intelligible given the focus on signs as revelatory. We do have a well-known touchpoint between the Synoptics and John, however, in John 6:15 and Mark 6:45 // Matt 14:22.

61. 1:43–44; 5:43; 7:36; 9:9. 5:19 and 8:26 are open to debate. Twelftree (*Jesus the Miracle Worker*, 96) interprets 5:19 as a command to silence (so also Theissen, *Miracle Stories*, 146). But silence seems to be the opposite of Jesus's intent—thus the man obeys (5:20). Similarly, Marshall, *Luke*, 341. The difference may be that the Decapolis is outside Jewish territory, with less threat of messianic preconceptions. Note: commands to demons are not included.

62. Luke 5:14 // Mark 1:43–44; 8:39 // Mark 5:19 [debatable]; 8:56 // Mark 5:43.

63. Matt 8:4 // Mark 1:43–44; Matt 17:9 // Mark 9:9. Additions: 9:30; 12:15–16.

64. First, it could be a church creation to explain why the multitudes did not accept Jesus—but the way Christians based apologetics on Jesus's miracles makes this unlikely, as they would probably want to emphasize Jesus's miracles (Harvey, *Constraints of History*, 113). Second, it could also largely be Mark's creation—yet it is found in other streams of tradition, and seeds may be found within the tradition. Räisänen ("Messianic Secret," 134) notes: "The tradition knew how Jesus sometimes

Jesus's ministry.[65] Thus, that Jesus might command silence after some miracles supports the idea that he did not seek miraculous authentication.

The second line of supporting evidence is the way faith in the Gospel traditions is usually seen *prior* to a miracle.[66] In fact, lack of faith is a hindrance (Mark 6:5 // Matt 13:58; cf. Mark 9:23–24; Matt 9:28–29). If faith usually comes before a miracle (e.g., Mark 2:5 parr.; 5:36 // Luke 8:50), how can miracles authenticate or create faith?

Returning to our main passage where Jesus refuses to give a sign (Mark 8:11–13 parr.), the complicated question of what constitutes "the sign of Jonah" in Q need not concern us (Luke 11:29 parr.). Our interest lies rather in the way Jesus refuses to validate himself with a miracle generally, and how this can be understood in light of my argument that Jesus *did* view miracles as authentication in some cases. Why would Jesus refuse to grant miracles if he viewed them as authentication?

Essentially our options are three: (1) incoherence, where the tension is evidence for inauthentic material; (2) a lexical distinction, where Jesus and his opponents are not referring to the same kind of phenomena; or (3) what we might call a "motivational" distinction, where Jesus might offer, based on the individual involved, miracles as authentication in some cases.

Option 1 is of course possible, but first it is preferable to see whether we can account for both lines of evidence as they stand. As in the case of the future or present kingdom in Jesus's preaching, a both/and view might be possible.[67]

Option 2 is promising. We note immediately that, in all four Gospels, Jesus never refers to his miracles as "signs," and neither do the authors of the Synoptics.[68] Beyond this, in all four Gospels there is an interesting literary placement of the request for a sign in contexts immediately after a miracle (Mark 8:11; cf. 8:1–10; Matt 12:38; cf. 12:22–32; Luke 11:16; cf. 11:14–15; John 6:30–31; cf. 6:14). This suggests that the request for "signs" anticipates a different kind of phenomenon.[69] One

---

withdrew into solitude, how he healed some people in private or in the presence of only a chosen few, etc." Cf. Luz, "The Secrecy Motif," 87. Furthermore, if this was Mark's goal, he bungled it—because the calls to miracle secrecy really emphasize the *failure* to keep Jesus's miracles secret. See ibid., 80; cf. Räisänen, "Messianic Secret," 133; Dunn, "Messianic Secret," 98–99.

65. Motivation includes a desire for privacy for those healed and avoiding a wrong perspective on his ministry (ibid., 94–95). The whole messianic secret motif also "reflects the complexity of life rather than the artificial complicatedness of a theory" (ibid., 117).

66. As Roskovec ("Miracle Worker," 883) writes, "Faith is only exceptionally a *result* of the event; it is usually its prerequisite." E.g., Mark 2:5 parr.; 5:34 parr.; 10:52 parr. For our purposes, the best treatment is by Yeung. In dealing with the phrase "your faith has healed/saved you," she considers Mark 5:24–34 parr.; 10:46–52 parr.; Luke 7:36–50; 17:11–19 (*Faith in Jesus and Paul*, 53–63, 170–95).

67. I discuss this in ch. 4.

68. John 4:48 and 6:26 might be implicit exceptions.

69. So, essentially, Davies and Allison, *Matthew*, 2:354; Edwards, *The Sign of Jonah*, 77–78. Thiessen (*Miracle Stories*, 296 n. 35) writes: "It is questionable whether the 'sign' in Mk 8:11f. can possibly refer to a miracle of Jesus of the sort described in the synoptic miracle stories. If it refers to something quite different, this tradition cannot simply be cited as an example of the relativisation of synoptic

major usage of "sign" in the Old Testament, especially when paired with "wonder," concerns the dramatic miracles of national deliverance at the exodus.[70] Similarly, Josephus's so-called sign-prophets seemingly promised this kind of large-scale confirmatory miracle.[71] In our passages, "from heaven" likely points in this direction, indicating something cosmic in origin or degree.[72] This would be different from the kind of miracles Jesus has been performing.[73]

But option 3 is also promising. Theissen puts it simply: "Rejection of the demand for signs is not a rejection of signs."[74] One could still see miracles having an authenticating function—rightfully understood and prioritized—and criticize a skepticism that demanded such a display before committing. More precisely, the question may be one of allegiance, a condition that might affect what Jesus did or how it was understood.[75] In this case, Jesus might have understood his miracles as signs, but his opponents did not recognize them as such.

We need not finally choose between options 2 and 3, since both may be operative. In either case, it is plausible to allow that Jesus viewed miracles as authentication in some sense but at the same time criticized a demand for miraculous proof—be it a "sign" on a cosmic scale or more "ordinary" healings.

---

miracles." Twelftree (*Miracle Worker*, 82) writes: "Also, readers can assume that the Pharisees are aware of Jesus' fame as a miracle worker." Linton ("The Demand for a Sign from Heaven," 113, 128) notes that most writers agree that the sign must be "of a special kind, greater than the other miracles," though he demurs. Roskovec ("Miracle Worker," 881–82) writes: "Only if Jesus' 'miracles' were not perceived as satisfactorily convincing 'signs' is it understandable that he was asked to provide such legitimization of his identity and claim." Hägerland (*Jesus and the Forgiveness of Sins*, 210–13) too distinguishes Jesus's miracles of healing from authenticating signs as referred to in Mark 8:11. So also B. Meyer, *The Aims of Jesus*, 158. Gibson ("Jesus' Refusal," 38–39 n. 8) surveys about fifty passages and writes that a sign is: (1) a public event, (2) happens on request, and (3) functions to either confirm a questioned prophecy or a person or action as "of God." These features are not always present in the passages (e.g., Judg 6:17 seems private), but his generalizations seem fair.

70. I discuss this in ch. 4.

71. E.g., *J. W.* 2.259–62; *Ant.* 18.85–87; 20.97–99.

72. Luz, *Matthew*, 2:216 n. 26. His examples include: Sib. Or. 3:786–806; 4 Ezra 4:52–5:13; 6:12–27. So also Keener, *Matthew*, 421. His examples include Josephus, *J.W.* 6.288–91. Davies and Allison (*Matthew*, 2:580) write: "Probably one should think of an unambiguous, eschatological sign, one so dramatic or cosmic in scope as to preclude the need for interpretation." Alternatively, "from heaven" might mean "from God," in which case they wanted a sign unambiguously divine. So also Guelich, *Mark 1–8:26*, 414.

73. As Twelftree (*Miracle Worker*, 82) argues: "The Pharisees are looking for a phenomenon quite different from the miracles so far described by Mark, something reminiscent of the authenticating miracles of the Old Testament prophets." So also Gibson, "Jesus' Refusal," 53. Similarly, Hooker, *Signs of a Prophet*, 18.

74. Theissen, *Miracle Stories*, 296.

75. As Sanders (*Historical Figure*, 168) writes: "The difference in his replies to requests for signs … may show the difference in audience: to his enemies he offered no signs, but those who had eyes to see would perceive that God was active in his ministry." Similarly, Merrill, "The Sign of Jonah," 23–24; Hagner, *Matthew*, 1:354; Eve, *Healer from Nazareth*, 100; Yeung, *Faith in Jesus and Paul*, 94. For those who might view Jesus as a faith healer, his refusal indicates an inability to heal in that environment. See Hägerland, *Jesus and the Forgiveness of Sins*, 210; M. Smith, *Jesus the Magician*, 14. Cf. Mark 6:5.

In summary, I have argued that there are several well-attested passages where Jesus appeals to miracles as somehow confirmatory (Luke 7:22 par.; 11:20 par.; 10:13 par.) and that this is coherent in light of the background material where miracles could be confirmatory. At the same time, however, we see that Jesus shows a certain reserve toward authenticating miracles and refuses to offer a sign—however defined. This is supported by the "miracle-secret" motif and how Jesus's healings were typically preceded by faith. It seems plausible that both lines of evidence could be true. There is no reason Jesus could not occasionally point to his miracles as demonstrations of God's favor but also qualify the evidential value of miracles and resist defining himself by such demonstrations.[76] Especially to the "insider" who came to him in faith, the miracles would serve as personal authentication.[77]

The Miracles of Jesus and a Lifestyle of Weakness

We find an interesting contrast with the miracles that demonstrated the authoritative power of Jesus in what we might call a lifestyle of weakness. Here we use "weakness" generally to summarize a pattern of hardship in Jesus's life and message. While this contrast between numinous power and personal weakness is suggested to us especially by Paul, we will see that it is also present for Jesus.[78] In Jesus's case, we have a kind of "cultural" weakness, whereby Jesus rejected power, wealth, and ease and instead followed a path of suffering and service.[79] We will explore this from a few different angles.

We see first that Jesus's ministry was marked by deprivation.[80] His was an itinerant ministry throughout Galilee and Judea (e.g., Mark 5:1; 7:24, 31; 8:27; Luke 13:34 par.; John 2:13, 23; 4:45; 5:1).[81] Crossan notes that a simpler option existed, with Jesus and his group settling down in one place and then making people seek them out.[82] Instead, they stayed on the move. This itinerancy led to an essential

---

76. As Seccombe (*The King of God's Kingdom*, 293) writes, "Although he refused requests to do signs proving his divine authorization, Jesus nevertheless performed a number of miracles whose chief purpose seems to have been to give a sign."

77. As Hooker (*Signs of a Prophet*, 77) notes: "He refused to perform *authenticating* miracles. . . . Yet for those who had the eyes to see, these miracles were also sufficient proof that Jesus was a 'true' prophet acting with authority from God, and thus *served* as 'authenticating miracles'—not, indeed, to outsiders, but to those who already believed in him."

78. The commonality of suffering has been argued before in the Jesus-Paul debate: Wolff, "Humility and Self-Denial," 145–60; Schoberg, *Perspectives of Jesus in the Writings of Paul*, 137–241.

79. Aspects of what Paul associates with the term *weaknesses* in 2 Cor 12:10 include the sorts of themes we will see in Jesus's life.

80. The term is Wolff's (See "Humility and Self-Denial," 145–50).

81. Ibid., 146.

82. Crossan (*The Historical Jesus*, 346) writes: "Neither Jesus nor his followers are supposed to settle down in one place and establish there a brokered presence. And, as healers, we would expect them to stay in one place, to establish around them a group of followers, and to have people come to them. Instead, they go out to people and have, as it were, to start anew each morning."

homelessness: "The Son of Man has nowhere to lay his head" (Luke 9:58).[83] Going hand-in-hand with this, Jesus never receives payment for his healings.[84] On the contrary, Jesus favors the poor—radically so.[85] Allison thus argues that Jesus was a millenarian ascetic:

> Jesus and those around him were of more than temperate character. They practiced a rigorous self-denial for religious ends. They chose to forsake money and live in poverty. They elected to leave their homes and wander about without sandals. They decided to abandon wives and business. And some of them at least adopted celibacy. Surely such governing of themselves with extraordinary restraint, such denial of the usual amenities average villages around them took for granted, deserves to be called "asceticism."[86]

Similar to this is a theme of humble service.[87] Jesus taught his disciples that they must renounce striving and honor and instead serve.[88] In many of these passages, we have eschatological reversal, where God elevates the station of the lowly.[89] Though some elements are debated, all the Gospels portray Jesus as serving or self-sacrificing.[90] We also find a pattern of suffering and a calling to follow Jesus unto death.[91] That Jesus predicted his own death (as in Mark 8:31 parr.) is of course

83. Wolff, "Humility and Self-Denial," 147. The Jesus Seminar (Funk and Hoover, *The Five Gospels*, 316) is favorable to authenticity. Twelftree (*Jesus the Exorcist*, 214) notes passages that show weak ties to family and home (Mark 3:21; 3:31–35; 10:28–30 parr.; Luke 11:27–28; 9:58 par.), though because of references to Jesus operating from Capernaum, he disputes the image of Jesus as homeless. Yet Wolff ("Humility and Self-Denial," 147) is probably right that Luke 9:58 par. displays Jesus's general experience. Similar is Luke 9:59–62 par.

84. Kahl, *New Testament Miracle Stories*, 146. Though as Eve (*Healer from Nazareth*, 122) writes, some recompense might be assumed, such as respect or hospitality. E.g., Luke 8:1–3; 10:7–9 par.

85. E.g., Mark 6:8–9 parr.; 10:17–22 parr.; 10:23–31 parr.; Luke 6:20–25 par.; 11:3 par.; 12:22–34 par.; 14:12–14, 33; 16:13 par. On this theme, see Wolff, "Humility and Self-Denial," 147–48; Dunn, *Jesus Remembered*, 516–26; B. Longenecker, "Good News to the Poor," 38–45.

86. Allison, *Millenarian Prophet*, 215. For objections to the label, in part because Jesus did not fast (Mark 2:18–22 parr.), see ibid., 211–16. "Jesus could have been ascetic in some respects . . . but not in others" (ibid., 211).

87. Again the term is Wolff's ("Humility and Self-Denial," 154).

88. E.g., Mark 9:33–37 parr.; 10:14–15 parr.; 10:35–45 parr.; Luke 14:7–14; 18:9–14; Matt 18:3–4; 23:8–12.

89. E.g., In passages already listed: Mark 10:31 parr.; Luke 14:11; 18:14; Matt 18:3–4; 23:12. Additionally, e.g.: Luke 6:20–23 par.; 6:24–26; 14:15–24 par.; 16:19–31. See Dunn, *Jesus Remembered*, 412–17. He writes: "Where we find such a consistent emphasis within the Jesus tradition we can scarcely doubt that it was an emphasis in Jesus' own preaching" (ibid., 417).

90. Famously so in Mark, most succinctly in 10:45. Though the expectation of death and ransom is debated, the reference to service is easier to corroborate as Jesus's attitude. See, e.g., Funk and Hoover, *The Five Gospels*, 95–96, 389 (though they assign it a gray rating). Matthew and Luke both include a version of this saying (Matt 20:28; Luke 22:27). The theme is also present in John, e.g., 13:1–15.

91. Wolff's heading is "Suffering Persecution" ("Humility and Self-Denial," 156). Schoberg calls it "Jesus' Challenge to Share His Fate" (*Perspectives of Jesus*, 137).

debated. But speaking more generally, there are reasons to believe that Jesus would be aware of the possibility or probability of death.[92] We also have multiple traditions in which Jesus's followers are called to embrace suffering, be faithful unto death, and even follow Jesus into death.[93]

For the most part, there is no connection in the Gospel traditions between Jesus's authoritative power in miracles and a lifestyle of weakness.[94] There are some examples, however.

First, the Gospel of Mark famously combines Jesus as a miracle worker with a path of weakness and suffering.[95] For this reason, Remus calls Jesus, in Mark's portrayal (and in all the Gospels), "a wounded healer."[96] The contrast is so extreme that some have argued that Mark is opposing a divine-man understanding of Jesus by deliberately opposing the image of a miracle worker.[97] While the juxtaposition of suffering and miracle working is an emphasis of Mark, given what we have seen above, the combination in Jesus's ministry seems fair to the evidence.[98]

Second, we have touchpoints in additional passages, though debates over historicity make them problematic. One example might be the Q account of Jesus's temptation, where he refuses a miracle to alleviate hunger (Luke 4:3–4 par.) and refuses an easier way to authenticate himself by miraculous demonstration (Luke 4:9–12 par.).[99] A second example might be Jesus's refusal to call for angels to save him (Matt 26:53).

Conclusion on Jesus

In this section, we have considered two tensions. The first concerns authentication. On the one hand, we have key passages where Jesus viewed his miracles as

92. Schoberg (*Perspectives of Jesus*, 138–47) argues this on the basis of: (1) the context of violence in Judea; (2) the death of John; and (3) the opposition that Jesus faced from different groups.

93. E.g., taking up one's cross (Luke 14:27 par.; Mark 8:34 parr.; Gos. Thom. 55:2). For arguments favoring authenticity, see ibid., 155–59. Cf., more generally, Borg, *Jesus: A New Vision*, 122 n. 65.

94. We will consider relevant background material in ch. 5.

95. See, e.g., Dawson, *Healing, Weakness*, 99.

96. Remus, *Jesus as Healer*, 38, 50–51.

97. E.g., Weeden, *Mark*. This thesis does not finally convince. See, e.g., Blackburn, Theios Anēr, 1–12, 263–66; Dawson, *Healing, Weakness*, 98. Chief for our purposes is how Mark seemingly treats the miracles positively. Theissen (*Miracle Stories*, 294) quips: "Can Mark really have told sixteen miracle stories solely in order to warn against belief in miracles?"

98. It is well-attested that Jesus was a miracle worker and one whose ministry and message were marked by deprivation, service, and suffering. These themes are attested in all Gospel sources, one way or another. We have seen already its juxtaposition in Mark. Kolenkow ("Paul and Opponents in 2 Cor 10–13," 363) writes that "'Q' emphasizes both miracles and the demand for following in suffering." E.g., Luke 7:1–10 par. (miracle); 14:27 par. (suffering). So too: M (26:53 [suffering chosen over possible miracle]); L (7:11–17 [miracle]; 9:52–56 [rejection]); and John (2:1–11 [miracle]; 12:27 [suffering]).

99. Yet authentication may not be the point of the latter temptation, since it is not portrayed as public. See Bock, *Luke*, 1:379–80.

demonstrating authoritative power (Luke 7:22 par.; 11:20 par.; 10:13 par.), a feature supported by broad Gospel themes. On the other hand, we have a strong tradition of Jesus's refusing to grant an authenticating sign (Mark 8:11–13 parr.), which is supported by the miracle-secret motif and the place of faith as usually prior to miracles. The second tension concerns how Jesus combined miraculous power with what might be called a lifestyle of cultural weakness (deprivation, humble service, and a call to suffering and death). Though this path called for a resolve that was anything but "weak," to an outside observer, Jesus's path would stand in marked contrast to a path of ease, comfort, and honor that would constitute a sort of triumphalism.

We suggest that these tensions should not be considered strong enough to call into question either set of evidence. One can easily see Jesus as pointing to his miracles as authenticating in some instances and refusing to do so in others. When we add the contrast of miraculous power with Jesus's lifestyle of personal weakness, it seems appropriate to call Jesus's miracles *(qualified) signs of authoritative power with a lifestyle of weakness.*

The Miracles of Paul as (Qualified) Signs of Authoritative Power with a Lifestyle of Weakness

When we reach Paul and the questions of authenticating miracles, we reach a diversity of opinion similar to what we saw concerning Jesus. Some scholars clearly see Paul making use of miracles to demonstrate the authenticity of his position as one sent from God.[100] Others just as strongly deny the point.[101] We will consider both streams of evidence before considering Paul's lifestyle of weakness.

The Miracles of Paul as Signs of Authoritative Power

We saw above that both Greco-Roman and Jewish backgrounds make intelligible the concept of miracles as authentication. With this still in mind, we return to our key passages, 2 Cor 12:12 and Rom 15:18–19, plus some additional evidence.

In ch. 2, we discussed 2 Cor 12:11–12 and alluded to various ambiguities. Two uncertainties bedevil discussions: the provocation of Paul's response and the origin of the phrase "signs of an apostle."

---

100. Sanders (*Paul,* 24) writes: "Paul performed miracles which established his authority as a true prophet or spokesman of God." So also Latourelle, *Miracles of Jesus,* 286–87; Garland, *2 Corinthians,* 529; Bultmann, *Second Letter to the Corinthians,* 231.

101. Like Fee (*God's Empowering Presence,* 888): "Not only does he not point to miracles as grounds for accepting either his gospel or his ministry, but on the contrary he rejected such criteria as authenticating ministry of any kind." So, essentially, Murphy-O'Connor, *Theology of the Second Letter,* 122–24.

First, then, what charge prompts Paul's response? That Paul's opponents found him insufficient is clear (2 Cor 10:1, 10; 11:5, 13:3), and this might involve Paul's miracles and experiences since he brings them up (12:1–4, 11–13)—though he might be responding to different criticism. The issues involved are complex and wider than miracles.[102]

One possibility, as noted in ch. 2, was that Paul's opponents accused him of being unable to perform miracles at all.[103] This is possible but perhaps undermined by Paul's somewhat low-key inclusion of miracles in reply. If the ability to perform miracles had been directly challenged, we might have expected a more focused rebuttal. A second, more plausible suggestion is that Paul's opponents criticized the *degree* of miraculous manifestations in Paul's ministry, with Paul appearing an insufficient pneumatic by comparison.[104] The expectation for manifestations of the Spirit could be part of a broader issue over the proper lifestyle of an apostle—with Paul's weakness, illness, and demeanor all against him.[105] A third related possibility was that it was Paul's inability to heal himself—despite being a healer—that was the problem.[106] This is compatible with some of the other options—and would make sense of how Paul is able to claim having experienced visions and having worked miracles and still receive opposition.

A fourth possibility is that miracles were not an issue of dispute at all. Kolenkow argues that *both* Paul and his opponents valued *both* miracles and suffering and that their dispute lies elsewhere.[107] In such a case, Paul could raise the topic of the miracles that accompanied his ministry unprompted by a specific challenge. Due to the inherent problems in mirror-reading, it is impossible to choose with confidence between these options—though a combination of the second and third possibilities, or alternatively the fourth alone, seems preferable. As we will see, however, a specific decision does not greatly affect our argument.

---

102. Sumney ("Studying Paul's Opponents," 14) summarizes four approaches for Paul's opponents in 2 Corinthians: advocates of torah boundary-markers for Gentiles, Gnostics, "divine men," and "pneumatics." Winter (*Philo and Paul among the Sophists*, 237–39) argues Paul was facing a Hellenistic sophist movement where Paul's oratory skills did not measure up.

103. As Haenchen (*Acts of the Apostles*, 113; cf. p. 563) argues on 2 Cor 12:12: "The exploits in question were so little out of the ordinary that his opponents flatly denied his ability to perform miracles."

104. See Georgi, *Opponents of Paul*, 236.

105. Sumney (*Identifying Paul's Opponents*, 177–78) concludes that the central issue in 2 Cor 10–13 is how the Spirit directs the lifestyle of an apostle; the opponents' view included a lack of difficulty, a performance of miracles, good speaking skills, and obvious superiority. Perhaps in this category belongs the suggestion of Twelftree (*Paul and the Miraculous*, 212–16) that Paul was not as actively involved in *initiating* miracles as were his opponents.

106. Jervell, "The Signs of an Apostle," 94. He writes: "Paulus ist ein kranker Wundertäter, Charismatiker und Pneumatiker" (Jervell, "Der schwache Charismatiker," 191–92; cf. pp. 190–98); cf. Holmberg, *Paul and Power*, 76–77.

107. Kolenkow, "Paul and Opponents," 364. Namely, issues of power and weakness in relation to leadership (pp. 365–66).

The second uncertainty in the passage concerns the origin of the term "signs of an apostle." Was it a standard held by the Corinthian congregation?[108] Did it come from the opponents?[109] Or was it Paul's own creation?[110] This too is impossible to know with confidence. Fortunately for our purposes, the answers to both these uncertainties do not greatly impact our argument. This is because, regardless of whether the phrase "signs of an apostle" and the issue of miracles were raised by the Corinthians, the opponents, or Paul, *within his apostolic defense, Paul still uses in a positive way both the phrase "signs of an apostle" and a claim to have performed miracles.*[111]

The way that Paul associates miracles with apostleship should not be missed.[112] As Aune writes, Paul presents his miracles here as legitimization for his position as apostle.[113] It is not the whole of that legitimization, of course. Paul will immediately chronicle his suffering and weaknesses—and he elsewhere appeals to resurrection appearances and successful church planting.[114] Yet the presence of God manifested in "signs, wonders, and powers" would also serve as confirmation that Paul was acting on behalf of God.[115] He was "not at all inferior" as an apostle (2 Cor 12:11), in part because of these miracles. Thus, Harris paraphrases: "The signs of genuine apostleship were clearly evident as I was working among you with the greatest of patient endurance. You saw the signs and wonders as well as other displays of God's power that all authenticate my apostleship."[116]

In Rom 15:18–19, we are once again in the context of a validation of Paul's apostolic mission. The tone is not immediately polemic, but 15:18–19 comes on the heels of Paul's description of himself as "a minister of Christ Jesus to the Gentiles" (15:16), and before Paul reveals what is probably the main purpose of

108. As suggested by Barrett, *Second Epistle to the Corinthians*, 321; Murphy-O'Connor, *Theology of the Second Letter*, 122.

109. As suggested by Käsemann, "Die Legitimität des Apostels," 477; cf. Betz, *Der Apostel Paulus*, 70–72.

110. As allowed by: Harris, *Second Epistle*, 874; Garland, *2 Corinthians*, 529.

111. It is thus difficult to understand the comment of Dunn (*Theology of Paul the Apostle*, 557 n. 138) that 2 Cor 11–12 (esp. 12:11–13) shows "Paul's misgivings about relying on 'signs and wonders' as proof of apostleship."

112. Of course, as discussed in ch. 2, Paul's two uses of σημεῖον here are not the same. The first, in "signs of an apostle" is probably broad and not referring only to miracles. Rather, it concerns the whole array of what should mark an apostle. The second use is clearly focused on miracles though, and in conjunction with δύναμις and τέρας presents miracles as one element of the "signs of an apostle."

113. A picture, as Aune (*Prophecy in Early Christianity*, 194) writes, "in continuity with the image of Jesus and the early Christian leaders depicted in Acts." He cites 2 Cor 12:12; Rom 15:19; Gal 3:5; 1 Thess 1:5; 1 Cor 2:4.

114. As mentioned in ch. 2, Twelftree (*Paul and the Miraculous*, 217) shows that Paul stresses other aspects of apostleship: seeing the Lord (1 Cor 9:1; 15:8–9), enduring hardship (2 Cor 11:23–27), and resultant churches (1 Cor 9:2; 2 Cor 3:2).

115. Cf. 1 Cor 4:20, which I will discuss in ch. 4.

116. Harris, *Second Epistle to the Corinthians*, 960.

his letter—that the Roman church might support him on his push further west (15:23–24). Echoes of trouble can be detected in 15:31.[117] Paul needs the Roman church to accept him and his gospel if they are to support his mission.

It is notable that we find a reference to Paul's miracles here in the middle of ch. 15—in practical terms, the climax of Paul's presentation of his ministry to a church unknown. Lest anyone doubt that Christ lay behind Paul's pioneering work to the Gentiles (15:18), God had set his seal of approval upon Paul's ministry—as it were—by testifying to it "by the power of signs and wonders, by the power of the Spirit of God" (15:19). Here Paul seems to use miracles as implicit authentication of his apostolic ministry in a broad sense.[118]

It is worthwhile to recall that in ch. 2 we noted how, in the passages where Paul is most unambiguous about his miracles (Rom 15:18–19; 2 Cor 12:12), he is also directly concerned with establishing his apostolic credentials.[119] Paul's association of miracles with the phrase "signs of an apostle" is of a piece with this. Part of his apostolic authentication comes in the form of miracles.[120]

One somewhat obscure passage may also support an evidential value for miracles. In 1 Cor 14:24–25, Paul writes that, if an unbeliever enters the worship service and witnesses prophecy in action, "he will worship God and declare that God is really among you." It is not necessary to negotiate all the difficulties in this passage.[121] I am rather interested in the "punchline" concerning an imaginary unbeliever witnessing prophecy. Here its effectiveness demonstrates the reality of Christian profession and authenticates believers as bearers of genuine divine revelation.

This may be significant. If Paul can envision a situation where an unbeliever witnesses prophecy and it leads him to faith, we are close to a situation where an unbeliever might witness another kind of miracle and reach the same conclusion. In the context, miraculous phenomena are not far from Paul's mind (12:9–10). While to modern ears there might be a dramatic difference between prophecy and miracles, in that prophecy sounds more "plausible," such a distinction probably does not hold for Paul. Both prophecy and miracles are equally divine works of the Spirit.[122]

---

117. And perhaps 15:23 (cf. 3:8; 6:1).

118. As Jewett (*Romans: A Commentary*, Hermeneia [Minneapolis: Fortress, 2007], 911) notes: "These signs authenticate his ambassadorial role, and the appropriateness of his addressing the varied Christian communities in Rome."

119. Gal 3:5 may belong here. See Kelhoffer, "The Apostle Paul," 170; Schreiber, *Paulus als Wundertäter*, 271–72.

120. As Jervell ("Signs of an Apostle," 94) writes: "By his miracles, among other things, Paul proves to be a legitimate apostle."

121. See, e.g., Dunn, *Jesus and the Spirit*, 230–32.

122. Twelftree (*Paul and the Miraculous*, 25; cf. p. 26) writes that prophecy is a matter of divine revelation for Paul, citing 1 Cor 14:6, 26; 2 Cor 12:1, 7; Gal 1:12; 2:2. "In this we see that Paul takes

But it might be unwise to push too far. After all, Paul's imagined scenario speaks of prophecy, not miracles—and he places miracles and healings *after* prophets in the list of 1 Cor 12:28.[123] It thus might be dangerous to equate the functions of prophecy and miracles too closely, though they may indeed belong the same category. For our purposes, then, 1 Cor 14:23–25 should probably remain only secondary evidence.

But if Paul sees some evidential value in miracles, akin to what he says of prophecy in 1 Cor 14:22, then we would have something similar to what he writes in 1 Cor 2:3–5. This is one of our debatable passages where Paul might refer to miracles: "I was with you in weakness and in fear and much trembling, and my speech and my message were not in plausible words of wisdom, but in demonstration of the Spirit and of power [ἐν ἀποδείξει πνεύματος καὶ δυνάμεως], so that your faith might not rest in the wisdom of men but in the power of God" (1 Cor 2:3–5).

Here Paul contrasts himself with the sort of rhetorical oratory that the Corinthians faulted him for lacking.[124] Instead, Paul emphasizes how his message was ἐν ἀποδείξει πνεύματος καὶ δυνάμεως.[125] It was this Spirit and power which marked his presentation to the Corinthians.[126]

Unfortunately, as Ashton writes, Paul is "maddeningly reticent about the nature of the spiritual power" referenced here.[127] On the one hand, it is easy to see why some understand a reference to miracles.[128] We have the colocation of Spirit and power, a pairing that takes place elsewhere for Paul in contexts of miracles (e.g., Rom 15:19; 1 Cor 12:9–10), and a miraculous demonstration of the Spirit's power would contrast nicely with rhetorical skill. On the other hand, many commentators do not see a reference to miracles.[129] Two primary reasons include the

---

revelation to be in the same orbit of the miraculous with healing and miracles." See also Kolenkow, "Relationships between Miracle," 1470–1506.

123. On the significance of this, see González, "Healing in the Pauline Epistles," 571.

124. On the essential issue here being one of insufficient rhetoric, see Lim, "Not in Persuasive Words," 146–47; cf. Winter, *Philo and Paul*, 143–64.

125. On translating the *hapax legomenon* and the likely hendiadys, see Fee, *First Epistle to the Corinthians*, 100. As Snyder (*First Corinthians*, 32) notes, Paul's insufficiency here actually follows a biblical pattern: Exod 4:10; Isa 6:5; Jer 1:6.

126. As Lim ("Not in Persuasive Words," 147) writes: "He asserts that his word and his preaching are based upon a demonstration, not of the rhetorical kind, but of the Spirit and of power."

127. Ashton, *Religion of Paul*, 163.

128. E.g., Kelhoffer, "Paul and Justin," 172; González, "Why the Silence," 566–67; Ashton, *Religion of Paul*, 165; Evans, "Paul the Exorcist and Healer," 364–65; Jervell, "Signs of an Apostle," 93; Lockwood, *1 Corinthians*, 86; Grosheide, *First Epistle to the Corinthians*, 61–62; Sanders, *Paul*, 24; Paget, "Miracles in Early Christianity," 135 n. 25; Nielsen, *Heilung und Verkündigung*, 201. So, seemingly, Peerbolte, "Paul the Miracle Worker," 195–96. Dawson (*Healing, Weakness*, 172) keeps "an open mind."

129. E.g., Garland, *1 Corinthians*, 87; Schreiber, *Paulus als Wundertäter*, 252; Ciampa and Rosner, *First Letter to the Corinthians*, 117–18; Thiselton, *First Epistle to the Corinthians*, 221–22. So, seemingly, Dunn, *Jesus and the Spirit*, 226–27; Fitzmyer, *First Corinthians*, 173–74. Fee (*First Epistle to the Corinthians*, 100) says a reference to miracles "is possible, but not probable."

emphasis on weakness in the context, and the apparently negative reference to Jews asking for a sign in 1:22.[130]

Twelftree presents the strongest argument for seeing miracles. As mentioned, "Spirit" and "power" occur together elsewhere with miraculous or strange phenomena.[131] The objection that Paul rejects the request for signs in 1:22 is not decisive.[132] Neither is the use of the singular δύναμις as opposed to plural.[133] Nor is the emphasis on weakness in the immediate context.[134] That Paul uses "demonstration" (ἀπόδειξις) also seems to imply something more than just speech.[135] Twelftree concludes: "The expression is a reference to miracles that accompanied and were the demonstration or proof of his proclamation."[136]

These arguments are strong, though certainty is elusive. We note, however, that this passage still supports our argument, at least to a degree, even if one decides that miracles are not in view. This is because, as noted in ch. 2, Paul closely associates miracles with the Holy Spirit. An association with the Holy Spirit *generally* could thus be seen to apply also to miracles *specifically*, because miracles are themselves manifestations of the Spirit. So, as seen even in a nonmiraculous view of 1 Cor 2:4, the Spirit still brings confirmation to Paul's message.[137] It is plausible that miracles, as clear manifestations of the Spirit, would bring similar confirmation.[138]

We have seen that, in our two key passages, Rom 15:18–19 and 2 Cor 12:12, Paul appeals to miracles as part of his apostolic defense. Secondary support can probably be found in the way prophecy is imagined to lead to conversion in 1 Cor 14:24, and also found in 1 Cor 2:4. Though Paul does not often raise the issue, this

130. E.g., ibid.; Ciampa and Rosner, *First Letter to the Corinthians*, 118.

131. His examples include: Luke 1:17, 35; 4:14; Acts 1:8; Rom 1:4; 15:19; 1 Thess 1:5 (Twelftree, *Paul and the Miraculous*, 196).

132. Ibid., 197. As we saw for Jesus, this request for a "sign" plausibly refers to different phenomena from healing or exorcism.

133. Ibid., 198. The plural would more clearly indicate miracles (see BDAG 263.3). Yet Twelftree (*Paul and the Miraculous*, 184, 198) shows that the singular can also be used for miracles (Mark 6:5; 9:39), though it is more often what *causes* miracles: e.g., Mark 5:30 par.; Luke 5:17; 6:19; 9:1; Acts 3:12; 4:7. An example of the latter in Paul is Rom 15:19. Twelftree (ibid., 198) argues that Paul does not use the plural in 1 Cor 2:4 because it might imply a contrast between the Spirit and miracles—and by using two singular terms they can form a hendiadys.

134. Ibid., 198–200. The contrast is between God's power and Paul's weakness. This may allow for *God* to demonstrate real power despite *Paul's* insufficiency.

135. Ibid., 200. BDAG (p. 109) puts it this way: "lit. *proof of spirit and power*, i.e. proof consisting in possession of the Holy Spirit and miracle-working power."

136. Twelftree, *Paul and the Miraculous*, 201.

137. Gunkel (*Influence of the Holy Spirit*, 81) says, though not of our verse: "The presence and activity of the Spirit in the world are for Paul a divine guarantee of the Christian faith."

138. This is one problem with an objection of Fee (*Empowering Presence*, 888) to miracles as authentication for Paul. After rejecting such a function, he writes: "The cross, with the subsequent resurrection, and the present gift of the Spirit was all the authentication he ever appealed to." The problem is that miracles would be part of the "present gift of the Spirit" and thus would also carry authenticating implications.

evidence should be sufficient to show that, at times, Paul was indeed willing to adduce miracles as authentication.[139]

The Miracles of Paul and a Resistance to Signs

We will pursue a counterpoint in two ways. First, we will address Paul's implicit rejection of the request for a sign (1 Cor 1:22–23). Second, we will show that Paul, in some striking ways, emphasizes "the word" over miracles.

First we consider 1 Cor 1:22–23. Here we have Paul, in his first salvo against the Corinthian preoccupation with worldly wisdom, appealing to the foolishness of the cross (1:18–25). In the midst of this, Paul writes: "For Jews demand signs [σημεῖα αἰτοῦσιν] and Greeks seek wisdom, but we preach Christ crucified, a stumbling block to Jews and folly to Gentiles, but to those who are called, both Jews and Greeks, Christ the power [δύναμιν] of God and the wisdom of God" (1 Cor 1:22–24).

It is interesting that, despite the main concern in this section of 1 Corinthians being the issue of "wisdom," Paul nonetheless includes a request for "signs," something seemingly unprovoked. One suspects that Paul uses the Jew-Greek contrast as a merism to include all humanity (cf. 1 Cor 10:32; 12:13), and while primarily addressing the presenting issue of wisdom in relation to the Greek world, he associates the Jewish world with what would have been a well-known sticking point—authenticating signs. In 1:24 we have God's answer, as it were, to both requests. Here Christ as "the wisdom of God" (1:24) clearly corresponds to the Greek desire for wisdom (1:22). Accordingly, it looks like Christ as "the power of God" (1:24) corresponds to the Jewish request (1:22). A request for a sign, therefore, seemingly involves power.

What does Paul have in mind by these signs? While he does not specify, most see some kind of authenticating miracle, perhaps cosmic or apocalyptic.[140] This makes sense based on the backgrounds discussed above.[141]

What is the relation of these signs to those in 2 Cor 12:12, where Paul treats the term positively? As in the case of Jesus, we have essentially three options. First, if

---

139. As Latourelle (*Miracles of Jesus*, 286) notes: "God reveals himself in the words of the message, and he 'authenticates' his revelation by the miracle-working power that he gives to his apostle." Ashton (*Religion of Paul*) is even stronger: "Without his mastery of spiritual gifts, his power to perform cures and miracles, his prophetic and interpretive skills, his speaking in tongues . . . Paul's authority, as he was only too aware, would vanish" (p. 211). Similarly: "Nor should we forget that he ascribes his success in winning converts to the most spectacular gift of the lot, the power to work miracles" (p. 210). Ashton is apparently thinking of passages like 1 Cor 2:4 (cf. p. 165).

140. E.g., Fee, *First Epistle to the Corinthians*, 77–78; Garland, *1 Corinthians*, 69; Twelftree, *Paul and the Miraculous*, 197; Ciampa and Rosner, *First Letter to the Corinthians*, 99. So, seemingly: Thiselton, *First Epistle to the Corinthians*, 170–71.

141. Exod 4; Josephus, *Ant.* 20.167–70. Cf. Mark 8:11–13 parr.

the references to signs are similar enough, it could mean a flat-out contradiction or development in thought, perhaps forced by Paul's opponents. Second, different kinds of phenomena might be in view despite the same terminology, with the Jewish request for signs envisioning something more cosmic, and with Paul using the same term to refer to (and reinterpret) more "mundane" healings or exorcisms.[142] Third, similar phenomena might be in view, with the difference being that signs might be given to those who ask aright but not to skeptics and naysayers.[143]

What is Paul's opinion of this request, however imagined? He rejects it, as least as articulated by the envisioned speakers.[144] Instead of a messianic sign of power, Paul offers a messiah powerless on a cross, a reversal causing Jews to stumble (1:23). Twelftree argues that Paul's response is intended to answer the two requests, one for a sign and one for wisdom. While the cross as God's wisdom answers the Greek's request for wisdom, the cross as God's power answers the Jewish request for a sign, preparing the way for a reference to miracles in the "demonstration of the Spirit and of power" in 2:4.[145]

Even if we were to grant this, Paul still seems to reject the demand for a sign in 1:22—at least as framed by the "askers." His preaching did not include the giving of the sort of signs envisioned here. This verse thus forms the primary evidence that Paul would resist either (1) an *authenticating function* for miracles, (2) *certain kinds of cosmic signs*, or (3) a *demand* for confirmatory signs.

Because we have, in some sense, an explicit rejection of authentication-by-miracle in 1 Cor 1:22–23, we can bring to bear some implicit evidence that might not be strong enough alone. This involves various ways in which Paul, as we saw in the case of Jesus, seems to downplay miracles or, in various ways, values gospel proclamation over the performance of miracles.

First, we *do* wish to note the relative scarcity of Paul's reference to performing miracles. Dawson summarizes, in terms of healings:

> A decision to be made is whether or not Paul's writing about healing is less than one would expect from the milieu in which he was working. He mentions his own miracle-healing in the authentic letters between two and five times. . . . Even if we were to accept the five as evidence of Paul presenting evidence of himself as a miracle-worker, this *is* a small number, taking into account the relatively large volume of the letters, the climate of first-century interest in miraculous healing, and the evidence of the synoptic gospels and Acts, which purport to present the situation

---

142. I discuss this in ch. 4.

143. Hans Conzelmann (*1 Corinthians*, 46 n. 75) distinguishes it like this: "Miracles are granted. To *demand* them is to prove one's wickedness."

144. It is possible to see Paul's description of Jews seeking signs and Greeks seeking wisdom as not necessarily negative but only as dangerous if taken too far. E.g., Thiselton, *First Epistle to the Corinthians*, 170.

145. Twelftree, *Paul and the Miraculous*, 197.

regarding divine healing immediately before, and contemporaneously with, Paul's mission. More importantly, it is clear that Paul does not stress the occasions when he did heal. There are *no* concrete examples in the letters, and no indication that healing was of primary importance to Paul in his proclamation of the gospel.[146]

Dawson is speaking only of healings and immediately goes on to note that Paul has access to charismatic gifts such as prophecy, tongues, and visions. Nor do I wish to counteract the arguments in ch. 2 that the performance of miracles was indeed important to Paul's ministry—even only on the basis of Rom 15:18–19 and 2 Cor 12:12—and that the lack of mention can be plausibly explained in various ways, including Paul's reticence to stress his own gifts, as well as the occasional nature of Paul's letters.

Yet at the same time, the relative scarcity of the topic in Paul does support a certain reserve with respect to Paul in terms of viewing miracles as authentication. Notably, where Paul is at pains to authenticate his apostleship in Gal 1–2, he makes no mention of miracles performed. We thus do not wish to overplay the evidence and claim that evidential miracles were more important in Paul's proclamation than in fact they were. In his letters, Paul only rarely appeals to miracles.

Far more often, we have Paul describing his apostolic ministry as one of preaching or proclaiming.[147] This means it is fair to say that, in terms of a ministry of word or miraculous deed, Paul seems to have emphasized the word.

A parallel might be found in how Paul speaks of baptism in 1 Cor 1:17.[148] We know baptism is important to Paul (e.g., Gal 3:27; Rom 6:3–4). Yet he is still able to say: "Christ did not send me to baptize but to preach the gospel" (1 Cor 1:17). Perhaps then, we might imagine and rephrase Paul as saying: "Christ did not send me to work miracles, but to preach the gospel." The latter is clearly primary for him.

In conclusion, how can we bring together the conflicting lines of evidence we have seen thus far in Paul? We argued first that Paul did at times mention miracles as authentication (e.g., Rom 15:18–19; 2 Cor 12:12; 1 Cor 2:4 [debatable]). Conversely, we argued for an implicit rejection of the request for a sign in 1 Cor 1:22, and gave supporting evidence that Paul did not emphasize miracles as authentication. The situation is similar to what we saw in Jesus, and the options are essentially the same. We can either reject completely one side or other of the evidence, or allow both strands and see Paul maintaining a balance. This latter option seems preferable. There is no reason not to see Paul as sometimes viewing miracles as authentication and at other times rejecting the demand for a sign or downplaying

---

146. Dawson, *Healing, Weakness*, 172.

147. E.g., Rom 1:9, 15; 10:8–17; 15:18–21; 1 Cor 1:22–23; 9:14–16; 15:11; 2 Cor 2:12–17; 4:5; 10:16; Gal 1:11–23; 2:2.

148. Suggested by Daniel B. Wallace in personal conversation, spring 2013.

miracles. If we wish to hypothesize how Paul would resolve this ambiguity, we might suggest that the motives of the audience would plausibly be at issue. To those who would demand to see a sign before they would believe, Paul would refuse (1 Cor 1:22).

The Miracles of Paul and a Mission of Servanthood and Suffering

We see in Paul an interesting contrast with a miracle-working ministry that in ways demonstrated authoritative power—namely, a lifestyle of weakness. We will consider the theme generally before turning to connections with miracles.

The experience of Paul's ministry was one of deprivation, itinerancy, and home-lessness.[149] Paul writes: "To the present hour we hunger and thirst, we are poorly dressed and buffeted and homeless, and we labor, working with our own hands" (1 Cor 4:11–12).[150] To avoid appearing like he was profiting from his proclamation, Paul earned his own way as an artisan when first preaching in a city (1 Cor 4:12; 9:18; 2 Cor 11:7; 1 Thess 2:9; cf. 1 Cor 9:12–14; 1 Thess 2:5).[151] Paul believed that this lifestyle showed him to be a true servant of God and Christ.[152] He writes, "As servants of God we commend ourselves in every way: by great endurance, in afflictions . . . sleepless nights, hunger" (2 Cor 6:4–5). "Are they servants of Christ? I am a better one—I am talking like a madman—with far greater labors. . . . in toil and hardship, through many a sleepless night, in hunger and thirst, often without food, in cold and exposure" (2 Cor 11:23, 27). Paul considered himself "as poor, yet making many rich; as having nothing, yet possessing everything" (2 Cor 6:10).

Paul also presents his approach to ministry as one of humble service.[153] Despite being free, he had enslaved himself to all (1 Cor 9:19). His purpose was to serve others: "For what we proclaim is not ourselves, but Jesus Christ as Lord, with ourselves as your servants [δούλους] for Jesus' sake" (2 Cor 4:5). He understood his free preaching of the gospel to the Corinthians as an act of self-humiliation (2 Cor 11:7).[154] He aimed to act for the betterment of others: "I try to please everyone in everything I do, not seeking my own advantage, but that of many, that they may be saved. Be imitators of me, as I am of Christ" (1 Cor 10:33–11:1). As in this last

---

149. I depend on Wolff ("Humility and Self-Denial," 145–46) throughout this paragraph. Wolff includes Paul's unmarried state (e.g., 1 Cor 7:7–8; "Humility and Self-Denial," 150–51). On Paul's concern to help the poor (e.g., Gal 2:10), see Longenecker, "Good News," 51–59; Dunn, "From Jesus' Proclamation to Paul's Gospel," in *Jesus, Paul, and the Gospels* (Grand Rapids: Eerdmans, 2011), 105–6.

150. On the hardships of working as an artisan, see Hock, *Social Context*, 34–37.

151. Wolff, "Humility and Self-Denial," 146. This also kept any patrons from dictating Paul's message.

152. Ibid.

153. The term is Wolff's, and again we depend on his treatment throughout this paragraph (ibid., 154). For evidence that Paul saw his ministry in light of Isaiah's "servant," see Schreiner, *Paul*, 47–49.

154. On how his work as an artisan would open him to mockery and shame, see Hock, *Social Context*, 35–37, 60.

reference, this selflessness was modeled on the example of Jesus (cf. Rom 15:3; Phil 2:4–8; 2 Cor 8:9).

Paul's ministry was also one of suffering, and this was crucial.[155] Paul's hardships are featured prominently (e.g., 1 Cor 4:11–13; 15:30–32; 2 Cor 4:8–11; 6:4–5; 11:23–28; 12:10; Phil 3:8–10). As Wolff points out, Paul mentions his suffering as part of gospel ministry in each of his undisputed letters. Paul describes these sufferings as *similar* to Jesus's sufferings (1 Thess 1:6, 2:14–15; 1 Cor 4:12–13; 2 Cor 6:8; cf. Rom 15:3), as well as somehow *connected* to Jesus's sufferings (2 Cor 1:5; 4:10; Gal 6:17; Phil 3:10; 2 Cor 13:4). In addition, a special measure of suffering is distinctive of apostles (1 Cor 4:9; 2 Cor 1:5; 2:14–17; 11:23).[156]

We noted that, in the Gospels, Jesus's numinous power is not often brought into explicit connection with patterns of weakness and suffering. This is not the case with Paul. In fact, 2 Cor 12:12 stands in immediate connection to Paul's most developed presentation of weakness. In the Fool's Speech (11:1–12:13), Paul answers his opponents on their own terms, though it is not his wish (11:17; 12:11). One accusation had been Paul's weakness (perhaps an illness, unimpressive presence, lack of oratory skills—or combination): "For they say, 'His letters are weighty and strong, but his bodily presence is weak, and his speech of no account'" (10:10). Instead of resisting this accusation, Paul embraces it: "If I must boast, I will boast of the things that show my weakness" (11:30). In response to the refusal of his request for relief from his thorn, likely an illness, Paul formulated an important view: "I will boast all the more gladly of my weaknesses, so that the power of Christ may rest upon me. For the sake of Christ, then, I am content with weaknesses, insults, hardships, persecutions, and calamities. For when I am weak, then I am strong" (12:9–10).[157] Here we also see that Paul associated with "weakness" the broader hardships we have described throughout this section, and not just physical infirmity.

Almost immediately, we have Paul's reference to miracles (12:12). Does this weakness contradict the presence of miracles that indicate an authoritative power? Paul does not see it that way, as the close juxtaposition of both phenomena shows. It is precisely because he is weak that the power of God can be displayed so unambiguously (cf. 4:7; 13:2–4). Paul's miracles thus did not contradict his emphasis on the cross, because Paul's miracles were not brought forth in a display of triumphalism or self-aggrandizement, but rather emerged from a context of weakness and suffering.[158]

---

155. As Schreiner (*Apostle of God's Glory*, 87) writes, and develops at length elsewhere in the same work: "Suffering was not a side effect of the Pauline mission; rather it was at the very center of his apostolic evangelism."

156. Wolff, "Humility and Self-Denial," 156–57.

157. On Paul's illness, see Dawson, *Healing, Weakness*, 191–203.

158. This point comes from Barrett (*Second Epistle*, 321): "Miracles were no contradiction of the *theologia crucis* he proclaimed and practiced, since they were performed not in a context of triumphant success and prosperity, but in the midst of the distress and vilification he was obliged to endure."

Which would Paul value more in demonstrating the validity of his apostolic position—faithfulness in weakness and suffering, or miracles? If forced to choose, we would of course select the former.[159] Yet this is probably a false dichotomy. There is no reason Paul could not value both, especially because Paul's "power" was not his own.[160] Thus, both deeds of power *and* a ministry of personal weakness marked an apostle in Paul's thinking.[161]

Conclusion on Paul

In this half of the chapter, we have considered two tensions regarding Paul's miracles. The first concerns miracles as authentication. On the one hand there is limited—but significant—evidence that Paul viewed his miracles as demonstrating authoritative power (2 Cor 12:12; Rom 15:18–19; 1 Cor 2:4). On the other hand, we do have Paul's negative response to an envisioned request for a sign (1 Cor 1:22–23), and Paul mentions miracles infrequently. The second tension concerns the issue of power and weakness. On the one hand, Paul's life was one of poverty, humble service, and weakness. On the other hand, he bore a numinous power that, in his interpretation, stood in marked contrast with—though also in some sense enabled by—that weakness.

We have suggested that it is not necessary to resolve these tensions. Paul could have viewed the power of God manifested in miracles as authentication and at the same time could have rejected demands for a sign (however defined). Neither is it necessary to pit Paul's weaknesses against the numinous power to which he had access, since in his mind they complemented each other (2 Cor 12:5–12). It seems fair then to understand Paul's miracles as *(qualified) signs of authoritative power with a lifestyle of weakness.*

Comparing Jesus and Paul

For this proposed significance of miracles, we indeed seem to have a family resemblance. We have evidence of both figures presenting miracles as authentication in some sense (e.g., Luke 7:22 par.; 11:20 par.; 10:13 par.; 2 Cor 12:12; Rom 15:18–19; 1 Cor 2:4). At the same time, both demonstrate a certain reserve on the subject, and both respond negatively to the request for an authenticating sign (e.g., Mark

159. Sanders (*Paul*, 25) writes: "Despite boasting of his 'power,' when pressed for signs of his apostolic authority Paul appealed more to 'weakness' than to miracles."

160. In a similar context, see 1 Cor 2:1–5. See also Twelftree, *Paul and the Miraculous*, 201.

161. As Schreiner (*Apostle of God's Glory*, 88) puts it: "Of course, signs and wonders were characteristic of Paul's ministry (2 Cor 12:12), but Paul believed that strength *in weakness* was even more distinctive of an apostolic ministry."

8:11–12 parr.; 1 Cor 1:22–23).[162] Alongside Paul's ability to work miracles, as Knowling writes, "There is a reserve in the appeal to miracles and in the place assigned to miracles, a reserve which characterizes St. Paul no less than his Master."[163]

In addition to these similarities, we also have the interesting case of both figures combining a ministry of miracles with a lifestyle of poverty, service, and suffering that we have generally labeled "weakness." Now, it may be doubted that "weakness" is the appropriate term, since the resolve and selflessness displayed by both Jesus and Paul indicate a real strength. From one perspective, this point may be freely admitted. Yet Paul would surely object and say that he contributed nothing save what God provided (e.g., 1 Cor 15:10; Gal 2:20). Paul was weak; God was powerful (2 Cor 12:9).

This concept of "weakness" can be understood easily enough in Paul's life, since he likely suffered from a physical ailment (e.g., 2 Cor 12:7). But it may be questioned how appropriate the term is when applied to Jesus's ministry. Is there really anything about Jesus that may be called "weak?" Here we again apply the term generally to a pattern of what may be considered "cultural" weakness—a life of deprivation, self-sacrifice, and humble service. Significantly, Paul himself associates these sorts of travails with his term *weakness* (2 Cor 12:10), so our applying the term to Jesus seems appropriate. In this line of thought, it may of course also be significant that Paul views the pre-resurrection existence of Jesus as one of weakness and service (2 Cor 13:4; Rom 15:8).

The similarity between Jesus and Paul in this matter of lifestyle has of course been noted by others. Schweitzer notes: "Jesus' saying that whosoever will be great shall be the servant of all . . . is not indeed handed down by Paul's pen, but it is exemplified in his life."[164] So too even the combination of this lifestyle with miracles, as seen in Kolenkow: "The combination of miracles and suffering which occurs in the gospels also characterizes Paul."[165] To what degree Paul is indebted to Jesus for this we will consider in ch. 5.

---

162. Both would probably also agree on faith being properly prior to a miracle (e.g., Mark 2:5 parr.; 5:36 par.; 1 Cor 12:9; 13:2).

163. Knowling, *Testimony of St. Paul*, 228. Parallels are also noted by Wenham, *Follower of Jesus*, 353–54; Nielsen, *Heilung und Verkündigung*, 201.

164. Schweitzer, *Mysticism of Paul*, 322. See Wenham, *Follower of Jesus*, 354–56. Wenham also sees an echo between 1 Cor 4:1–5 and Jesus's parable of the stewards in Matt 24:45–51 par. (ibid., 312).

165. Kolenkow, "Paul and Opponents," 363 n. 27.

CHAPTER 4

Signs of the New Age

This section will explore how the miracles of Jesus and Paul demonstrated the presence of eschatological fulfillment. For each figure, we will explore the theme generally before turning to miracles.

The Miracles of Jesus as Signs of the New Age

Here we deal with the subject of Jesus and eschatology, a hotly contested issue.[1] Some favor portraits of Jesus that downplay futuristic eschatological expectation in a traditional sense.[2] Others maintain that Jesus had a thoroughgoing futuristic eschatology.[3] The most plausible perspective seems to be one that accounts for both strands of evidence within the Gospels, with present and future elements combining to form the tension of an inaugurated eschatology.[4] But for our purposes, we need not solve all these disputes. Our interest lies in how Jesus understood himself to be living in the period of eschatological fulfillment.

Jesus's Ministry and the New Age

As both Allison and Dunn have noted, one of the safest ways to proceed in assessing historical-Jesus material is to look for broad patterns.[5] Scattered across the Jesus

---

1. For summaries of the debate, see Theissen and Merz, *Historical Jesus*, 240–45; Fletcher-Louis, "Jesus and Apocalypticism," 3:2877–2909; Powell, *Jesus as a Figure*, 233–35. For possibilities in defining eschatology, see Caird, *Language and Imagery*, 243–71; Wright, *Jesus and the Victory of God*, 208.

2. E.g., Dodd, *Parables of the Kingdom*, 21–59; Caird, *Language and Imagery*, 243–71; Crossan, *The Historical Jesus*, 238–60; Borg, "A Temperate Case," 47–68; Borg, *Conflict, Holiness*, 256–71.

3. E.g., Schweitzer, *Quest for the Historical Jesus*, 315–54; Sanders, *Historical Figure*, 169–88; cf. p. 178; Allison, "A Plea for Thoroughgoing Eschatology," 651–68; Allison, *Constructing Jesus*, 31–164; Ehrman, *Apocalyptic Prophet*, 125–62; cf. pp. 176–81.

4. E.g., with some variations, Jeremias, *Parables of Jesus*, 115–230; Kümmel, *Promise and Fulfillment*, 154–55; Bornkamm, *Jesus of Nazareth*, 90–95; Perrin, *Kingdom of God*, 185–201; Ladd, *A Theology of the New Testament*, 61–67; Ladd, *Jesus and the Kingdom*, 322; Dunn, *Jesus Remembered*, 466–67; Wright, *Jesus and the Victory of God*, 467. Significantly, both future and present sayings of Jesus are usually considered authentic (Theissen and Merz, *Historical Jesus*, 253). Cf. Sanders, *Historical Figure*, 178.

5. Dunn, *Jesus Remembered*, 332; Allison, *Constructing Jesus*, 10–17.

traditions we have multiple lines of evidence showing that Jesus saw in his ministry the presence of the age of eschatological fulfillment.

The obvious place to begin is with the kingdom of God. On the one hand, most of Jesus's references to the kingdom refer to the future.[6] Yet alongside this stands evidence of Jesus understanding the kingdom as present. The sense of Mark's summary of Jesus's preaching, "The time is fulfilled, and the kingdom of God is at hand" (Mark 1:15), is that the climactic time has arrived.[7] The kingdom is hidden like a pearl, ready to be found (Matt 13:44–46).[8] The kingdom was present among Jesus's hearers (Luke 17:20–21).[9] In some distinctive way, the kingdom was present with Jesus in contrast with John the Baptist (Luke 7:28 par.; 16:16 par.)[10] The parables of growth show that the kingdom has begun, though in a surprisingly unimpressive form (e.g., Mark 4:30–32 parr.; Matt 13:33 par.).[11] The parable of the banquet (Luke 14:15–24) shows the kingdom was not delayed because of Jewish opposition.[12] Outsiders were going into the kingdom (Matt 21:28–32; 22:1–10; Luke 14:16–24).[13]

Beyond kingdom references, other patterns point to the time of eschatological fulfillment. The time of Jesus was what the prophets had awaited (Luke 10:23–24 par.).[14] Something greater than Jonah and Solomon was present (Luke 11:31–32 par.).[15] The current generation would experience decisive judgment (Luke 11:49–51 par.), and to reject Jesus's message was to suffer worse than Sodom (Luke 10:13–15 par.).[16] The need to settle accounts with the judge was pressing (Luke 12:57–59 par.).[17] John the Baptist was the Elijah to come (Mark 9:13 par.). In terms of piety,

---

6. Bock and Simpson, *Jesus the God-Man*, 29. The discussion of Dunn (*Jesus Remembered*, 406–37), both kingdom specific and conceptual, includes: the kingdom as drawn near (e.g., Mark 1:15 par.; 13:28–29 parr.; Luke 10:9 par.); the prayer for the kingdom to come (Luke 11:2 and par.); impending eschatological reversal (Luke 6:20–23 par.; 11:31–32 par.; 13:28–29 par.); impending suffering (Mark 13:8–13 parr.; Luke 9:57–62 par.); impending judgment (Luke 10:12–15 par.; 17:26–35 par.; 19:11–27 par.); future reward (Mark 8:33–37 parr.; Luke 14:16–24 par.; 22:28–30 par.); parables of crisis (e.g., Mark 13:33–37 parr.); and the kingdom as imminent (Luke 18:8; Mark 9:1 parr.; 13:30 parr.; Matt 10:23). Theissen and Merz (*Historical Jesus*, 253) note that this evidence occurs in Mark, Q, M, L, and in Thomas (though this future eschatology is rejected by Jesus in Thomas).

7. Dunn, *Jesus Remembered*, 437–38; Wright, *Jesus and the Victory of God*, 471–72. On difficulties concerning this verse see Meier, *Mentor, Message*, 433–34. Cf. Luke 4:18; Matt 4:17.

8. Dunn, *Jesus Remembered*, 442–43.

9. Bock, *Luke*, 2:1416–19; cf. Meier, *A Marginal Jew*, 2:430.

10. Dunn, *Jesus Remembered*, 445–55; Meier, *A Marginal Jew*, 2:403. In whatever way we understand Luke 16:16 par., the kingdom is somehow present.

11. So, similarly, Bock and Simpson, *Jesus the God-Man*, 30–31; Theissen and Merz, *Historical Jesus*, 261.

12. Bock and Simpson, *Jesus the God-Man*, 32.

13. Schoberg, *Perspectives of Jesus*, 244.

14. Meier, *A Marginal Jew*, 2:434–39.

15. Dunn, *Jesus Remembered*, 439–41.

16. Wright, *Jesus and the Victory of God*, 329.

17. Ibid., 327.

fasting was inappropriate since the bridegroom was present (Mark 2:18–20 parr.).[18] New wineskins were needed (Mark 2:21–22 parr.).[19] All of this was to be a cause of celebration.[20] What are the implications of all this? The kingdom must be close—if not already present.[21]

Jesus's Miracles and the New Age

How do Jesus's miracles fit into this? We are helped in that certain passages concerning Jesus's miracles have traditionally been key in arguing for the kingdom as somehow present in Jesus's ministry. We will consider the issue from a variety of angles.

Healing as Expected Restoration

The language of eschatology is, at its most basic, "the language of hope."[22] As such, eschatology envisages divine intervention in differing ways.[23] Various traditions within Israel contained different hopes and expectations.[24] I will thus use the term *restoration* very generally to encompass a wide variety of possible acts of God, whether national, personal, political, spiritual, literal, figurative, or a mixture.[25]

Since one of the great hindrances to human well-being—especially in an age of primitive medical care—would be sickness, injury, and death, it comes as no surprise that the prophets envisioned healing as part of God's restoration.[26] For example, light from the sun and moon will increase "when the LORD binds up the brokenness of his people, and heals the wounds inflicted by his blow" (Isa 30:26). In the day of Zion's restoration, "no inhabitant will say, 'I am sick'; the people who dwell there will be forgiven their iniquity" (Isa 33:24). The prophet reassures:

---

18. Meier, *A Marginal Jew*, 2:439–50.

19. Dunn, *Jesus Remembered*, 441–42.

20. E.g., Luke 15:6, 9; 7:34 par.; Matt 13:44–46 (Wenham, *Paul*, 49–50).

21. As Bock and Simpson (*Jesus the God-Man*, 31) put it, referring to only parts of the evidence we have surveyed: "All of this suggests that if the kingdom has not come, it is very, very close."

22. Schoberg, *Perspectives of Jesus*, 248.

23. For common themes among millenarian movements, see Allison, *Jesus of Nazareth*, 78–94; cf. pp. 152–56.

24. See, e.g., Schoberg, *Perspectives of Jesus*, 248–49, 302–21. Some of what he mentions are: restoration of Davidic rule (Amos 9:1–12); return from exile (Isa 45:13; 48:20; 49:8–12, 24–26; 51:11, 14); rebuilt temple (Ezek 40–48); an influx of foreign wealth to Jerusalem (Isa 60:1–14; 61:5–6); God ruling as king of the earth (Zech 14:9); resurrection (metaphorically: Ezek 37:1–14; literally: Isa 26:19; Dan 12:2–3); and out-poured Spirit (Isa 59:21; Ezek 39:29).

25. Our interest is thus not *precision* in terms of referent but rather the kinds of language and imagery used to express hope for God's intervention and then how this language is picked up by Jesus and the New Testament authors. It can be difficult to define "restoration," as anticipated in the prophets. Complicating matters, later writers could also interpret literally what was originally intended as figurative, and vice versa.

26. See Harvey, *Constraints of History*, 116–17.

"Then the eyes of the blind shall be opened, and the ears of the deaf unstopped; then shall the lame man leap like a deer, and the tongue of the mute sing for joy" (Isa 35:5–6; cf. 29:18–19; 42:7). To the righteous, 1 Enoch says, "But you, who have experienced pain, fear not, for there shall be a healing medicine for you" (96:3).[27] The later 4 Ezra speaks of a paradise "whose fruit remains unspoiled and in which are abundance and healing" (7:53[123]).[28] Jubilees 23:29–30 includes healing as part of the glorious future: "All their days will be days of blessing and healing. And then the LORD will heal his servants."[29]

So we see a rich scriptural background for the idea that God's restoration would include healing. Yet, as Harvey points out, people would not need to remember these prophecies to see a connection between miracles and God's restoration, since Jesus's miracles showed him combating age-old enemies like sickness and death.[30] Yet beyond such an intuitive connection between Jesus's work and general hope for God's intervention and restoration, we also have explicit connections between healing and fulfilled Scripture.

Our key passage is Jesus's reply to John's messengers (Luke 7:22 par.), which we discussed in ch. 2 with reference to Jesus's miracles initially realizing God's gracious inclusion of outsiders. Here we are concerned with how Jesus's answer showed the presence of the age of eschatological fulfillment. By alluding to Old Testament expectation for healing at the time of restoration (Isa 35:5–6; 61:1 [LXX]; and perhaps 29:18–19; 42:7, 18; 26:19), Jesus was claiming that the time of fulfillment had arrived.[31] That these expectations were alive and well in Jesus's day can be seen from 4Q521 2 II:

> [for the heav]ens and the earth will listen to his anointed one, [and all th]at is in them will not turn away from the precepts of the holy ones. Strengthen yourselves, you who are seeking the Lord, in his service! *Blank* Will you not in this encounter the Lord, all those who hope in their heart? For the Lord will consider the pious, and call the righteous by name, and his spirit will hover upon the poor, and he will renew the faithful with his strength. For he will honour the pious upon the throne

27. Isaac, *OTP* 1:76.

28. Metzger, *OTP* 1:541. Cf. the even later 2 Bar. 73:1–7.

29. Wintermute, *OTP* 2:102.

30. As Harvey (*Constraints of History*, 117) explains: "It is rather that Jesus appeared to be demonstrating the possibility of overcoming those constraints and limitations—including even death—which were felt instinctively to stand as an intractable and inexplicable barrier in the way of mankind attaining to a better world."

31. Dunn (*Jesus Remembered*, 450) writes that the inclusion of lepers in Q 7:22 is surprising, since it is absent in Isaiah (though see Evans, *Matthew*, 235–36). However, as Marshall (*Gospel of Luke*, 292) notes, there may be a connection to Elisha: 2 Kgs 5; cf. Luke 4:27. Hieke ("Q 7,22," 183) writes that since some eschatological hopes involved Elisha and Elijah, the healing of leprosy (as Elisha did) is "an indirect eschatological motif."

of an eternal kingdom, freeing prisoners, giving sight to the blind, straightening out the twis[ted.] And for[e]ver shall I cling [to those who h]ope, and in his mercy [...] and the fru[it of...]... not be delayed. And the Lord will perform marvelous acts such as have not existed, just as he sa[id, for] he will heal the badly wounded and will make the dead live, he will proclaim good news to the poor and [...]...[...] he will lead the [...]... and enrich the hungry. [...] and all...[...][32]

Here we see that Jesus's claims could be intelligible as an answer to John.[33] Kvalbein argues that the language of healing and sickness in Isaiah and 4Q521 is figurative for the need of restoration of the people.[34] If so, when Jesus applies these passages in Isaiah to his own literal healings, the healings pick up the connotations of God's eschatological restoration.[35] Yet, while these passages transparently have metaphorical implications, it would be wrong to force an either/or choice between the literal and figurative, since both are mutually reinforcing.[36] Either way, here is a *pesher* type of interpretation where Jesus applies the Scriptures to his own day.[37] The Kingdom of God has come upon the recipients of Jesus's miracles.[38]

32. Martínez and Tigchelaar, eds., *The Dead Sea Scrolls Study Edition*, 2:1045.

33. Collins ("The Works of the Messiah," 112) argues that 4Q521 shows these expectations to be the work of the Messiah, though understood as a prophetic figure, not royal. Accordingly, Dunn (*Jesus Remembered*, 449) writes: "With such evidence it is no longer satisfactory to argue that the Q list was composed with hindsight in the light of resurrection faith. On the contrary, we can deduce that an expectation was current at the time of Jesus to the effect that the coming of God's Messiah would be accompanied by such marvellous events, in fulfillment of Isaiah's prophecies."

34. See Kvalbein, "Wonders of the End-Time," 87–110. Support for a figurative meaning comes from the later targums, which sometimes interpret the healings nonliterally. For example, Isa 35:5 is interpreted as blindness and deafness toward the law (Chilton, *Isaiah Targum*, 69–70). See Kvalbein, "Wonders of the End-Time," 95; Hägerland, *Jesus and the Forgiveness of Sins*, 197.

35. As Kvalbein ("Wonders of the End-Time," 109) writes, when Jesus appeals to these Scriptures, "the miracles of Jesus are given a meaning far beyond the concrete physical and social relief to the (relatively few) persons who were healed. They are signs of the eschatological renewal of the whole people of God promised in the Scripture." Meier (*A Marginal Jew*, 2:134) notes the significance of Jesus alluding to passages from Isa 24:1–27:13, a section "which speaks of Yahweh's redemption of his people Israel on the great 'day of the Lord,'" and from Isa 56–66, "which speaks of the glory of a restored Jerusalem after the return of the exiles from the Babylonian captivity."

36. See Rodríguez, "Re-framing End-Time Wonders," 219–40. Similarly, as Hieke ("Q 7,22," 178 n. 17) writes, "How is an eschatological renewal worthwhile, if there are still sick people, blind, deaf, lame? To read the eschatological promises 'only' as metaphors lets these powerful texts faint and sound rather cynical." On millenarian language being taken literally, see Allison, *Millenarian Prophet*, 157–67.

37. Bovon, *Luke*, 1:282–83. As Bock (*Luke*, 1:668) notes, "These events show the presence of the eschaton." This coheres with Jesus's Nazareth sermon in Luke 4:16–21.

38. As Twelftree (*Jesus the Miracle Worker*, 272) puts it, "The import of this saying of Jesus is not that people are being prepared for the new age or made eligible for entry. Rather, it is that as the eschaton has come, these individuals are experiencing it in their lives." Of course, wrapped up in all this is the presence of Jesus himself as the bringer of all these fulfillments. If these things are happening through Jesus, and these are the things to which Isaiah pointed, then here is another sign of the presence of the kingdom—the presence of the king. As Seccombe (*The King of God's Kingdom*, 193)

As I will discuss below, Sanders is well known for doubting that Jesus viewed the kingdom as present. Nevertheless, Sanders is still able to say that Jesus "probably saw his miracles as indications that the new age was at hand. *He shared the Evangelists' view that he fulfilled the hopes of the prophets—or at least that these hopes were about to be fulfilled.*"[39]

Exorcism as the Defeat of Satan

If eschatology is the language of hope, which manifests itself in relation to various challenges to human well-being, it is no surprise that eschatological expectation can extend beyond the removal of physical evil (sickness and injury) to include the removal of spiritual evil (however envisioned). Accordingly, some Jewish eschatological expectation anticipated the defeat of Satan and evil, and this forms an important background for Jesus's exorcisms.

Evans has helpfully laid out the evidence.[40] In the OT, the clearest picture of the rule of God opposing the rule of spiritual evil is in Daniel, where angelic "princes" stand behind the various kingdoms opposed to God (Dan 10:13–14; cf. 2:44–45; 7:18–27). Alongside healing, Jubilees envisions an end to spiritual evil: "There will be no Satan and no evil (one) who will destroy" (23:29; cf. 50:5).[41] In 1 Enoch, the evil angel Azaz'el is bound for judgment (10:4–6) and finally faces God's "Elect One," who "sits in the throne of glory and judges Azaz'el and all his company, and his army, in the name of the Lord of the Spirits" (55:4).[42] In the Testament of Moses we read, "Then his kingdom will appear throughout his whole creation. Then the devil will have an end. Yea, sorrow will be led away with him" (10:1).[43] Similar themes may be found at Qumran.[44]

---

writes concerning Jesus as the bringer of Isaiah's good news (as in, e.g., Luke 4:18): "We see that his presence was part of the fulfilment. It is not just that he proclaimed the coming or presence of the kingdom as a prophet or commentator might. He, the announcer, is part of the fulfilment, for he is the promised courier."

39. Sanders, *Historical Figure*, 168.

40. Craig A. Evans, "Exorcisms and the Kingdom," 151–79. I depend on his treatment throughout this paragraph.

41. Wintermute, *OTP* 2:102.

42. Isaac, *OTP* 1:38.

43. Priest, *OTP* 1:931.

44. 1QS IV 18–26 anticipates that God will be "ripping out all spirit of injustice" from within men, and he will remove "the defilement of the unclean spirit" (Martínez and Tigchelaar, eds., *The Dead Sea Scrolls Study Edition*, 1:79). Twelftree (*Jesus the Exorcist*, 219) includes this passage among those showing "the binding of the powers of evil or the demise of Satan." This passage probably indicates the former, since it seems to envision a struggle within human hearts (cf. 1QS IV 23, "Until now the spirits of truth and injustice feud in the heart of man"). 1QM XVIII 1–15 envisions a day "when the mighty hand of God is [r]aised against Belial . . . when the hand of the God of Israel is raised against the whole horde of Belial" (Martínez and Tigchelaar, eds., *The Dead Sea Scrolls Study Edition*, 1:141–43). Yet this seems to envision an actual physical battle (see 1QM XVIII 2, "when they pursue Assyria;

This background helps us understand our key passage (Luke 11:20 par.), where Jesus speaks of his exorcisms (εἰ δὲ ἐν δακτύλῳ [Matt: πνεύματι] θεοῦ [ἐγὼ] ἐκβάλλω τὰ δαιμόνια, ἄρα ἔφθασεν ἐφ᾽ ὑμᾶς ἡ βασιλεία τοῦ θεοῦ). This passage is important because it can give us Jesus's understanding of his exorcisms and connects them with the presence of the kingdom.[45]

This saying is generally well regarded in terms of historicity.[46] Whether the original was "finger" or "Spirit" does not greatly impact our argument, since the presence of eschatological power is implied either way.[47] If "finger" is original (as most argue), we have a clear allusion to the exodus, where deliverance comes by the "finger of God."[48] If "Spirit" is original, we have a reference to the Holy Spirit, which in some Jewish eschatological thinking would be poured out in the final days.[49]

In either case, Jesus sees in his exorcisms the presence of the kingdom of God. The saying emphasizes the power of the kingdom as operative in the *present* days of Jesus's ministry.[50] This is the most natural way to take ἔφθασεν.[51] This implication is intelligible in light of the backgrounds where the defeat of evil was expected in the time of fulfillment.

---

the sons of Japhet shall fall without rising; the Kittim shall be crushed"). Witmer (*Jesus, the Galilean Exorcist,* 127) suggests the reference may be indicating exorcism or some kind of miracle.

45. Theissen and Merz (*Historical Jesus,* 258) call this passage "the main evidence for a present eschatology."

46. I discuss this in ch. 3.

47. So also Dunn, *Jesus Remembered,* 460. Whichever is original, Schoberg (*Perspectives of Jesus,* 274) writes: "It is clear that he understood himself to be living at a climactic time in the history of Israel." Marshall (*Luke,* 475) writes that "The meaning is the same in both versions."

48. Δάκτυλος θεοῦ (Exod 8:15 LXX). "Just as at that time there was a prelude to the exodus in the miracles of Moses, so in the exorcisms today there is a prelude to the liberation of Israel through the kingdom of God" (Theissen and Merz, *Historical Jesus,* 260). There are other uses of the phrase "finger of God" in the Old Testament as well (e.g., Exod 31:18; Deut 9:10; Ps 8:4 [MT]). For arguments for "finger" as original, see Meier, *A Marginal Jew,* 2:410–11. For a helpful study on the background and meaning of "finger of God" in this passage, see Woods, *The 'Finger of God'.* He argues for the originality of "finger of God" in Q and argues that the phrase in Luke 11:20 has a double significance: both "deliverance power" as seen in Exod 8:19 and the "covenantal revelation" of God's law as seen in Deut 9:10 (e.g., pp. 158–68, 245–46).

49. A theme we will address below. For arguments for "Spirit" as original, see Nolland, *Luke,* 2:639–40.

50. Davies and Allison (*Gospel According to Saint Matthew,* 2:340) write: "The Greek implies the presence of the kingdom: it has already, in some sense, come."

51. So also Meier, *A Marginal Jew,* 2:412–13. BDAG (p. 1053) has: "To get to or reach a position," "*have just arrived,*" "*arrive,*" "*reach.*" See Rom 9:31; 2 Cor 10:14; Phil 3:16. For Aramaic reconstruction, see Meier, *A Marginal Jew,* 2:423. Bock (*Luke,* 2:1080) notes what is decisive is how ἐπί is combined with a personal object. Kümmel (*Promise and Fulfillment,* 107) says it is "exegetically untenable" to understand this verse to refer simply to the nearness of the kingdom. See also G. R. Beasley-Murray, *Jesus and the Kingdom of God* (Grand Rapids: Eerdmans, 1986), 78–79. Dodd (*Parables of the Kingdom,* 29) writes: "The 'eschatological' Kingdom of God is proclaimed as a present fact, which men must recognize, whether by their actions they accept or reject it."

This interpretation of the exorcisms coheres with other passages.[52] In the preceding charge that Jesus exorcises by demonic power, Jesus portrays Satan's opposition as a kingdom, implying that he is pitted against it (Mark 3:22–26 parr.).[53] Jesus implies he is the robber stealing from Satan (Mark 3:27 parr.).[54] This saying supports the view that in Jesus's exorcisms the eschatological defeat of Satan had begun.[55] The defeat of Satan via exorcism is also found in the vision of Satan's defeat (Luke 10:18).[56] To these we can add Luke 7:22–23 (par.), where much the same point is made of Jesus's healings.[57]

E. P. Sanders is known for questioning whether Jesus saw the kingdom as present. He says about our passage and Jesus's response to John's messengers: "I have never been able to see in these passages what others do: the claim that, in Jesus' own view, the kingdom was *fully present* in his actions."[58] Yet we are not claiming the kingdom was fully present. That the kingdom was predominantly future for Jesus is clear. The question is whether it was present in some inaugurated form.

Sanders further appeals to general uncertainty: "The principal sayings which support the view that the kingdom was present in Jesus' work are not absolutely firm, either with regard to their original context or their precise wording—both of which are essential to the arguments based on them."[59] While he is right about lacking certainty, his skepticism is too strong. Meier responds by arguing that these complaints could be brought against any Gospel tradition, and that no finding of historical-Jesus study will be beyond all doubt—we aim rather for findings that are "solidly probable."[60]

So can we say it is "solidly probable" that Jesus saw in his exorcisms the presence of the kingdom? It seems we can. As noted above, when Jesus says of his exorcisms, ἔφθασεν ἐφ' ὑμᾶς ἡ βασιλεία τοῦ θεοῦ, the most natural understanding is that the rule of God was present, as Meier argues:

---

52. Meier, *A Marginal Jew*, 2:417–22.

53. See Dunn, *Jesus Remembered*, 458. Beyond this, even if Jesus used Satan's power to accomplish his exorcisms, Twelftree (*Jesus the Exorcist*, 106) writes: "Jesus' exorcisms would still mark the destruction of Satan and his kingdom."

54. "The strong man had been already disabled; that was why his possessions . . . could be liberated from his control" (Dunn, *Jesus Remembered*, 460–61).

55. Dunn, "Matthew 12:28/Luke 11:20," 43.

56. Bock, *Luke*, 2:1080; Theissen and Merz, *Historical Jesus*, 258; Dunn, *Jesus Remembered*, 461. Notably, the Jesus Seminar (Funk and Hoover, *Five Gospels*, 321) rates it pink.

57. Dunn, "Matthew 12:28," 43–44. Yet of course there is still a "not-yet" element of this defeat. See Twelftree, *Jesus the Exorcist*, 220–24, 227–28.

58. Sanders, *Historical Figure*, 177. He goes on to take the saying as a warning to Jesus's opponents that the kingdom was imminent.

59. Sanders, *Jesus and Judaism*, 140; cf. p. 158.

60. "The problem is that the same objection could be leveled against almost any saying of Jesus used to establish any aspect of his teaching. . . . We cannot ask that our views be 'absolutely firm'; all we can hope is that they are solidly probable in representing the substance of what Jesus said on a particular issue" (Meier, *A Marginal Jew*, 2:422). See also on this, Dunn, "Matthew 12:28," 47.

To decide, without any special basis in the text, that *ephthasen* is a "prophetic" or "proleptic" aorist ignores the precise argument about and explanation of Jesus' exorcisms that this verse purports to give. Such an appeal to a prophetic or proleptic aorist cannot help but look like special pleading, geared to avoiding an unwelcome theological conclusion about the presence of the kingdom of God in Jesus' ministry.[61]

Sanders argues that the aorist could be proleptic (a coming "determined," not "accomplished"), citing for example the Testament of Abraham where the cup of death "came" (ἔφθασεν) to Abraham and yet he lived for many chapters (A 1:3).[62] Yet Meier says Sanders has misunderstood the symbolism. The coming of the cup of death does not refer to dying itself—rather, it is the *drinking* of the cup of death that would signify dying (cf. Mark 14:36 parr.).[63]

But even if we allow Sanders this possibility, it is clear that Jesus *associated* his exorcisms with the kingdom's coming (in whatever degree).[64] What would be the sense of the saying if the kingdom were only imminent? The exorcisms were occurring *in the present*. The power of God's rule and God's kingdom worked deliverance *in the present*. In the end, rejecting the *presence* of God's rule while acknowledging the presence of the *power* of God's rule is too fine.[65] One way to speak of the *presence* of God's rule would be to speak of the *power* of God's rule. Sanders admits as much: Jesus "thought that the power of God was present."[66] Beyond this, "The kingdom in the full eschatological sense could not be present, nor could it be entirely entered into by individuals, but the meaning of the word can be stretched so that one can talk of the kingdom, in the sense of God's power, as present and as extended to individuals in the present."[67]

61. Meier, *A Marginal Jew*, 2:412. It also ignores the point of the illustration that follows in Luke 11:21–22. The Stronger One is present!

62. Sanders, *Jesus and Judaism*, 134; T. Ab. A 1:9; Stone, *The Testament of Abraham*, 2.

63. Meier, *A Marginal Jew*, 2:413.

64. As Twelftree (*Jesus the Exorcist*, 218) puts it, "whether or not that 'coming' was imminent, taking place or realized."

65. See, similarly, Beasley-Murray, *Kingdom of God*, 76–77.

66. Sanders, *Jesus and Judaism*, 153.

67. Ibid., 236–37. Similarly, Perrin (*Rediscovering the Teaching of Jesus*, 67) notes: "The hotly debated question as to whether this implies that the Kingdom is to be regarded as present, inbreaking, dawning, casting its shadows before it, or whatever, becomes academic when we realize that the claim of the saying is that certain events in the ministry of Jesus are nothing less than *an experience* of the Kingdom of God." This too is how we can think through the insightful suggestion of Caragounis ("Kingdom of God," 3–23, 223–38) that the kingdom of God came after the crucifixion. Even if this may be granted, the healings and exorcisms are extensions of the power of that kingdom working earlier in the ministry of Jesus. Caragounis essentially argues that this is what distinguishes Jesus's exorcisms from those of his Jewish compatriots—Jesus's exorcisms grow out of Jesus's role as the self-giving Son of Man who brings the kingdom by sacrifice (pp. 236–37). Thus, either way, the exorcisms and healings of Jesus are *present* workings of the eschatological Kingdom of God, which may

Again, we reiterate that the point is not that the kingdom of God is fully present in Jesus's ministry.[68] The presence of God's rule in Jesus's exorcisms is not the consummation or fullness of the kingdom (which is still treated as future), but rather the inauguration of the kingdom's presence.[69]

This passage does not stand alone, nor even only with passages concerning miracles. As seen above, this view of the exorcisms of Jesus coheres with other traditions where the kingdom is somehow present. A case in point are the parables, where the kingdom is already working.[70] Dunn summarizes the argument for the present understanding of Luke 11:20 (par.) on the basis of coherence by pointing to two categories: (1) passages that show Jesus's ministry as aligning with Isaianic eschatological fulfillment, and (2) passages that show Jesus's ministry as prophetic and empowered by the Spirit of God.[71] "In view of the diversity and range of these traditions, the most obvious conclusion is that the conviction of eschatological fulfillment in Jesus' ministry belongs to the bedrock of the tradition."[72]

The Spirit as Eschatological Gift

A third aspect of Jesus's miracles that shows the presence of the new age concerns the Holy Spirit. While references to the Spirit in Jesus's ministry are not numerous, they are nonetheless significant. This is especially so for us because of the Spirit's prominence in Paul. As mentioned above, one eschatological hope concerned the coming of the Spirit. In the Old Testament, this expectation sometimes takes the form of an outpouring of the Spirit on God's people (Isa 32:15–18; 44:1–5; Ezek 37:1–14; Joel 3:1–5 [MT]) and sometimes through a Spirit-anointed figure (Isa 11:1–11; 42:1–4; 61:1–4).[73] The new age comes with a bestowal of the Spirit

---

be present or near or inaugurated to a variety of possible degrees, depending on which scholar's suggestion one finds most persuasive.

68. As Allison (*Constructing Jesus*, 100–101) writes, "To affirm that the kingdom has arrived is not to say that it is already all that it will be."

69. As Luz (*Matthew*, 2:204) writes: "It is present, but it retains its transcendence or its future." Luz is speaking of the kingdom in Matthew, including our verse.

70. So also Beasley-Murray, *Kingdom of God*, 77.

71. Dunn, "Matthew 12:28," 45. (1) Luke 10:2 par.; Luke 7:28 par.; Luke 16:16 par.; Luke 11:31–32 par.; Luke 10:23–24 par. Luke 17:20–21. (2) Luke 6:20 par.; 7:22 par. (cf. Luke 4:16–21); Mark 3:28–29 parr.; 6:4 parr.; 6:14–15 parr.; 8:28 parr.; 14:65 parr.; Matt 21:11, 46; Luke 13:33; 24:19; John 6:14; 7:40, 52.

72. Ibid.

73. Matthias Wenk, "Holy Spirit," 388. With a focus on backgrounds concerning Paul's pneumatology, Finny Philip (*The Origins of Pauline Pneumatology*," 32–76) treats what he considers: (1) key exilic and postexilic passages (2) that focus on the Spirit coming on the whole people in the new age and (3) that potentially affect Gentiles: Ezek 36:26–27; 37:1–14; 39:29; Isa 32:9–20; 44:1–5; Joel 3:1–2 [MT]. Other potentially significant passages include: Ezek 11:19; 18:31; Isa 28:5–6; 59:21; 61:1; Zech 12:10. See generally, e.g., Neve, *The Spirit of God*, 54–85; Montague, *Holy Spirit*, 33–60; Hildebrandt, 91–103; Ma, *Until the Spirit Comes*, 209–13.

as part of God's work of restoration.[74] Later references to the Spirit fall into the same categories of a specially anointed figure (e.g., 1 En. 49:2–3; 61:1–11; 62:1–12; Pss. Sol. 17:37; 18:7–8; 1Q28b V, 24–26; 4Q161 III, 10–19; 4Q521) and concerning people more generally (e.g., T. Benj. 8:2; T. Sim 4:4; Jos. Asen. 8:9 (11); 19:10–11; Philo *Gig.* 24; *Virt.* 212–19; 1QHa VI, 11–13;VIII 10–20 XV, 6–7).[75]

Several passages among the Jesus traditions are pertinent on this point.[76] Immediately fruitful is a return to Luke 7:22 (par.). We saw that there are good reasons to accept this as Jesus's interpretation of his miracles of healing, and here Jesus's response draws on the imagery of Isa 61:1 in bringing good news to the poor, and, in the LXX, sight to the blind (καὶ τυφλοῖς ἀνάβλεψιν). The significance for our point is that the imagery and activity of Isa 61:1 is immediately preceded by, and dependent on, the speaker being anointed with the Spirit (πνεῦμα κυρίου ἐπ᾽ ἐμέ οὗ εἵνεκεν ἔχρισέν με).[77]

As Dunn argues, support for a connection between Jesus and Isa 61:1 also comes from the beatitudes of Luke 6:20–21 (par.). In the wording of μακάριοι οἱ πτωχοί [τῷ πνεύματι] and μακάριοι οἱ κλαίοντες/πενθοῦντες, we have a direct allusion to Isa 61:1–2 (πνεῦμα κυρίου ἐπ᾽ ἐμέ οὗ εἵνεκεν ἔχρισέν με εὐαγγελίσασθαι πτωχοῖς [61:1]; παρακαλέσαι πάντας τοὺς πενθοῦντας [61:2]).[78] Since these beati-

---

74. As Ma (ibid., 210) writes: "The coming of the new age is attributed to the 'outpouring' of the spirit from above ([Isa] 32.15). The long-awaited day of restoration will be ushered in by the overwhelming presence of the רוח."

75. Wenk, "Holy Spirit," 388–89. Cf. Sjöberg ("πνεῦμα κτλ.," *TDNT* 6:384–86), who adds T. Jud. 24:3; T. Levi 18:11 as examples of the Spirit falling on the people. Not all the references listed by Wenk are eschatological. Isaacs (*The Concept of Spirit,* 82–85) argues that an eschatological role for the Spirit was rare in Diaspora and Palestinian Judaism. Yet Philip (*Origins of Pauline Pneumatology,* 119; cf. pp. 81, 84) notes that some Second Temple texts do pick up and continue expectation derived from passages such as Ezek 36:26–27; Joel 3:1 [MT], and Isa 44:3, applying them to the age to come, e.g., Jub. 1:23; 4 Ezra 6:26–28, cf. 3:20. He also points to Qumran as an eschatological community (e.g., CD 3.13–20; 7.9–8.2; 1QS 5.7–24; 9:3; 4Q504–506) which holds an emphasis on the Holy Spirit (e.g., 1QS 3.6–12; 9.3–5; 1QH 16.11–13 [ibid., 86]); cf. Schoberg, *Perspectives of Jesus,* 317–19. For differing treatments of the understanding of the Holy Spirit in Second Temple sources, see Menzies, *Empowered for Witness,* 49–101; Turner, *Power from on High,* 82–137; Wenk, *Community-Forming Power,* 56–118; Cho, *Spirit and Kingdom,* 14–51.

76. We have already discussed Luke 11:20 (par.) above, where if "Spirit of God" were deemed original, we have an important connection between Jesus and the working of exorcisms by the Spirit. Unfortunately, we decided that, for our purposes, it is too difficult to determine with certainty which is original, and a majority of scholars seem to prefer "finger of God." Yet again, the close parallels between the phrases make them essentially synonymous. Dunn (*Jesus and the Spirit,* 46) writes: "The equation, finger of God = power of God = Spirit of God, is one which arises directly out of the Hebrew understanding of God's action . . . and one which was obvious to either Matthew or Luke when he altered the Q original." Dunn points to Exod 3:20; 8:19; Ezek 3:14; 8:1–3; 37:1; Ps 8:3; cf. 33:6; 1 Kgs 18:12, cf. 2 Kgs 2:16; 1 Chr 28:12; cf. 28:19; Isa 8:11.

77. In Jesus's view, his power of healing and proclamation was, as Dunn (ibid., 61) puts it, "the eschatological Spirit operating in and through him."

78. Ibid., 55. Similarly, Marshall, *Luke,* 249; Davies and Allison, *Matthew,* 1:443; Hagner, *Matthew,* 2 vols., WBC 33 (Dallas: Word, 1993, 1995), 1:91–92.

tudes are generally well regarded historically, we have here evidence that Jesus interpreted his ministry through the lens of Isa 61:1.[79]

A possible connection between Jesus and Isa 61:1–2 is also seen in Luke 4:16–21, where Jesus explicitly applies the prophet's words to himself. Yet this passage is problematic, since Jesus's words are often considered to be Luke's work (cf. Mark 6:1–6).[80] On the other hand, Jesus's sense here is not appreciably different from Luke 7:22 (par.), which is better regarded historically.[81] Even if Jesus's words are seen as coming from Luke's hand, we should acknowledge they are a fair summary of Jesus's attitude in light of the passages just discussed (Luke 6:20b par.; 7:22 par.).

Additional evidence may come from the descent of the Spirit and the allusion to Isa 42:1 at Jesus's baptism (Mark 1:9–11 parr.).[82] While strong arguments can be made for the historicity of Jesus's baptism itself, it is a harder business to corroborate the vision or voice from heaven.[83] However, if Jesus considered himself a prophet (e.g., Mark 6:4 parr.) a call or vision would be in line with some Old Testament prophets (e.g., Ezek 1:1).[84] Similarly, as Dunn writes, if Jesus had a special sense of sonship with God and was conscious of bearing the Spirit in a significant way, this probably took final form somewhere toward the beginning of Jesus's ministry.[85] The baptism timing fits this nicely. The imagery of a dove is also a curious choice if simply a created detail, since no symbolic significance can be easily identified.[86] Yet for our purposes, this passage should probably remain secondary.

Another debatable passage is Jesus's warning about blaspheming the Spirit (Mark 3:28–29 parr.). The difference between Mark's "children of men" and Q's "Son of Man" need not concern us, since we are interested in the "punchline."[87] More serious is the possibility of the saying having been originally independent of

79. For example, the Jesus Seminar (Funk and Hoover, *The Five Gospels*, 289, 138) rates them red in Luke and pink in Matthew.

80. So, e.g., Dunn, *Jesus and the Spirit*, 54; Fitzmyer, *Gospel According to Luke*, 1:527; Funk and Hoover, *The Five Gospels*, 279.

81. Bock, *Luke*, 1:397–98. Cf. Marshall, *Luke*, 179–80.

82. On the allusion to Isa 42:1, see Davies and Allison, *Matthew*, 1:336–39; Bock, *Luke*, 1:341–44.

83. For the historicity of the baptism itself, see, e.g., Webb, "Jesus' Baptism," 95–108; Meier, *A Marginal Jew*, 2:100–105. On difficulties concerning the vision, see, e.g., ibid., 106–9.

84. Webb, "Jesus' Baptism," 110–11. Similarly, Borg (*Jesus*, 42) writes: "Like them, his ministry began with an intense experience of the Spirit of God." Bock (*Luke*, 1:338) notes that Jesus's baptism experience seems more than just a prophetic call.

85. "Such distinctive and defining characteristics of Jesus' own sense of mission presumably crystallized at some point. The most obvious candidate for that 'point' was presumably the beginning of Jesus' mission, or at least the stage at which Jesus' mission assumed a character distinctive from that of the Baptist's" (Dunn, *Jesus Remembered*, 376). So also, to differing degrees: Webb, "Jesus' Baptism," 110; Marcus, "Jesus' Baptismal Vision," 513.

86. See Webb, "Jesus' Baptism," 111.

87. On how both plausibly grew from an original generic singular in Aramaic, see, e.g., Dunn, *Jesus and the Spirit*, 49–50.

its exorcism context in Mark and Matthew, since this would mean it may not have been connected with Jesus's miracles.[88] Of course, it is also often argued that this saying was created by the church.[89] Yet the emergence of the saying in the context of an exorcism dispute is plausible, and this is clearly how Mark intends us to read it.[90] If Jesus uttered such a saying with any reference to himself, it would be additional evidence of the Spirit's presence.[91] Yet because of the uncertainties, for our purposes this passage should probably be considered secondary corroboration.

While there are few references to the Spirit in the Synoptic Gospels, we have two fairly firm passages in which Jesus understands his ministry as connected to the Spirit-endowed figure of Isa 61:1 (Luke 6:20b par.), one of which occurs in the context of miracle working (Luke 7:22 par.). A variety of debatable passages may strengthen a connection between Jesus's ministry and the Spirit (Mark 3:28–29 parr.; Luke 11:20 par.; Luke 4:16–21; Mark 1:9–11 parr.). Dunn is confident enough to say that we may know for sure that Jesus saw himself as bearing the Spirit.[92] This should probably not be too controversial. So, against the backdrop of some expectation of an outpouring of the Spirit in the days of eschatological fulfillment, a connection between Jesus and the Spirit adds corroboration for understanding Jesus's miracles of healing and exorcism as signs of the presence of that fulfillment.

Conclusion on Jesus

This section should be the least controversial of this study. It is widely agreed that Jesus's ministry was colored by eschatological fulfillment and that Jesus's understanding of the kingdom was not only future, but also something inaugurated. The healings and exorcisms of Jesus form a major part of this evidence, and—while not beyond dispute—it is widely agreed that Jesus saw in his miracles the presence of the age of eschatological fulfillment. The connection Jesus saw between his ministry and the Spirit-empowered figure of Isa 61:1 strengthens this association. The

---

88. In Luke 12:10 and Gos. Thom. 44 it occurs apart from this context. Cf. Did. 11:7.

89. At least in part, e.g., Boring, "The Unforgivable Sin," 276–77; Luz, *Matthew*, 2:201–2. The Jesus Seminar (Funk and Hoover, *The Five Gospels*, 51) rates it black. On the other hand, Davies and Allison (*Matthew*, 2:344–45) see an origin in Jesus.

90. See Dunn, *Jesus and the Spirit*, 52.

91. Bock (*Luke*, 2:1143) notes that the commonality among the saying's settings in the three Synoptics is "the rejection of allegiance to Jesus." On the other hand, it could have been a general warning apart from any specific connection to Jesus—though this seems less likely. Dunn (*Jesus and the Spirit*, 52–53) explains the significance of this passage as: (1) Jesus's consciousness of wielding the power of the eschatological Spirit; (2) Jesus's knowledge that the power's source was God; and (3) Jesus's unique "consciousness of eschatological empowering" seen in the seriousness of the unforgivable status of the act of rejecting his exorcism.

92. As he writes, "It is certain that Jesus believed himself to be empowered by the Spirit" (*Jesus and the Spirit*, 63).

miracles of Jesus's ministry, then, would form dramatic evidence of the eschatological coming of God.[93]

The Miracles of Paul as Signs of the New Age

We now consider how miracles performed in the course of Paul's ministry might be connected with eschatology. Similar to my approach with Jesus, we will first consider the theme of eschatological fulfillment in Paul's ministry generally before turning to miracles.

Paul's Ministry and the New Age

Paul's eschatology can be summarized in the familiar slogan, "already-but-not-yet."[94] This is a modification of the common Jewish division of time, "this age" and "the age to come," where (in Paul's case) the age to come is thought to have been inaugurated so the present new age overlaps with the old age.[95] On the one hand, the future "not-yet" element of Paul's eschatology is clear. Christians await the appearance of Jesus (1 Thess 1:10), all creation longs for liberation (Rom 8:22), and Paul himself desires to be with Christ (Phil 1:23). Concerning metaphors of salvation, Christians await adoption and redemption (Rom 8:23), a final sanctification (Rom 6:19), the righteousness of final justification (Gal 5:5), the full inheritance ensured by a deposit (2 Cor 5:5), the full harvest implied by the firstfruits (Rom 8:23; 1 Cor 15:23), and future salvation itself (1 Cor 3:13–15). In 2 Cor 11:2, as Dunn writes, conversion is pictured more like a betrothal than a marriage.[96]

On the other hand, we are more interested in the "already" aspects of Paul's eschatological thinking. Did he think that the age of eschatological fulfillment had already begun? We will consider just a few themes.[97]

93. Speaking merely of exorcisms, Evans ("Exorcisms and the Kingdom," 176) writes: "In short, for Jesus and his following, the exorcisms offered dramatic proof of the defeat and retreat of Satan's kingdom in the face of the advancing rule of God." Much the same could be said of Jesus's healings and of his consciousness of the eschatological Spirit.

94. See, e.g., Cullmann, *Christ and Time*, 81–93; Furnish, *Theology and Ethics in Paul*, 115–35; Beker, *Paul the Apostle*, 135–63; Dunn, *The Theology of Paul the Apostle*, 461–98; Schoberg, *Perspectives of Jesus*, 282–331; Wright, *Paul and the Faithfulness of God*, 477–80, 500, 1101–28.

95. See sources in previous note, as well as Sasse, "αἰών, κτλ.," *TDNT* 1:202–7. Examples of this usage, mentioning either one age or both, include: 2 Esd 7:50, 112–13; 8:1–2; 1 En. 48:7; 71:15; 2 En. 43:3 [J]; 50:2; 61:2; 65:8; 66:6; 2 Bar. 15:7–8; 44:8–15; T. Levi 10:2; T. Benj. 11:3; 4 Ezra 4:2; 6:9; 7:47, 112–13; 8:1; 9:19; Mark 10:30 par.; Luke 16:8; 20:34; Matt 12:32. Paul never uses the complete paired saying in an undisputed letter (cf. Eph 1:21), but he does speak of "this age" (Rom 12:2; 1 Cor 1:20; 2:6, 8; 3:18; 2 Cor 4:4; cf. Gal 1:4).

96. Dunn, *Theology of Paul*, 466–67.

97. Omitting most notably the eschatological Spirit, a theme we will take up below.

Immediately we note that most of the metaphors of salvation that Paul treats as future he also in some sense treats as present. Christians already cry out as though they have been adopted (Rom 8:15), possess the firstfruits (Rom 8:23), have received the deposit (2 Cor 5:5), have been redeemed (Gal 3:13), sanctified (1 Cor 6:11), justified (Rom 5:1), and saved "in hope" (Rom 8:24). While Paul longs to be with Christ, he has already died and been buried with him (Rom 6:4).[98]

As with Jesus, while the kingdom is something predominately future in Paul (1 Cor 6:9–10; 15:24, 50; Gal 5:21; 1 Thess 2:12 [debatable]), Paul in two cases treats the kingdom as somehow present. In the context of the weak and the strong in Rome, Paul writes, "The kingdom of God is not a matter of eating and drinking but of righteousness and peace and joy in the Holy Spirit" (Rom 14:17). Here the kingdom is associated with three (or four) elements of present Christian experience.[99] The *present* nature of that association is similar to how Paul warns his opponents in Corinth of his coming and says οὐ γὰρ ἐν λόγῳ ἡ βασιλεία τοῦ θεοῦ ἀλλ᾽ ἐν δυνάμει (1 Cor 4:20). Here the issue is power *present* in Paul's ministry, a power he understands as that of the kingdom of God.[100] We will return to this below.

We can also see the presence of the age of eschatological fulfillment in how Paul treats his days as the climactic time of salvation history. God had sent his son "when the fullness of time had come" (Gal 4:4). Paul applies storylines from the Old Testament to Christian believers and says, "They were written down for our instruction, on whom the ends of the ages has come" (1 Cor 10:11). Similarly, after citing Isa 49:8, he says, "Behold, now is the favorable time; behold, now is the day of salvation" (2 Cor 6:2).[101] The present world is "passing away" (1 Cor 7:31), and in the world clock of God's salvation, "the night is far gone; the day is at hand" (Rom 13:12). Because of Christ's death and resurrection, union with him means

---

98. Ibid., 467.

99. E.g., Phil 3:9; Rom 15:13. Examples of those seeing the presence of the kingdom include: Cranfield, *Epistle to the Romans*, 2:717; Moo, *Epistle to the Romans*, 57 n. 40; Schreiner, *Romans*, 740; Wright, *Paul and the Faithfulness of God*, 481. Johnston, "'Kingdom of God' Sayings in Paul's Letters," 152–55. Dunn (*Romans*, 2:822) notes the parallel with Jesus's exorcisms and table fellowship: "In both cases it is the powerful activity of the Spirit which is regarded as the manifestation of God's final rule." Accordingly, as Schmithals (*Der Römerbrief*, 506) writes, in Rom 14:17, righteousness, peace, and joy are all eschatological gifts. That the kingdom is associated with the Holy Spirit, which is connected with the presence of the New Covenant in 2 Cor 3, indicates Paul is making a reference to the kingdom as somehow present and not just a gnomic statement.

100. Examples of those seeing the presence of the kingdom include: Fee, *God's Empowering Presence*, 120; Bauckham, "Kingdom and Church," 15; Witherington, *Jesus, Paul*, 56; and seemingly, Fitzmyer, *First Corinthians*, 225. Cf. Johnston, "Kingdom of God," 149–52. The way it is contrasted with speech and with a power that will be displayed when Paul arrives shows that a gnomic sense is not intended but rather a reference to the presence of the kingdom in some sense.

101. See Jackson, *New Creation in Paul's Letters*, 125–27. Furnish (*Theology and Ethics*, 126–27) writes, "He does not mean that salvation has now been manifested in all its aspects . . . but that the decisive event of salvation—the death and resurrection of Christ—has already occurred and is already effective."

"new creation" has come (2 Cor 5:17), both individually and cosmically—and it is this inaugurated new creation that really matters (Gal 6:15).

In terms of his ministry, Paul was also conscious of being a minister of a/the new covenant (διακόνους καινῆς διαθήκης, 2 Cor 3:6), in contrast to the old covenant (2 Cor 3:14; cf. 1 Cor 11:25). This fulfilment of Old Testament expectation (e.g., Jer 31:31–33) is of a piece with how Paul saw the rejection of Israel and the entry of Gentiles into the people of God as nothing short of the fulfillment of Old Testament prophecy (Rom 9:25–33), a fulfilment which would lead in turn to the jealousy and restoration of Israel (Rom 11:11–32).

A major theme featured in discussions of Paul's "already-but-not-yet" thought is Jesus's resurrection.[102] Because Paul (and fellow Christians) understood the resurrection of Jesus as the beginning of the eschatological resurrection, and not just resuscitation to normal life, Jesus's raising meant the final resurrection had begun and thus also the age to come.[103] Evidence for the eschatological connection can be seen most clearly by how Jesus's resurrection is called the firstfruits of the resurrection (1 Cor 15:20).[104] His resurrection was the beginning of the great resurrection.[105] Fulfillment of the eschatological expectations had begun, with the center of that action having already taken place in Jesus's death and resurrection—though of course the final fulfillment was yet to come.[106]

I have touched briefly on these themes but sufficiently to show that, though Paul clearly held to a "not-yet" final fulfillment, he understood himself to be working in an "already" time of eschatological fulfillment where the blessings of the new age were already being felt. Why is this significant for our study? It suggests Paul

---

102. E.g., Cullmann, *Christ and Time*, 81–84; Furnish, *Theology and Ethics*, 124, 134, 168–71; Dunn, *Theology of Paul*, 240, 463; Wright, *Paul and the Faithfulness*, 551–52.

103. Yet Schoberg (*Perspectives of Jesus*, 302–14) helpfully shows that Jesus's resurrection *alone* would not be enough for Paul and the other Christians to readjust their eschatological thinking to the already-but-not-yet. More likely is that the teaching of Jesus informed their interpretation. He argues that the resurrection alone would not bring about this eschatological understanding because: (1) the Jewish people expected a *general* resurrection; (2) no judgment accompanied Jesus's resurrection; and (3) Jesus did not remain present on a restored earth like might be expected if the end of the age had come (ibid., 314).

104. As Beker (*Paul the Apostle*, 163–81) argues, the connection between Jesus's resurrection and the final apocalyptic resurrection can be seen in how eager Paul is to persuade the Corinthians that Jesus's resurrection entailed a future *general* resurrection (1 Cor 15). If divorced from a future resurrection of believers, Jesus's resurrection would lose its apocalyptic connection—something nonnegotiable for Paul.

105. In much Jewish thought occurring at the dividing point between this age and the age to come. See, e.g., Josephus, *Ag. Ap.* 2.217–18; *J.W.* 3.374; 2 Bar. 30:1–5; Apoc. Mos. 13:2–5. See Wright, *The Resurrection of the Son of God*, 176–81, 200–206.

106. As Jackson (*New Creation*, 102) writes more eloquently: "Paul inverts the future oriented hope of God's actions described with new creation language in Jewish writings into an eschatological system where the epicenter of God's cosmic earthquake was located in the past; and, at the same time, he maintained an expectation for the consummation of that action in the future."

would likely understand all aspects of his ministry to be colored by eschatological significance, and specifically for our purposes, miracles. This suggestion will be strengthened when we consider the eschatological nature of the Spirit.

Paul's Miracles and the New Age

We have seen that Paul's thinking was informed by the conviction that the new age had been inaugurated. We will now consider the eschatological significance that Paul might have associated with miracles, discussing first the eschatological nature of the Spirit generally before turning to the language of "signs and wonders" that occurs in two of our key passages. Finally, we will consider a possible connection between Paul's miracles and the presence of the eschatological kingdom (1 Cor 4:20).

The Eschatological Spirit

In ch. 2, I argued that, for Paul, miracles should be understood as one aspect of the working of the Spirit (e.g., Rom 15:19; 1 Cor 12:9–11; Gal 3:5). This is important, because an eschatological connection to the Spirit might lend a similar connotation to miracles performed through the Spirit. Paul's understanding of the outpoured Spirit as an eschatological event is prominent.[107] In fact, attempts to explain the "already" half of Paul's eschatological tension often highlight the Spirit, alongside, of course, resurrection. In terms of eschatological understanding, the presence of the Spirit was critical here for Christian thought.[108] The eschatological significance of the Spirit's presence is intelligible against the Jewish backgrounds, some of which, as we saw above, anticipated an outpouring of the Spirit as part of God's restoration (e.g., Isa 32:15–18).

Paul describes the Spirit as a seal and deposit (2 Cor 1:21–22; 5:5), as well as firstfruits (Rom 8:23)—in each case a pledge of future and full eschatological fulfillment.[109] It was the experiential presence of the Spirit that assured the believer that the power of the new age was operative. Unsurprisingly, the coming of the

---

107. For example, the first chapter of Fee's synthesis section is entitled "The Spirit as Eschatological Fulfillment" (*Empowering Presence*, 803–26). In the chapter Dunn (*Theology of Paul*, 416–19) has on the Spirit, his first subsection after the introduction is "The Eschatological Spirit." See also Hamilton, *The Holy Spirit and Eschatology in Paul*.

108. As Dunn (*Theology of Paul*, 418; cf. pp. 469–70) writes: "In eschatological terms, this experience of the Spirit was as decisive for the Christians' self-understanding as was Jesus' resurrection." See also, e.g., Furnish, *Theology and Ethics*, 129–35; Fee, *Empowering Presence*, 803–6; Schoberg, *Perspectives of Jesus*, 314–21. Yet, as in the case of Jesus's resurrection, Schoberg argues that the experience of the Spirit alone would not have been enough to convince Christians to adopt the already-but-not-yet tension (p. 321).

109. Fee, *Empowering Presence*, 806–8. In each of these metaphors, as Dunn (*Theology of Paul*, 469) puts it, "The eschatological tension, we may say, is set up precisely because the Spirit is the power of God's final purpose already beginning to reclaim the whole person for God."

Spirit was seen as scriptural fulfillment. An example of this is Gal 3:14, which we have already discussed in ch. 2. Here Paul speaks of the "blessing of Abraham" as coming to Gentiles and immediately describes the blessing as receiving "the promised Spirit through faith."[110]

The outpouring of the Spirit as an element of Old Testament fulfillment can also be seen in 2 Cor 3:6–18, where we have Paul's sole explicit reference to the new covenant apart from the traditional material in 1 Cor 11:25.[111] Paul's statement here in 2 Corinthians presupposes the enactment of the promise of Jer 31:31–34, with Christ as its mediator and Paul one of its administrators.[112] The nature of this covenant is said to be not of the letter (οὐ γράμματος) but of the Spirit (ἀλλὰ πνεύματος). While this could conceivably be taken to refer to a literal reading versus an allegorical reading, or to a legalistic interpretation of the law versus how God intended it, it seems best to view the contrast as being between the Mosaic law as something outward and domineering versus God's new way of working through the inward power of the Spirit inside the believer's heart.[113] The connection to Jer 31:31–34 seems clear, where it is God himself who will work within hearts. Yet by referring to the Spirit, we also recognize the giving of the Spirit as part of the new covenant, as described in passages such Ezek 36:26–27. That Paul continues to refer to the Spirit throughout the passage (2 Cor 3:8, 17–18) shows that the Spirit is integral to his understanding of the new dispensation.[114]

For Paul, then, the Spirit's presence was eschatological and a sign of the presence of eschatological fulfillment.[115] Miracles wrought by the Spirit would then be manifestations of the eschatological Spirit. This makes it likely that Paul would understand miracles performed in his ministry as signaling the arrival of the eschaton.

Signs and Wonders and the Exodus

That Paul saw elements of eschatological fulfillment in the miracles he performed is strengthened by how Paul twice describes them using the terminology "signs

---

110. As discussed in ch. 2, most interpreters think Paul equates the Spirit here with the blessing of Abraham, though some suggest justification (3:8).

111. Cf., e.g., Gal 4:21–31, which presupposes an old covenant in contrast to the new, without using those exact words (Furnish, *2 Corinthians*, 198).

112. Harris, *The Second Epistle to the Corinthians*, 270–71.

113. Thrall, *Second Epistle to the Corinthians*, 272–75.

114. Fee (*Empowering Presence*, 812 n. 18) notes that the Spirit is also connected with covenant implicitly in Gal 4:29 (cf. 4:24) and alluded to in Rom 2:29 (cf. Deut 30:6); 7:6. Nielsen (*Heilung und Verkündigung*, 205) writes that for Paul, the presence and working of the Spirit meant the presence of the New Covenant, as in 2 Cor 3:4–18.

115. Furnish (*Theology and Ethics*, 130) puts it like this: "As in late Judaism and even already in the Old Testament itself (e.g., Joel 2:28–29) the sign of the inbreaking of the eschaton was to be the coming of the Spirit in power, with attendant wonders, so also in Paul the Spirit signifies the coming of the new age."

and wonders" (σημεῖον, τέρας; Rom 15:19; 2 Cor 12:12). We will explore some of the backgrounds concerning this phrase and its use in our passages.

Behind these Greek terms for "signs and wonders" are the Hebrew terms אות and מופת, which together in the Old Testament usually refer to the exodus out of Egypt.[116] Additional occurrences of the Greek σημεῖα and τέρας in the LXX and Apocrypha are similar.[117] Of course the phrase can also refer to God's redemptive actions for his people beyond just the exodus (e.g., Jer 32:20–21; Isa 8:18; Joel 3:3 [MT]).[118] In nonbiblical Greek usage, the phrase "signs and wonders" can have connotations of superstition.[119] Perhaps for this reason, Josephus avoids the phrase completely when describing the exodus (instead using simply σημεῖα [e.g., *Ant.* 2.274, 276, 280]), and the way he uses "wonders and signs" to describe what imposters predicted also looks negative (e.g., *Ant.* 20.168).[120] Philo uses "signs and wonders" only twice, and in both cases it refers to the signs of the exodus (*Mos.* 1.95; *Spec.* 2.218).[121] Usage elsewhere in the New Testament can be negative (e.g., Mark 13:22 par.; John 4:48 [debatable]; 2 Thess 2:9) or positive (Acts 2:19, 22, 43; 4:30; 5:12; 6:8; 7:36 [exodus miracles]; 14:3; 15:12; Heb 2:4).

For our purposes, Twelftree presents the most helpful treatment of the expression and its significance to Paul.[122] Twelftree is likely right that, for Paul, the most important usage of the phrase "signs and wonders" would be that of the LXX, which predominantly uses it with reference to the exodus account.[123] Twelftree suggests that with the addition of δυνάμεσιν in 2 Cor 12:12, we see Paul qualifying the term "to echo the redemptive exodus miracles" as found in the LXX of Deut 9:29; 26:8, which speaks of God's deliverance with "great strength," "outstretched arm," and "powerful hand."[124] While some parallel may be found here, a better

---

116. Rengstorf, "Σημεῖον κτλ.," *TDNT* 7:216, listing Exod 7:3; Deut 4:34; 6:22; 7:19; 13:2–3; 26:8; 28:46; 29:2; 34:11; Isa 8:18; 20:3; Jer 32:20–21; Pss 78:43; 105:27; 135:9; Neh 9:10, with Deut 13:2–3; 28:46; and Isa 8:18 as exceptions (7:216 n. 102; cf. 7:210 n. 65). To the list of exceptions we can add, in Aramaic, Dan 3:32–33; 6:28. The way in which this phrase focuses on the exodus is parallel with how, as Eve (*The Healer from Nazareth*, 8) points out, miracles discussed across the surviving Jewish literature mostly concern the time of the exodus and, less so, the conquest.

117. Rengstorf, *TDNT* 7:221, discussing Bar 2:11; Sir 36:5 (using θαυμάσια); Wis 8:8; 10:16; Dan (Θ) 4:2; 6:28. Additional usages in the LXX include: Exod 7:9; 11:9–10; Deut 11:3; Esth 10:3[6].

118. Kee, *Medicine, Miracle*, 11.

119. E.g., Polybius, *Hist.* 3.112.8; Plutarch, *Alex.* 75.1; Appian, *Bell. civ.* 2.36; 4.4; Aelian *Var. hist.*, 12.57. See Rengstorf, *TDNT* 7:206–7.

120. See ibid., 7:224–25; Eric Eve, *The Jewish Context of Jesus' Miracles*, 30–31. Eve (p. 33) notes that Josephus does use τέρας elsewhere: in *Ant.* 2.265; 4.43, 291; 20.168 (cf. 10.28, 232); as "miracle" in *J.W.* 1.331; 5.411; as "portent" in *J.W.* 1.28, 377; 378; 4.287; 6.288, 295. Twelftree (*Paul and the Miraculous*, 209) points to usage of the phrase to describe portents of warning before the war: *J.W.* 1.28; 6.288–309.

121. Rengstorf, *TDNT* 7:222.

122. Twelftree, *Paul and the Miraculous*, 209–12. See also Rengstorf, "Τέρας," *TDNT* 8:113–26; Rengstorf, *TDNT* 7:200–69; McCasland, "Signs and Wonders," 149–52; Weiß, *Zeichen und Wunder*.

123. Twelftree, *Paul and the Miraculous*, 210.

124. Ibid. Deut 9:29: Καὶ οὗτοι λαός σου καὶ κλῆρός σου οὓς ἐξήγαγες ἐκ γῆς Αἰγύπτου ἐν τῇ ἰσχύι σου τῇ μεγάλῃ καὶ ἐν τῷ βραχίονί σου τῷ ὑψηλῷ. Deut 26:8: Καὶ ἐξήγαγεν ἡμᾶς κύριος ἐξ Αἰγύπτου

example than 2 Cor 12:12 would be Rom 15:19, where Paul uses the singular of δύναμις instead of the plural as in 2 Cor 12:12. Though Rom 15:19 would be a better example, it would only be a conceptual parallel because we still do not have δύναμις used in Deut 9:29 and 26:8. Twelftree provides a lexical link in his best example, Bar 2:11, which we saw briefly in ch. 2: "And now, O Lord God of Israel, who brought your people out of the land of Egypt with a mighty hand (ἐν χειρὶ κραταιᾷ) and with signs and wonders (καὶ ἐν σημείοις καὶ ἐν τέρασιν) and with great power (καὶ ἐν δυνάμει μεγάλῃ) and outstretched arm (καὶ ἐν βραχίονι ὑψηλῷ), and made yourself a name that continues to this day." Here we have a passage similar in ways to both Rom 15:19 and 2 Cor 12:12.[125] Paul's usage of these three words in conjunction is "almost certainly a deliberate recalling of the miracles of Moses associated with the exodus."[126] To put the point another way, the only occurrences in the LXX of δύναμις together with σημεῖα and τέρας are in the context of the exodus.[127]

This is significant, because it seems many Jews believed that God's future saving acts would be parallel with those of the past—the ultimate example being the exodus. Eve gives several examples.[128] The Wisdom of Solomon focuses on the exodus and its miracles (e.g., 8:8; 10:16; chs. 11–19).[129] Particularly, 5:17–23 anticipates a future saving act of God that is reminiscent of the nature wonders during the plagues and sea crossing.[130] 1QM 11.9–10 refers to the sea crossing in a section focused on the hope that God will similarly overcome his enemies: "You shall treat them like Pharaoh, like the officers of his chariots in the Red Sea."[131] This repetition of the exodus appears to also be the logic behind how the false prophets, which Josephus describes, called their followers to the desert (*Ant.* 20.97, 167–68).

αὐτὸς ἐν ἰσχύι μεγάλῃ καὶ ἐν χειρὶ κραταιᾷ καὶ ἐν βραχίονι αὐτοῦ τῷ ὑψηλῷ καὶ ἐν ὁράμασιν μεγάλοις καὶ ἐν σημείοις καὶ ἐν τέρασιν.

125. Similar to Rom 15:19 in the use of the singular δύναμις and similar to 2 Cor 12:12 in the order of σημεῖα and τέρας followed by a form of δύναμις.

126. Twelftree, *Paul and the Miraculous*, 210.

127. Beyond Bar 2:11, Exod 7:3–4 is the second possible occurrence—though it is possible that δύναμις refers to God's armies, as in the Hebrew. The reference could be understood as referring to power, however: ἐξάξω σὺν δυνάμει μου τὸν λαόν μου.

128. Eve, *Healer from Nazareth*, 9–10.

129. Eve, *Jewish Context*, 88–89.

130. "Shafts of lightning will fly with true aim, and will leap from the clouds to the target, as from a well-drawn bow, and hailstones full of wrath will be hurled as from a catapult; the water of the sea will rage against them, and rivers will relentlessly overwhelm them; a mighty wind will rise against them, and like a tempest it will winnow them away. Lawlessness will lay waste the whole earth, and evildoing will overturn the thrones of rulers" (5.21–23). Eve (ibid., 93) admits that this passage is vague enough to refer to other biblical miracles (e.g., Josh 10:11), but argues that overall the connections with the exodus are stronger and that the last verse of the book, 19:22, is a promise that God may repeat his former works. Here it is: "For in everything, O Lord, you have exalted and glorified your people, and you have not neglected to help them at all times and in all places" (Wis 19:22).

131. Eve, *Healer from Nazareth*, 8–9; Martínez and Tigchelaar, eds., *The Dead Sea Scrolls Study Edition*, 1:131.

4 Ezra 13:43 envisions a new exodus, complete with miraculous signs for the ten lost tribes: "At that time the Most High performed signs for them, and stopped the channels of the river until they had passed over."[132] 2 Baruch 29:8 anticipates the reappearance of manna: "And it will happen at that time that the treasury of manna will come down again from on high, and they will eat of it in those years because these are they who will have arrived at the consummation of time."[133] Sirach 36:6–9 asks God: "Give new signs, and work other wonders; make your hand and right arm glorious. Rouse your anger and pour out your wrath; destroy the adversary and wipe out the enemy" (cf. 36:1–17), which sounds similar to descriptions of the exodus elsewhere (e.g., Bar 2:11; Deut 4:34; 2 Kgs 17:36; Ps 136:12; Jer 32:21).[134]

The importance of all this is that when Paul uses the phrase "signs and wonders" to describe his miracles, he is implying that they are connected to the eschatological fulfillment of a new exodus.[135] In other words, in Paul's view, his miracles had an eschatological meaning. Schreiner writes: "Here the signs and wonders accomplished through Paul are tokens of the inauguration of the new age."[136] This connection to the exodus, and thus an eschatological significance to Paul's miracles, is strong in both Rom 15:19 and 2 Cor 12:12.[137] Some even fit this eschatological

132. Metzger, *OTP* 1:553.

133. Klijn, *OTP* 1:631.

134. Eve, *Healer from Nazareth*, 10.

135. Twelftree (*Paul and the Miraculous*, 217–18) writes: "As the miracles of Moses were the means of salvation for those involved, and also the miracles of Jesus were the realization of salvation for the supplicant, so Paul saw the apostolic miracles, including of his ministry, having the same function: miracles were realized soteriology." For arguments that the language of "signs and wonders" would have been known to Paul's recipients, see Schreiber, *Paulus als Wundertäter*, 211–12.

136. Schreiner, *Romans*, 768. Käsemann (*Commentary on Romans*, 394) writes that the two terms form a unity and "designate the experience of the divine presence in mighty eschatological acts." The background to our phrase, as Dunn (*Romans*, 2:863) puts it, "shows how deeply Paul's thought here is rooted in salvation-history (the eschatological exodus of the gospel out of Palestine into the world as of the same epochal significance as the original Exodus)." See, similarly, Schreiber, *Paulus als Wundertäter*, 202, 219–21; Jewett, *Romans*, 910–11; Thrall, *Second Epistle to the Corinthians*, 2:840. Speaking of the language of signs and wonders describing the miracles, Schreiber (*Paulus als Wundertäter*, 219) suggests, "Sie klassifizieren die Zeit des jungen Christentums als eschatologische Heilszeit." Hultgren (*Paul's Letter to the Romans*, 544) writes: "In all of this Paul is declaring that there is a similarity between what transpired at the exodus—and implicitly in the ministries of Jesus and other apostles—and in his own ministry as an apostle.... He speaks of God's power at work at the close of the age. The eschatological gift of the Spirit is being poured out." For a similar perspective on "signs and wonders" in Acts, see Rengstorf, *TDNT* 7:241.

137. This connection with the exodus is strengthened in 2 Cor 12:12, because earlier in the Corinthian correspondence (1 Cor 10:1–11) Paul has compared the Corinthians to the wilderness generation (Ciampa and Rosner, *The First Letter to the Corinthians*, 580). An eschatological connection is strengthened in Rom 15:19 because of the passage's emphasis on the Gentile mission (15:8–18), which Paul understood as connected to ultimate fulfillment (11:15, 25–32). Dunn (*Jesus and the Spirit*, 112; cf. Dunn, *Romans*, 2:864) writes that Paul's Gentile mission, "is of crucial eschatological significance, for only when 'the full number of the Gentiles has come in' will Israel be saved and the resurrection harvest be successfully concluded." Moo (*Romans*, 893) writes that "Paul may then choose to illustrate his apostolic work with ["signs and wonders"] in order to suggest the salvation-historical significance

understanding of miracles into Paul's "already-but-not-yet" tension, in that Paul's description of miracles being done "in all endurance" (2 Cor 12:12) demonstrate the need for hardship and suffering despite the presence of the new age's "signs and wonders."[138]

We have argued that Paul's miracles suggest eschatological fulfillment and that this connection between miracles and fulfillment can be seen first in Paul's understanding of the Spirit as an eschatological gift, and second, in Paul's usage of the phrase "signs and wonders." The final step will be to consider a passage that possibly makes a connection between Paul's miracles and the eschatological kingdom.

Kingdom and Power

In 1 Cor 4:20, Paul might explicitly connect the working of miracles with the presence of the kingdom, much like Jesus did in Luke 11:20 (par.). In the context of those who had grown "arrogant" (ἐφυσιώθησαν) as though Paul would not come to Corinth (1 Cor 4:18), Paul writes that he would indeed come and says, "I will find out not the talk of these arrogant people but their power [δύναμιν]" (4:19). He then explains: Οὐ γὰρ ἐν λόγῳ ἡ βασιλεία τοῦ θεοῦ ἀλλ᾽ ἐν δυνάμει (4:20). Here is one of Paul's (relatively) infrequent references to the kingdom of God, a theme more prominent in the Synoptic traditions.[139] We have already stated that this passage is a Pauline example of the eschatological kingdom as something already operative.

Our present interest is what Paul means by δύναμις. Some understand it to mean miracles; Bauckham, for example, thinks it includes exorcisms and miracles.[140]

---

of his own ministry. For Paul is not just another apostle; he is *the* apostle to the Gentiles, the one chosen to have a unique role in opening up the Gentile world to the gospel." Hultgren (*Romans*, 544) is similar: "The history of God's saving activity is being carried out as Gentile peoples are being incorporated into the people of the God of Israel, the God of the whole world." One is tempted to hear echoes of eschatological realization in Paul's πεπληρωκέναι τὸ εὐαγγέλιον τοῦ Χριστοῦ (15:19), though his point may be only geographical.

138. Fee, *Empowering Presence*; cf. Schreiber, *Paulus als Wundertäter*, 220–21.

139. Rom 14:17; 1 Cor 6:9–10; 15:24, 50; Gal 5:21; 1 Thess 2:12. We must stress the *relative* nature of the theme's infrequency in Paul for two reasons: (1) Paul does use the term with enough sufficiency to show he was aware of it and that it was not an unimportant concept; and (2) as Thompson (*Clothed with Christ*, 205) shows, Paul's usage is no less frequent than other New Testament epistles, where outside Paul's letters and Revelation, βασιλεία only occurs 5 times: Heb 1:8; 11:33; 12:28; Jas 2:5; 2 Pet 1:11, with Heb 1:8 being an Old Testament citation and Heb 11:33 concerning kingdoms generally. For treatments of the theme in the context of the Jesus-Paul debate, see Wenham, *Follower of Jesus*, 34–103; Thompson, *Clothed with Christ*, 200–207; Witherington, *End of the World*, 51–74.

140. He writes that the passage "most likely refers to exorcisms and other manifestations of miraculous power in Paul's ministry" (Bauckham, "Kingdom and Church," 15). So also Evans, "Paul the Exorcist and Healer," 364–65; Chrysostom, *Hom. 1 Cor.* 14.3. Hays (*First Corinthians*, 75) suggests a miracle of punishment: "Presumably Paul expects that if necessary God will unleash some manifestation of the power of the Spirit that will humble the arrogant ones. (One thinks, for example, of the story of Elijah's triumph over the prophets of Baal [1 Kings 18:20–40], a story that Paul elsewhere connects to his own apostolic vocation [Rom 11:2–4])." Allo (*Première Épitre aux Corinthiens*, 80) understands Paul's reference as being to "oeuvres de puissance."

Most scholars, however, do not see miracles in view here.[141] Twelftree gives the strongest argument for miracles.[142] He argues that the key to understanding 1 Cor 4:20 is how Paul uses "power" with "kingdom of God" to define his message.[143] Twelftree first argues, as we mentioned in ch. 2, that πνεῦμα and δύναμις are essentially synonyms in Paul, so when Paul uses δύναμις the thought of πνεῦμα would not be far behind, and the reader would likely think back to 1 Cor 2:4, where Paul described his message using both terms (a passage that Twelftree also argues includes miracles).[144] Twelftree then argues that, because (1) Paul's casual use of "kingdom of God" shows it was a common term for the gospel for him and his readers, (2) early Christians remembered Jesus's association of the kingdom with miracles (e.g., Luke 11:20 par.), and (3) the Christianity Paul joined had a tradition of believers performing miracles while announcing the kingdom of God (e.g., Luke 10:9 par.), "it would be surprising if any early Christian readers did not associate Paul's collocation of kingdom and power or Spirit with the miraculous," and "it is quite probable that . . . Paul intended his readers to see in the word 'power' a reference to the miraculous."[145] It is important to note, however, that in the end, Twelftree does not see an exclusive reference to miracles in 1 Cor 4:20. This is because, if Paul had wanted to be that specific, he could have used "signs and wonders" or the plural of δύναμις.[146]

How shall we assess this argument for a reference to the miraculous in 1 Cor 4:20? It is tempting for our thesis to see here an explicit link between miracles and the eschatological kingdom. Yet it is probably safer to keep our conclusions modest, since Paul is not precise. We should likely understand the power Paul describes as the power of the gospel or the power of the Holy Spirit.[147] At the same time, however, this passage does provide evidence for Paul's miracles carrying implications of eschatological fulfillment. We should note that (1) the point here seems to

141. Either by explicitly rejecting a reference to miracles (e.g., Thiselton, *The First Epistle to the Corinthians*, 377; Fitzmyer, *First Corinthians*, 226), or by not even mentioning it (e.g., Barrett, *A Commentary on the First Epistle to the Corinthians*, 118; Fee, *The First Epistle to the Corinthians*, 208–9, however, cf. p. 100; Lockwood, *1 Corinthians*, 156; Garland, *1 Corinthians*, 148). Spencer ("The Power in Paul's Teaching," 51–61) understands δύναμις as referring to Paul's sufferings.

142. In his discussion, Twelftree (*Paul and the Miraculous*, 202–4; cf. pp. 180–87, 192–201) essentially ties 4:20 with two other disputed passages, 1 Cor 2:1–5 and 1 Thess 1:5.

143. Ibid., 203.

144. Ibid., 183, 203. E.g., Rom 1:4; 15:13, 19; 1 Cor 2:4; 5:4; Gal 3:5; 1 Thess 1:5; 2 Cor 6:6–7. For connections in Paul between the Spirit and the kingdom, see Gunkel, *The Influence of the Holy Spirit*, 82–85; Bauckham, "Kingdom and Church," 15.

145. Twelftree, *Paul and the Miraculous*, 203–4; cf. pp. 114–16, 125–27, 192–201. One difficulty is that we have the singular δύναμις instead of the plural, but as we saw in ch. 3, this is not decisive. See ibid., 184. E.g., Mark 6:5; cf. Rom 15:19.

146. He writes: "Therefore, for Paul, while the kingdom of God could be equated with the power (of God) or the miraculous, [the kingdom] was more than the miracles" (ibid., 204).

147. Barrett (*First Epistle to the Corinthians*, 118) understands it as: "The power of the Holy Spirit." Fee (*First Epistle to the Corinthians*, 209) considers it: "The *power* of the Spirit." Lockwood (*1 Corinthians*, 156) calls it: "God's saving power in the crucified and risen Christ."

be the connection between the kingdom and a supernatural power, capability, or enablement, and (2) since Paul elsewhere speaks of miracles in connection with the Spirit, his gospel, and δύναμις (e.g., Rom 15:19), the associations made here between the kingdom of God and power more *generally* can plausibly apply to miracles as *specific manifestations* of that power. In other words, if Paul associates the kingdom with power, he would also associate the kingdom with miracles as particular expressions of that power. This is intelligible because, as Godet explains concerning the use of δύναμις in Rom 15:19, Paul's miracles are a matter of "the (divine) power breaking forth in signs."[148]

So, how does 1 Cor 4:20 connect miracles with eschatological fulfillment? It is not because power in Paul always refers to miracles, which need not be the case. Rather, the connection is plausible because in this passage the kingdom is associated with the presence of supernatural power, capability, or enablement, and miracles would be specific occasions of that supernatural power, capability, or enablement working in the present (e.g., Rom 15:19). If for Paul, the *power* that sometimes erupts in miracles has a connection to the kingdom of God, so plausibly would *miracles* deriving from that power.

Conclusion on Paul

This section began by highlighting how Paul was aware of ministering in the age of already-but-not-yet fulfillment, something widely acknowledged among scholars. I then argued that the miracles of Paul had an eschatological meaning in that their presence would be understood as signs of the presence of the age of eschatological fulfillment. This was pursued along three lines. First, the presence of Spirit itself had eschatological implications, and thus miracles associated with the Spirit would share the same connotations. Second, Paul's use of the phrase "signs and wonders" to describe his miracles gives them connotations of eschatological fulfillment via connections with the expectation of a new exodus (Rom 15:19; 2 Cor 12:12). Third, in 1 Cor 4:20, Paul connected the presence of divine power with the presence of the eschatological kingdom, a divine power that elsewhere he describes as bringing forth miracles (Rom 15:19; 1 Cor 12:9–10). This evidence should be sufficient to see Paul's miracles as manifestations of, or evidence for, eschatological fulfillment.

Comparing Jesus and Paul

We now examine similarities between Jesus and Paul. Whether Paul was indebted to Jesus for his understanding we will consider in the next chapter. More generally, there does seem to be a family resemblance in that Jesus and Paul both were

148. Godet, *Commentary on St. Paul's Epistle to the Romans*, 2:373.

conscious of ministering in the age of fulfillment—but with major features awaiting fulfillment. This can be conveniently seen in how the kingdom of God was something clearly future for both Jesus and Paul (e.g., Luke 11:2 par.; Gal 5:21) but already operative somehow in the present (e.g., Luke 11:20 par.; 1 Cor 4:20), as Witherington notes: "The correspondence in outlook about both the present and future *basileia* in the Jesus and Pauline tradition is quite remarkable."[149]

Turning specifically to miracles, there is strong evidence that both Jesus and Paul saw their miracles as signs of eschatological fulfillment. This can be seen in Jesus by how (1) his healings fulfilled some Old Testament expectations for national and personal restoration, (2) his exorcisms demonstrated the eschatological defeat of Satan, and (3) his miracles were connected with the presence of the eschatological Spirit.

A similar understanding can be seen in Paul, though by a different route. An eschatological significance to Paul's miracles can be seen by how (1) Paul's miracles were connected with the eschatological Spirit, (2) the phrase "signs and wonders" at two critical points (Rom 15:19; 2 Cor 12:12) interprets Paul's miracles as part of an eschatological new exodus (in that the language of the first exodus is applied to the Spirit's work in the present), and (3) at one point Paul connects the presence of divine power with the presence of the eschatological kingdom (1 Cor 4:20), a power that elsewhere produces miracles (Rom 15:19).

Two points of connection are especially strong. First, both Jesus and Paul connected their miracles with the Spirit whose presence indicated the age of eschatological fulfillment. As Dunn writes: "In both the Jesus tradition and Paul, the Spirit's present activity is an experience already of the kingdom whose consummation is not yet."[150] Second, both figures connected the presence of the kingdom with the presence of God's power. The clearest place to see this in Paul is 1 Cor 4:20, where, if perhaps not mentioning miracles directly, we at least have a significant thematic connection with the eschatological implications of Jesus's miracles (i.e., the present power of the kingdom; e.g., Luke 11:20 par.).[151]

Though Paul never says so directly, and rarely discusses them in his occasional letters, we have seen enough evidence to show that the miracles of Paul's ministry would ring with notes of eschatological fulfillment, just like the miracles of Jesus. Here we have a significant family resemblance. Nielsen sees the connection: "This means that Paul also saw healing in an eschatological perspective and held the most important aspect of the understanding of healing which we know from Jesus."[152]

---

149. Witherington, *End of the World*, 74.
150. Dunn, "Jesus Tradition in Paul," 1:179.
151. See Wenham, *Follower of Jesus*, 73. See also Twelftree, *Paul and the Miraculous*, 127, 204.
152. Nielsen, *Heilung und Verkündigung*, 210 (my translation).

CHAPTER 5

Paul and the Miracles of Jesus: Knowledge, Continuity, and Dependence

It is time to bring the threads of this study together. So far, I have argued for a family resemblance between Paul and Jesus in terms of a general similarity as miracle workers, as well as regarding three shared sign functions or significances, in which miracles (1) in some sense initially realized the gracious inclusion that both Jesus and Paul proclaimed, (2) served as (qualified) signs of authoritative power combined with a lifestyle of weakness, and (3) implied the presence of eschatological fulfillment. At this point, three issues must be addressed. First, did Paul know about Jesus's miracles? Second, how much final continuity is there between Jesus and Paul as miracle workers? Third, how plausible is it that Paul depends on Jesus for the family resemblances we have considered? Unfortunately, we have less evidence for some of these questions than for many issues discussed in preceding chapters. Though my suggestions will thus be necessarily tentative at several points, they will nonetheless prove suggestive for the Jesus-Paul debate.

Paul's Knowledge of the Miracles of Jesus

The first step to arguing for a similarity in miracles that will carry weight in the Jesus-Paul debate is to consider whether Paul even knew about Jesus's miracles. As is well-known, Paul makes no explicit references to Jesus's miracles.[1] Though certainty is impossible, we will argue that Paul probably did know of Jesus as a miracle worker. We will first consider the issue in terms of general probability, then specific channels by which Paul could have learned of Jesus's miracles, and finally, possible allusions that Paul might make to them. We will also then suggest reasons for Paul's silence on the miracles of Jesus.

---

1. See, e.g., Schweitzer, *Mysticism of Paul*, 73; Walter, "Paul and the Early Christian Jesus-Tradition," 60–61; Furnish, "The Jesus-Paul Debate," 43.

General Probability from the Widespread Miracle Tradition

Here our argument is simple.[2] As addressed in ch. 2, miracles are pervasive in the Jesus tradition, and he was known not only as a teacher but also as a miracle worker.[3] The significance of this pervasive tradition is that *if anyone knew anything about Jesus in the 30s and 40s CE, it is likely they also had at least heard of Jesus's miracles.*[4] With regard to the saying traditions, Patterson notes that, while Paul says he was unknown to the churches of *Judea* (Gal 1:22), this does not include Galilee, Damascus, Cilicia, or Arabia—all areas that Paul moved in during the years after his conversion (Gal 1:16–17, 21), which concerns a long time in a rather small locale: "To think that Paul came into the ranks of the Jesus movement in this region and yet had no contact with those early Christians who used and preserved the tradition of Jesus' sayings seems almost inconceivable."[5] We can make the same point about the miracle traditions.[6] In light of all this, we can say that Paul probably was aware of miracles performed by Jesus.[7]

Specific Possible Avenues

Through what channels might knowledge of Jesus's miracles have come to Paul? We will consider a few possibilities. First, he might have learned of Jesus's miracles before his conversion. Twelftree argues that the Pharisees were centered in Jerusalem, and so Paul would have had to spend significant time in the city as

2. For the likelihood that Christian communities would be interested in Jesus's life beyond just the kerygma, see Dunn, "Jesus Tradition in Paul," 1:170–73.

3. This should be no surprise, since as Theissen and Merz (*The Historical Jesus*, 302) put it, "The sensational is the first to draw attention to itself."

4. Theissen and Merz (ibid., 298–99) write that the miracle tradition was not emphasized in all of early Christianity. Nevertheless, they give Gos. Thom. as an example, before discussing Paul's silence on Jesus's miracles, noting though that Gos. Thom. 14 knows of the *disciples* as miracle workers.

5. Patterson, "Paul and the Jesus Tradition," 30. Cf. Fjärstedt, *Synoptic Tradition in 1 Corinthians*, 35; Moles, "Jesus the Healer in the Gospels," 167. We can also emphasize Paul's time in Antioch in this vein (Thompson, *Clothed with Christ*, 65). Yet Patterson's statement needs to be qualified somewhat by the fact that Galilee was part of the Roman province of Judea (see Longenecker, *Galatians*, 41). On the other hand, there is also even the possibility that Judea here is being used *exclusive* of Jerusalem itself. For some discussion of this, see, e.g., Burton, *Epistle to the Galatians*, 63–64.

6. And some of the saying tradition refers to Jesus's miracles (e.g., Luke 10:13 par.).

7. Twelftree (*Paul and the Miraculous*, 119) summarizes: "Given what we have seen of the place of miracles in the ministry of Jesus and the mission of his followers, it is very plausible that Paul had heard about the miracles of Jesus and his first followers, along with their significance." Dawson, *Healing, Weakness*, 182. Intriguingly, Moles ("Jesus the Healer," 117–82) even argues that a naming pun (common in the ancient world, he argues) exists between Ἰησοῦς and ἰάομαι. This is another way Jesus's miracles of healing would be well-known. Speaking of the Gospels and Acts, Moles (p. 172) writes: "How would pagan readers react to the Jesus-healer punning of these texts? They would certainly see it and hear it." Moles (p. 173) admits few examples in Paul, though he suggests Rom 5:6–21. Yet: "Since Ἰησοῦς, to Hellenising Jews and Greek Christians, actually *means* 'healer,' the puns I have argued for . . . will *always* be there, whether actively or only just below the surface" (p. 174).

part of his education.[8] Porter is very bold concerning the implications of this line of argument: "The question that must be asked, logic seems to dictate, is not just whether it is possible that Paul and Jesus would have, almost literally, run into each other, but how it would have been possible for them not to have known of each other."[9] Beyond this alignment of time and geography, Paul claims to have been a persecutor of the church (Gal 1:13, 23). This suggests that Paul would have had motivation and opportunity to learn about Jesus and his practices.[10] Because Jesus was renowned as a miracle worker, it is unlikely that a dedicated opponent like Paul would have been unaware of claims or rumors of miracles—though Paul probably would have rejected them as sorcery or deception.[11] It is worthwhile to remember that the miracle tradition most assuredly radiated outward from Palestinian Jewish circles, and it is not necessary to look to Greek influences by way of origin.[12] This entire line of argument is bolstered considerably if one finds persuasive Porter's arguments that Paul and Jesus actually met in person during Jesus's ministry.[13]

What about after Paul's conversion? Although Paul is concerned to show his independence in Galatians (e.g., 1:1–17), he shows himself indebted to Christian tradition at numerous other points (e.g., 1 Cor 11:2, 23–25; 15:1–11).[14] Some awareness of Christian tradition about Jesus as a miracle worker seems more probable than not. Beyond what Paul would have known about Jesus while a persecutor, Hengel, Wedderburn, Simmons, and Schoberg have argued convincingly that it is the "Hellenists" of Acts 6—Greek-speaking Jewish Christians who were located in Jerusalem and, later, Antioch—that form a link between Jesus and Paul in terms of historical connection and tradition.[15] It is this group that particularly seems to have fallen under persecution (Acts 8:1, 4–6; 11:19), including persecution by Paul (Acts 7:58; 8:1–3; 9:1–2; cf. Gal 1:13; Phil 3:6), and it is to this group that Paul attaches himself (Acts 9:20–26; 11:20–26; 13:1; Gal 1:17, 21–24; cf. 2 Cor 11:32–33; Gal 2:11–12; Acts 21:3–9).[16]

---

8. Twelftree, *Paul and the Miraculous*, 47; following Hengel, *The Pre-Christian Paul*, 56–62. Porter (*When Paul Met Jesus*, 12–25) argues along similar lines.

9. Ibid., 22.

10. Again, Porter (ibid., 25) is even stronger: "I find it difficult to believe that somewhere along the way, a serious-minded and increasingly zealotic Pharisee such as Paul would not have sought out and hence met Jesus." Akenson (*Saint Saul*, 171–72) observes this on Paul as a persecutor: "Whatever else that may have entailed, he certainly was in position to learn a lot about Yeshua." So, less strongly, Dodd, *Apostolic Preaching*, 17.

11. As in Luke 11:15 par.; b. Sanh. 43a; Origen, *Cels.* 1.38.

12. See Blackburn, Theios Anēr, 263–66.

13. Porter, *When Paul Met Jesus*, passim.

14. On his relation to tradition, see Schoberg, *Perspectives of Jesus in the Writings of Paul*, 123–26.

15. Hengel, *Between Jesus and Paul*, 1–29; Wedderburn, "Paul and Jesus: Similarity and Continuity," 117–43; Simmons, *A Theology of Inclusion in Jesus and Paul*, 88–152; Schoberg, *Perspectives of Jesus*, 64–136; cf. Räisänen, "The 'Hellenists,'" 149–202.

16. See Hengel, *Acts and the History*, 76–77; Simmons, *Theology of Inclusion*, 104–5; Schoberg, *Perspectives of Jesus*, 70–71, 84–85. Significantly, Acts 9:29 has Paul focusing on outreach in Jerusalem

Significantly, it is this group that probably first translated the Jesus traditions into Greek.[17] If so, it would allow Paul to stand in close connection with those responsible for the transmission of many miracle traditions. For example, Dunn argues that Mark 2:1–3:6, which includes a healing performed by Jesus (3:1–5), is a unit of pre-Pauline, Hellenistic-Christian tradition, and an example of the kind of material that they would transmit and that would support the emphases of both the Hellenists and Paul.[18] Also significantly, Acts remembers this group—exemplified by Stephen and Philip—as charismatics who performed miracles (e.g., 6:3–5, 8; 8:5–13, 26–40; 13:1; 21:8–9).[19] Thus, as Schoberg and others argue that the Hellenists mediated to Paul the traditions of Jesus's table fellowship, so too we can expect the Hellenists to have mediated knowledge of the Jesus miracles and the importance of Spirit-wrought miracles.[20]

Beyond the Hellenists of Acts 6, we know that Paul also had significant contact with Palestinian Jewish Christian leaders and apostles. As Twelftree notes, Paul knew of the twelve, Peter, and James (1 Cor 15:5–7); had met Peter, John, and James personally (Gal 1:18–19; 2:9; cf. 2:2); and had significant contact with Barnabas (1 Cor 9:5–6; Gal 2:1, 9, 13).[21] Paul's fifteen-day stay with Peter is significant (Gal 1:18).[22] Akenson points out that as much as Paul might have learned, Peter and James would also have been interested in what Paul knew and taught:

to Hellenists—in this case Greek-speaking, non-Christian Jews. One supposes this is essentially the group of which Paul was a part while a persecutor.

17. Either in Jerusalem, (Hengel, *Between Jesus and Paul*, 27–29) or Antioch (Thompson, *Clothed with Christ*, 65). It would be the Hellenistic Jewish Christians who would have been the first to need the Jesus traditions in Greek.

18. Dunn, "Mark 2.1–3.6," 412–13. "In short, the tradition behind Mark 2.15–3.6 provides an invaluable bridge between Jesus and Paul" (p. 413). Yet see the hesitations of Räisänen ("The 'Hellenists,'" pp. 197–201).

19. See, e.g., Philip, *Origins of Pauline Pneumatology*, 155. Hengel (*Between Jesus and Paul*, 18–19; cf. Hengel, *Acts and the History*, 73, 78–79) argues that this charismatic activity is one reason for their persecution. Yet see Räisänen, "The 'Hellenists,'" 172–74; Schoberg, *Perspectives of Jesus*, 85–86. Räisänen ("The 'Hellenists,'" 174) argues that "pneumatic experiences were probably something which united 'Hebrews' and 'Hellenists.'" Hengel (*Acts and the History*, 78) points out that we know of Phillip's daughters also from Papias, who mentions miracle stories connected to them; see Eusebius, *Hist. eccl.* 3.39; cf. 3.31.

20. Cf. Philip, *Origins of Pauline Pneumatology*, 217–23; Kollmann, "Paulus als Wundertäter," 95. For the place of the Spirit's reception for the Hellenists, with accompanying miracles, see Wedderburn, "Similarity and Continuity," 138. On Paul's emphasis on acceptance of Gentile outsiders, Wedderburn (pp. 142–43) suggests: "This is a conviction which he had inherited from the Hellenists whom he had once persecuted for holding it; they in turn had considered it to be in harmony with the ways and attitude of Jesus, and they and Paul had seen it confirmed by the outpouring of God's spirit."

21. Twelftree, *Paul and the Miraculous*, 119. Knowling (*Testimony of St. Paul to Christ*, 502) also discusses Andronicus and Junias (Rom 16:7), who had been Christians before Paul. Fraser (*Jesus and Paul*, 99) adds Mark and Silas.

22. A point particularly emphasized by Dunn ("Relationship between Paul and Jerusalem," 463–66). Of course, the comment of Dodd (*Apostolic Preaching*, 17) is well-known: "We may presume they did not spend all the time talking about the weather." Hengel (*Acts and the History*, 85) writes: "The

In more than a fortnight of intensive discussion with Peter he must have been tutored in all the basic actions and sayings of Yeshua as Peter knew them. Further, Saul obviously was being examined not only on his own character, but on his knowledge and ideology. The one-time audience with Yacov, direct heir to the headship of the Yeshua-faith, has the appearance of a *viva voce* examination of a doctoral candidate by a stern External Examiner. Saul passes, manifestly: he knows his Yeshua and his interpretations are within the acceptable boundaries of the plasticities of the time.[23]

Akenson's analogy is, of course, anachronistic, but it makes his point nicely.

Potential Touchpoints within Paul

Various scholars have argued that Paul alludes to Jesus's miracles at points in his letters.[24] While space does not allow detailed treatment, we will briefly consider some potential contacts. Wenham suggests that (1) Paul's references to "the affection of Christ Jesus" (σπλάγχνοις Χριστοῦ Ἰησοῦ) in Phil 1:8 might allude to stories of Jesus's healings, which use σπλαγχνίζομαι (e.g., Mark 1:41; Mark 6:34 // Matt 14:14; Mark 8:2 par.; Matt 20:34); and (2) Paul's reference to aiding "the weak" (τῶν ἀσθενῶν) in 1 Thess 5:14 might have similar significance, since ἀσθενής also occurs in the Gospel accounts of healing (e.g., Mark 6:56; Matt 10:8; Luke 5:15).[25] These are, however, only tenuous connections. More plausible is Wenham's argument that the reference to mountain-moving faith (ἐὰν ἔχω πᾶσαν τὴν πίστιν ὥστε ὄρη μεθιστάναι) in 1 Cor 13:2 shows Paul's knowledge of Jesus's saying on faith (Mark 11:22–23 // Matt 21:21; Luke 17:6 // Matt 17:20), especially since Paul discusses (plausibly) miraculous faith in the near-context (1 Cor 12:9).[26] Yeung adds that Paul's relative frequency in citing Jesus's sayings in 1 Corinthians also heightens the possibility of an allusion here.[27] Twelftree hesitates to accept the Wenham/Yeung argument because Paul could instead be picking up on a common proverbial phrase.[28] While this is a significant point, a connection to Jesus seems slightly more probable than not in this saying, given (1) the prominence of the saying in Christian tradition (Q and Mark), (2) Paul's other citations of Jesus in

---

two most significant figures in earliest Christian history will have exchanged views on what interested them; I myself feel that for Paul this will have included the Petrine tradition about Jesus, which, as is shown by the role of Peter in all the Gospels, was the dominant one in the Greek-speaking communities of the Roman empire."

23. Akenson, *Saint Saul*, 172.

24. Once again, the most helpful treatment is by Twelftree (*Paul and the Miraculous*, 118–48).

25. Wenham, *Paul*, 351–52.

26. Ibid., 81–83. Cf. Yeung, *Faith in Jesus and Paul*, 30–33; Pokorný, "Words of Jesus in Paul," 4:3459.

27. Yeung, *Faith in Jesus and Paul*, 30–31.

28. Twelftree, *Paul and the Miraculous*, 129. E.g., b. Ber. 64a; b. Sanh. 24a.

1 Corinthians, and (3) the presence of what appears to be miraculous faith nearby in the literary context (1 Cor 12:9).

This point may be strengthened by arguments that Paul knew Q, especially the mission discourse of Luke 10:1–16 (par.).[29] The saying on workmen being worth their wages in 1 Cor 9:14 is often accepted as a saying of Jesus later found in Luke 10:7 (par.).[30] Some see other Pauline allusions to this discourse and argue that Paul knew the whole discourse.[31] If it is probable that Paul was aware of the mission discourse, Paul would probably also be aware of the tradition of the Twelve being sent out with authority to heal and perform miracles: "Heal the sick in it and say to them, 'The kingdom of God has come near to you'" (Luke 10:9; cf. Matt 10:8). Wenham argues: "If Paul knew that the apostolic mission was a miracle-working one, he must have thought of Jesus' mission in similar terms."[32] If this be accepted, then Paul's reference to "signs of an apostle" in 2 Cor 12:12 is even more understandable. If Paul knows that Jesus sent his messengers to perform miracles of healing, it makes it likely Paul knew of Jesus as a miracle worker—since it seems unlikely to understand Jesus sending out followers to heal if Jesus himself did not.[33]

Romans 15:18–19 is likewise suggestive. Here Paul says that it is Christ who accomplished everything through him, including miracles. This makes the most sense if Paul is aware that Jesus also performed miracles.[34] One additional possibility also presents itself. In Rom 15:8, Paul knows of Christ as "a servant to the

29. On the likelihood of Paul's knowing blocks of Q and/or the mission discourse, see Bruce, *Paul and Jesus*, 70–71; Fjärstedt, *Synoptic Tradition*, 66–77; Allison, "The Pauline Epistles," 1–32; Allison, "Paul and the Missionary Discourse," 369–75; Wenham, *Follower of Jesus*, 190–96; Allison, *The Jesus Tradition in Q*, 54–60, 104–19; Twelftree, *Paul and the Miraculous*, 120–24. For arguments to the contrary, see Tuckett, "1 Corinthians and Q," 607–19; Tuckett, "Paul and the Synoptic Mission Discourse?" 376–81; Neirynck, "Paul and the Sayings of Jesus," 265–321. Somewhat by contrast, Porter (*When Paul Met Jesus*, 159) suggests that Paul might have actually overheard Jesus speak the Luke 10:7 saying in person.

30. See, e.g., Dungan, *The Sayings of Jesus*, xxxii; Wenham, *Follower of Jesus*, 192; Blomberg, "Quotations, Allusions, and Echoes of Jesus in Paul," 137–38.

31. See, e.g., Wenham, *Follower of Jesus*, 190–200. For example, two of these potential allusions by Paul include "the right to eat and drink" (1 Cor 9:4; cf. Luke 10:7–8) and "whoever disregards this, disregards not man but God" (1 Thess 4:8; cf. Luke 10:16). Allison (*Jesus Tradition*, 56) puts the argument for Paul's knowledge of the whole discourse another way: "1 Corinthians 9 not only cites a line which appeared in Q's missionary discourse (1 Cor 9:14 = Q 10:7b: the worker is worthy of reward) but also alludes to the broader Q context for that line. This implies that Paul knew some version of the missionary discourse."

32. Wenham, "The Story of Jesus Known to Paul," 308.

33. Wenham, *Follower of Jesus*, 351. See Resch, *Der Paulinismus und die Logia Jesu*, 528. The point is the same in 2 Cor 12:12 even if one rejects Paul's knowledge of the mission discourse, though perhaps somewhat lessened.

34. Twelftree (*Paul and the Miraculous*, 124) again writes: "It is reasonable to propose that this statement has force only if Paul held the view that Christ conducted miracles." Cf. Wenham, *Follower of Jesus*, 351; Kim, "Jesus, Sayings of," 486; Matheson, "The Historical Christ of St. Paul," 274; Schlatter, *Theology of the Apostles*, 191.

circumcised" (Χριστὸν διάκονον γεγενῆσθαι περιτομῆς).[35] In Rom 15:16, Paul calls himself "a minister of Christ Jesus to the Gentiles" (λειτουργὸν Χριστοῦ Ἰησοῦ εἰς τὰ ἔθνη). Despite the lexical change from διάκονος to λειτουργός, there might be a parallel here.[36] If this similarity holds, and *Paul* performs miracles as part of his mission to Gentiles (Rom 15:18–19), does this imply a knowledge of *Jesus* performing miracles as part of his mission to Israel? Although somewhat tenuous, this line of argument may not be without some merit.

Another possible touchpoint is 1 Cor 4:20, where we see a close connection in Paul between the kingdom of God and δύναμις, a theme reminiscent of Luke 11:20 (par.). Some accordingly see a knowledge of the miracle tradition here, like Kim: "Thus Paul reveals, though allusively, his knowledge of a narrative tradition about Jesus as a miracle worker."[37] None of these potential contacts is certain. Yet if, as argued above, we grant an initial likelihood of Paul knowing about Jesus's miracles even before considering these touchpoints, the probabilities grow very strong.

Why the Silence?

While space constraints forbid in-depth discussion, it is worthwhile to consider why—if he knew about Jesus's miracles—Paul makes no reference to them. It could be, of course, that Paul is actively opposed to a miracle working Jesus.[38] Yet on this suggestion it is difficult to understand how Paul could treat positively the working of miracles in his ministry and churches (2 Cor 12:12; Rom 15:18–19; 1 Cor 12:10; Gal 3:5).[39] The two most important suggestions for Paul's silence on Jesus's

---

35. Significantly, here is a place where Paul refers to the precrucifixion ministry of Jesus that shows he had an awareness of something apart from Jesus's death. See Wright, *People of God*, 408–9.

36. Akenson (*Saint Saul*, 228–29) suggests this similarity. He writes that here, "One has Saul's life in a compressed moment: (1) he is in subordination to Jesus Christ as far as his faith and message is concerned, but (2) his own mission to the Gentiles is a simulacrum of Yeshua's mission to the children of Israel."

37. Kim, "Jesus, Sayings of," 487. See also Wenham, *Follower of Jesus*, 73; Twelftree, *Paul and the Miraculous*, 203–4.

38. As argued variously by Kuhn, "Der irdische Jesus bei Paulus," 317–20; Georgi, *The Opponents of Paul*, 271–83; cf. pp. 170–74; Robinson, "Kerygma and History in the New Testament," 59–63; Koester, "*GNOMAI DIAPHOROI*," 150–53; Koester, "One Jesus and Four Primitive Gospels," 189–90. For various arguments against these suggestions, see Goppelt, *Theology of the New Testament*, 2:45, though cf. 2:45–46; Thompson, *Clothed with Christ*, 75; Pokorný, "Words of Jesus," 4:3449; Sumney, *Servants of Satan*, 79–133. On divergent suggestions concerning the ἄλλον Ἰησοῦν of 2 Cor 11:4, see Furnish, *2 Corinthians*, 500–501; Thrall, *Second Epistle to the Corinthians*, 2:667–70; Harris, *Second Epistle to the Corinthians*, 744.

39. The counterargument would probably be that Paul understood Jesus's life prior to resurrection as one of weakness and that this is incoherent with a powerful miracle worker. As Harvey (*Jesus and the Constraints of History*, 98–99) notes, one could take Paul's description of Jesus's humiliation in Phil 2:5–11 as implying the impossibility of performing miracles. Harvey cites Bultmann for this, though this is not precisely Bultmann's point, who admits that Jesus performed miracles (Bultmann, *Theology of the New Testament*, 1:27). Along the lines of Harvey's suggestion, Georgi (*Opponents of Paul*, 274–76) argues that, for Paul, the *weakness* of Jesus's earthly phase corresponds to the weakness

miracles—and minimal reference to the Jesus tradition generally—concern the genre of Paul's letters and their occasional nature. Both of these factors help us alleviate the problem of why Paul does not bring up Jesus's miracles.[40]

First, Paul's letters are occasional, and as such, he apparently had little pressing need to recall Jesus's miracles.[41] We remind ourselves of the oft-made observation that if the Corinthians had not abused the Lord's Supper, Paul would not have mentioned it—and some might assume his churches were unacquainted with it.[42]

Second, the letter genre was apparently not one to which early Christians turned to convey Jesus traditions.[43] The silence of Paul's letters actually matches the silence of other early Christian letters. Thompson is helpful on this point. Of all the letters he considers, only 2 Peter, Ignatius, Barnabas, and perhaps Hebrews refer to occasions in Jesus's life before his passion, and only Barnabas refers to Jesus's miracles generally.[44] What is the significance of this? We should not be surprised that Paul does not often bring up incidents in Jesus life, including miracles.[45] This was simply not done often in early Christian letters, for whatever cluster of reasons explains the general silence.[46]

Thus, we can assume that Paul conveyed more traditions about Jesus's life and death than references in his letters demonstrate. Hengel's words are often quoted:

> In the ancient world it was impossible to proclaim as Son of God and redeemer of the world a man who had died on the cross, i.e. had suffered the shameful death of a common criminal, without giving a clear account of his activity, his suffering and his death. Those to whom the earliest Christian missionaries preached were no less curious than we are today. Certainly, they too will have wanted more information about the man Jesus.[47]

---

of Paul's apostolic ministry; see, e.g., 2 Cor 4:10–11. But if this holds, and Paul *does* claim to work miracles within the weakness of his ministry (2 Cor 12:12), does this not imply that Paul could understand the same for the earthly phase of Jesus? Georgi (p. 281) acknowledges that Paul refers to his own miracles in 2 Cor 12:12.

40. Eve (*The Healer from Nazareth*, 83) puts it nicely: "The negative argument (that Paul is ignorant of any tradition of Jesus' miracles) is considerably weakened both by the genre of Paul's surviving letters and by the overall paucity of any kind of Jesus tradition in what he wrote. Paul's surviving writings are occasional letters written to address specific problems; they are not the entire content of his preaching about Jesus Christ, and, more specifically, they are not narratives."

41. See, e.g., Barnett, *Paul: Missionary of Jesus*, 20–21; cf. González, "Healing in the Pauline Epistles," 573.

42. E.g., Wenham, "Story of Jesus," 297.

43. See Allison, "Pauline Epistles," 21–23.

44. Thompson, *Clothed with Christ*, 61. Eve (*Healer from Nazareth*, 78) notes that the letters of the Apostolic Fathers are also largely silent about Jesus's miracles. An example, however, is Barn. 5:8.

45. As Thompson (*Clothed with Christ*, 62) writes, "It is unrealistic to expect Paul to refer to events in Jesus' life prior to the Passion, especially to particular miracles."

46. For more on some of these reasons, see Blomberg, *Making Sense of the New Testament*, 84–88.

47. Hengel, *Acts and the History*, 43–44. This echoes Machen ("Jesus and Paul," 562): "A missionary preaching that included no concrete account of the life of Jesus would have been preposterous.

Conclusion on Paul's Knowledge

What can we say in summary concerning Paul's knowledge of Jesus as a miracle worker? In light of (1) the general probabilities, (2) avenues by which Paul could have learned of Jesus's miracles, (3) potential touchpoints in the letters of Paul, and (4) plausible explanations for Paul's silence, it seems very probable that Paul knew of Jesus's miracles. In fact, Dawson might not be unjustified in calling Paul's knowledge of Jesus's healing miracles a "near-certainty."[48] This has significant implications for Paul's continuity with, and imitation of, Jesus as a miracle worker—to which we now turn.

Paul's Continuity with Jesus as a Miracle Worker

In this study, we have argued for continuity—or family resemblance—between Jesus and Paul in two ways. First, in part of ch. 2, we considered how both figures were miracle workers for whom we have strong historical corroboration, as well as how miracles accompanied the ministries of both. Second, in the rest of ch. 2, as well as in chs. 3–4, we investigated three sign functions or significances that seem to be associated with the miracles of both Jesus and Paul: their miracles were signs of a gracious inclusion of outsiders, (qualified) signs of authoritative power with a lifestyle of weakness, and signs of the new age.

These three sign functions correspond loosely to the shared convictions between Jesus and Paul as argued by Schoberg.[49] Because miracle working was a practical aspect of the ministry of each, miracle working is a further parallel to add alongside Wolff's similarities.[50] Significantly, we have also argued that it is likely that Paul knew of Jesus's miracles.

The claim that a crucified Jew was to be obeyed as Lord and trusted as Saviour must surely have provoked the question as to what manner of man this was. It is true that the gods of other religions needed to be described only in general terms. But Christianity had dispensed with the advantages of such vagueness. It had identified its God with a Jew who had lived but a few years before. Surely the tremendous prejudice against accepting a crucified criminal as Lord and Master could be overcome only by an account of the wonderful character of Jesus." Similar is Fjärstedt (*Synoptic Tradition*, 35), who says that, not long after Paul, we find "the gospel tradition in a form that bears clear signs of having been transmitted for some time, and also signs of the use of single pieces of tradition in the churches, particularly in gospel-preaching, apologetic discussion, catechetical instruction etc. If this kind of tradition was unknown to Paul, the leading missionary of the period, and not used by him, where was it? By whom was it used?"

48. Dawson, *Healing, Weakness*, 207.

49. "Jesus's Table Fellowship with Tax Collectors and Sinners" // "Paul's Welcome of the Gentiles"; "Jesus's Challenge to Share His Fate" // "Paul's Participationist Language"; and "Jesus's Ministry in the Context of New Creation" // "Paul's New Creation Eschatology" (Schoberg, *Perspectives of Jesus*, v).

50. "Deprivation"; "Renunciation of Marriage"; "Humble Service"; and "Suffering Persecution" (Wolff, "Humility and Self-Denial," 145–60).

We now need to turn our attention to a recent argument for ultimate *discontinuity* between Jesus and Paul as miracle workers—as found in Twelftree's *Paul and the Miraculous*. This is particularly important since, in many respects, we have followed Twelftree's arguments throughout this study.

Supporting in ways my first point on Jesus and Paul as both being miracle workers, Twelftree argues that miracles are central to any understanding of Paul.[51] Twelftree accomplishes this especially by broadening the category of the "miraculous" to include things such as prophecy, revelations, tongues, and divine protection.[52] Here and there, Twelftree also makes statements that can be taken to support aspects of the sign functions I have adduced.[53]

Yet in a few key respects, Twelftree argues finally for a significant *dissimilarity* between Jesus and Paul on the issue of miracles. He makes much of the fact that Paul, technically and grammatically, never claims to have worked a miracle.[54] Part of Twelftree's evidence lies in Paul's use of the *passive* voice (e.g., 2 Cor 12:12), and from this Twelftree suggests that Paul did not actively attempt to perform miracles, but rather, God worked miracles as Paul preached: "It is Paul's use of the passive and in never laying claim to performing miracles that we see his view: in the event of—or coincidental with—proclaiming the gospel the Spirit comes, obvious in the miracles that God performs. . . . In the coming of the gospel Paul saw himself doing the speaking and God performing miracles."[55]

Twelftree sees this in tension with Acts, which presents Paul as actively initiating miracles: "The image of the apostle of faith set out by Luke is of a powerful and prolific miracle worker, so unlike that of Paul's letters. . . . Luke has made Paul into a miracle worker not unlike Jesus. In this Luke proves to be an unreliable witness in seeking the historical Paul's involvement in the miraculous."[56] "It is not unreasonable to suggest that Paul would have repudiated Luke's portrait of him as a miracle-working apostle."[57]

My contention is that this is an over-reading of the evidence, and thus, it is unnecessary to pit the image of Paul in the epistles against the Paul of Acts. I will argue this by four avenues: (1) generally, there is not enough evidence in Paul's letters to make Twelftree's distinction; (2) specifically, Paul's use of the passive is not decisive; (3) Twelftree's understanding of "miracle worker" is too narrow; and (4) Acts may instead be seen as corroboration, not contradiction.

---

51. Twelftree, *Paul and the Miraculous*, 323.

52. Ibid., 308–9, 313–14; cf. pp. 20–26.

53. E.g., on gracious inclusion: ibid., 217–18; on signs of authority: 216, 315; on signs of the new age: 217–18, 204.

54. "Paul never claimed to perform miracles" (ibid., 317). "Paul clearly did not see himself as a miracle worker" (p. 318).

55. Ibid., 318–19. Cf. Kollmann, "Paulus als Wundertäter," 81–82; Alkier, *Wunder und Wirklichkeit*, 241.

56. Twelftree, *Paul and the Miraculous*, 311.

57. Ibid., 317 n. 17.

First, we do not have enough evidence in Paul's undisputed letters to say that the image of Paul as actively initiating miracles in Acts is exaggerated. As we have faced throughout this study, Paul only infrequently mentions his miracles—clearly only in 2 Cor 12:12 and Rom 15:18–19. To argue from such a limited set of evidence that Paul did not actively initiate miracles and that he would only preach and God would supply miracles is tenuous at best.[58] It is just as conceivable from the evidence in the epistles that Paul could be involved in miracles as described in Acts and discuss them as he does in Romans and 2 Corinthians.

This brings us to my second line of argument, namely, Paul's use of the passive in 2 Cor 12:12 is not decisive. Could Paul actively command a demon to come out (Acts 16:18) or be involved in raising a seemingly dead man (Acts 20:10), and still speak of events in the passive such as in 2 Cor 12:12?[59] It is difficult to know why this could not be. The reason for the passive could either be humility, or the related understanding that the power was not his but God's.[60] Both options fit the context of 2 Cor 12. Perhaps instructive is the very next verse (12:13): "For in what were you less favored than the rest of the churches, except that I myself did not burden you?" (εἰ μὴ ὅτι αὐτὸς ἐγὼ οὐ κατενάρκησα ὑμῶν). Here the emphasis is squarely on Paul's actions, and Paul even transitions grammatically to the active voice.

Further support for my point comes from Rom 15:18. Here Paul writes, "I will not venture to speak of anything except what Christ has accomplished through me [κατειργάσατο Χριστὸς δι' ἐμοῦ] to bring the Gentiles to obedience—by word and deed [λόγῳ καὶ ἔργῳ]." As Dunn puts it, "Anything achieved has been done by Christ; but the agency is Paul's."[61] Notably, Paul himself spoke the words, as implied in 15:19 ("I have fulfilled the gospel of Christ") and made explicit in 15:20 ("I make it my ambition to preach the gospel"), yet he credits Christ as the real actor (15:18).[62] Accordingly, when he speaks of "the power of signs and wonders" and "the power of the Spirit of God" in the same passage, it seems likely that Paul was the intermediate agent. Yet to say "I performed signs and wonders" would be inappropriate because of how the power was clearly God's and not Paul's. To put it

---

58. Of course this is not the whole of Twelftree's evidence. For example, he also argues from Paul's disputed letters that Paul was not remembered as a miracle worker (ibid., 302–3). Yet we have discussed earlier in this chapter the arguments of Thompson and others that Christians typically did not convey miracle stories in the genre of epistles. A silence of miracles in epistles thus should not surprise us (Twelftree says as much [pp. 301–2]). Beyond this, Acts remembers Paul as a miracle worker, and this evidence is potentially as early as some of the letters Twelftree adduces, which he views as pseudonymous, such as Ephesians or 2 Thessalonians (see pp. 276–80). Admitting the point is Twelftree's title for his chapter on Acts: "Luke: Paul's Earliest Interpreter" (p. 229).

59. These miracles in Acts Twelftree (ibid., 271) accepts as probably and possibly historical, respectively.

60. For general options on the passive, see Wallace, *Greek Grammar beyond the Basics*, 437–38.

61. Dunn, *Romans*, 2:862.

62. Twelftree (*Paul and the Miraculous*, 319) recognizes this point: "Paul saw himself doing the speaking and God performing the miracles—though, even his words could be seen as the accomplishments of Christ (Rom. 15:18)."

another way, if Paul could attribute his *speech* to Christ—which certainly involved conscious action on Paul's part—Paul could also attribute *miracles* to the Spirit or Christ despite his own agency being involved at some level.

More evidence comes from the Gospels and suggests that we should not over-emphasize the passive construction in 2 Cor 12:12. In two of our key passages for Jesus, the grammar does not present Jesus as the subject. In Luke 7:22 (par.), "the blind receive their sight" (ἀναβλέπουσιν), "the lame walk" (περιπατοῦσιν), "lepers are cleansed" (καθαρίζονται), "the deaf hear" (ἀκούουσιν), and "the dead are raised up" (ἐγείρονται). In Luke 10:13 (par.), Jesus refers to "the mighty works done in you" (αἱ δυνάμεις αἱ γενόμεναι ἐν ὑμῖν). *Even if these were the only passages where Jesus addressed miracles*, would we be justified in thinking that he took no initiatory or significant role because he is not the grammatical subject? Would we be justified in thinking that he was not a miracle worker? Not necessarily. There would not be enough evidence to make that distinction. A similar case holds for Paul.

My third argument is that Twelftree's understanding of "miracle worker" is too narrow. He writes, "Even when he could have won an argument by it, Paul did not assert that he had performed miracles (2 Cor 12:11–13). In this his critics were right: Paul was not a miracle worker, let alone a great miracle worker."[63] This is a perplexing statement, because as we have argued earlier—and as Twelftree himself does—Paul *is indeed* here claiming miracles as part of his ministry.[64] True, Paul's grammar does not make him the subject of the action. Plausibly, Paul would rather credit God with these miracles. But to say this disqualifies Paul from being a miracle worker is to insist on too narrow a distinction.[65]

Is Jesus a miracle worker only because he, at times, claims the power himself (e.g., Luke 13:32)? Would Jesus be disqualified if we only had passages where he attributes miraculous power to God or the Spirit? Two examples come to mind: "Go home to your friends and tell them how much the Lord has done for you, and how he has had mercy on you" (Mark 5:19); "If it is by the finger of God that I cast out demons, then the kingdom of God has come upon you" (Luke 11:20). This would hardly disqualify Jesus as a miracle worker.

Even if we were to grant Twelftree's point that Paul did not actively initiate miracles, and that God spontaneously brought them about as part of Paul's preaching, to say this means Paul was not a miracle worker goes too far. This is especially the case when the silence of Paul's self-presentation is pitted against Acts. Beyond this,

---

63. Ibid., 318.

64. Ibid., 208–18. Twelftree is differentiating the situations because of Paul's use of the passive and Paul's (proposed) lack of initiating miracles.

65. Note how Twelftree (ibid., 218) puts it: "Paul . . . challenges the Corinthians to recall that though he may not have been actively involved in them, salvific authenticating miracles—most probably not unlike those known in the Jesus tradition—characteristically did take place among them in association with his ministry (12:12)."

if God did not spontaneously bring miracles about through most early Christian preaching, the term is still meaningful.

My fourth line of evidence, accordingly, is that we can see Acts as corroboration rather than contradiction. Instead of pitting a Paul who drives out demons and prays for healing (Acts) against a Paul who preaches while God occasionally causes healings and exorcisms to occur (Twelftree's reading of Paul's letters), it seems just as plausible to use Acts to help us understand Paul's practice. This should especially be the case because Twelftree cautiously accepts the exorcism of Acts 16:16–18, the connection to exorcisms in 19:13, and the raising in 20:7–12 as probably or potentially having roots in historical Paul. Somewhat curiously, Twelftree also accepts 14:3, "So they remained for a long time, speaking boldly for the Lord, who bore witness to the word of his grace, granting signs and wonders to be done by their hands," and uses it to corroborate his thesis: "Paul was a preacher, and it was God who was credited with the miracles."[66] I would agree with his assessment of Acts 14:3, but this passage does not support his overly precise distinction between a Paul who initiates miracles and a Paul who passively watches miracles occur.

In the end, I agree with a reviewer of Twelftree's book, who writes that Twelftree's findings are "overly-cautious."[67] This is particularly so, in my view, in terms of similarity between Jesus and Paul. I agree rather with the author of an endorsement on the back of Twelftree's book: "[Twelftree's] focus on the miraculous locates Paul even closer to his Galilean master, and the often-assumed divide between Jesus and Paul is bridged from a rather unexpected angle."[68] It seems that there is more similarity between Jesus and Paul on the place of miracles than Twelftree allows.

Yet while Twelftree is overly cautious at points, one exception is his suggestion that Acts is a falsification because it has Paul initiating miracles. Here Twelftree is actually not cautious at all but puts too much weight on the ambiguities of Paul's few references to miracles in his undisputed letters. Here *more* caution is in order, and Luke's account in Acts may prove more helpful than Twelftree allows.

Paul's Dependence upon Jesus

I have argued that Paul likely knew of Jesus's miracles, and that there is significant practical and theological continuity between Jesus and Paul as miracle workers. What can we say now about Paul's historical *dependence* on the example of Jesus for these family resemblances?[69] This is a difficult question, not only because

---

66. Ibid., 271.

67. Litwak, review of *Paul and the Miraculous*, 635.

68. Roland Deines, quotation on back cover of *Paul and the Miraculous*.

69. One issue bears clarifying here. When addressing this issue of dependence, my thesis statement for this study says that the continuities between Jesus and Paul "suggest that Paul deliberately

dependence is harder to demonstrate than similarity, but particularly because our evidence for miracles is sparse on the Pauline side.[70]

By way of reminder, the methodology of this entire study attempts to model the approach of Schoberg, who, in seeking to argue for continuity between Jesus and Paul, follows a strategy of (1) arguing for the authenticity and significance of a particular feature in the Jesus tradition, (2) demonstrating a family resemblance between Jesus and Paul on that point, and (3) looking for a convincing explanation for why Paul was indebted to Jesus for that family resemblance instead of some other influence.[71] By necessity, this third step might look different for each sign function, since the issues might be rather different in each case. Schoberg elaborates: "Regarding the third point, depending on the evidence available, the emphasis may be on tracing the historical connection between Jesus and Paul, or on ruling out the possibility of other influences on Paul."[72] The first option involves looking for a "bridge" between Jesus and Paul that we might be able to see. The second option essentially involves the exploration of dissimilarity from backgrounds, because the more distinctive Jesus is against the backgrounds, the more likely Jesus's influence can be seen on Paul. For the sake of putting all options on the table, we will consider each option for our three sign functions.

The difficulties with dissimilarity as a criterion are also worth bringing up again at this point. To make perhaps the strongest case for historical continuity, we would ideally employ a version of the criterion of double dissimilarity of historical-Jesus studies, where the common element proposed for both Jesus and Paul is dissimilar to Hellenistic and Jewish backgrounds as well as Christian tradition prior to Paul. Yet the problems of this criterion are well-known, particularly in that it results in a Jesus divorced both from the Jewish Scriptures and from the Christian movement that Jesus started.[73] There is also the issue of our knowledge of the ancient world being incomplete—we might not be in the strongest position to decide what might or might not have been a widespread idea. The criterion

---

imitated Jesus in the performance of miracles." How should this proposed dependence be envisioned? Did Paul wake up one day and "decide" to become a miracle worker? How "deliberate" is this imitation, if one accepts it? It seems to best to see the situation being somewhere between the two extremes of pure human volition on the one hand and absolute divine direction on the other. Perhaps prophecy is a parallel case. Prophets are empowered by the Spirit (1 Cor 12:7–10), but the prophet still has some measure of control (1 Cor 14:32). Paul would surely acknowledge the Spirit's direction on him in working miracles, but if Paul knew that apostles worked miracles and that Jesus worked miracles, it would be possible for Paul to also follow this divinely directed course of action in deliberate imitation of the example he knew from Christ.

70. For example, as Witherington (*Jesus, Paul and the End of the World*, 45) writes: "It is one thing to point out similarities between the thought of Jesus and of Paul on a given matter, but it is quite another to establish a definite case of dependency of Paul on Jesus."

71. Schoberg, *Perspectives of Jesus*, 16–17.

72. Ibid., 17.

73. See, e.g., Dunn, *Jesus Remembered*, 82–83.

is also particularly problematic for the Jesus-Paul debate on the Christian side, because, as Paul most likely never met Jesus, he would by necessity depend on Christian tradition for much information about Jesus's life. Related to this, inquiring whether Paul adopted a practice or belief *because it was consciously grounded in the historical Jesus* instead of merely *because it was present in Christian tradition he found* is usually a question that creates too fine a distinction to be addressed.

Because of these difficulties, at points we face significant challenges in arguing for Paul's dependence on Jesus in terms of miracle working. Our suggestions will thus need to be somewhat tentative at points. We will nonetheless proceed according to a threefold strategy to explore Schoberg's third step of investigation. First, for each of our sign functions, we will briefly consider Greco-Roman and Jewish background material with an eye for dissimilarity.[74] This helps us in places where a specific dependency between Jesus and Paul on an issue might be difficult to see. Second, instead of looking for dissimilarity on the Christian side, we will rather consider whether a plausible bridge might exist for each sign function's presence in Paul. Such a connection is more important for our purposes than discontinuity, and the existence of some kind of bridge is very plausible.[75] Third, after discussing a potential bridge, we will see what evidence can be marshaled to argue that Paul was dependent on the example of Jesus for our themes.[76] This will end up looking different in each case due to the various issues and dynamics involved.

It is worthwhile to consider a different way of framing the issue, however. It is important to remember that, for our purposes, the similarities we have demonstrated for Jesus and Paul remain significant *even if we cannot find hard and fast evidence for Paul's dependence on Jesus.* These similarities point to a real congruity between Jesus and Paul on the very practical issue of miracle working, as well as on three significant theological family resemblances. Somehow, these emphases were incorporated by Paul, even if we cannot see how. So these similarities *do* point to a significant alignment between both figures even if the causal connections can only be glimpsed at times.

74. For the handiest access to the relevant backgrounds material on miracle workers, see Cotter, *Miracles in Greco-Roman Antiquity*, passim; Eve, *The Jewish Context of Jesus' Miracles*, passim; Blackburn, *Theios Anēr*, 13–96; Kahl, *New Testament Miracle Stories*, 56–62; Meier, *Mentor, Message, and Miracles*, 576–601; Twelftree, *Paul and the Miraculous*, 31–105; Koskenniemi, *Old Testament Miracle-Workers*, passim; Keener, *Miracles*, 1:35–82.

75. As Dunn ("Bridge between Jesus and Paul," 397) argues: "There is, after all, a considerable *a priori* plausibility in the working hypothesis that there was *some* bridge between Jesus and Paul, some group of individuals through whom at least some of the Jesus-tradition was mediated to Paul, whether we specify the Hellenists in particular, or include also Peter (Gal. 1.18) and other unnamed disciples."

76. Again, this is essentially the methodology of Schoberg (*Perspectives of Jesus*, 16–17), whereby he first establishes the authenticity and importance of each block of material, looks for family resemblance, and then seeks to show the likelihood of Jesus as the source of Paul's emphasis. We are focusing now on this third step.

Signs of Gracious Inclusion

In ch. 2, I argued that Paul and Jesus both combined a miracle working ministry with a message of gracious inclusion of outsiders. Is Paul dependent on Jesus for this? On the issue of dissimilarity to backgrounds, a few observations are salutary. As we noted in ch. 3, somewhat surprisingly, there is a paucity in our records of miracle workers for the period in which we are most interested (300 BCE–150 CE).[77] Major names are Vespasian, Ḥanina, Ḥoni, Eliezer, the "sign-prophets" of Josephus, and Apollonius.[78] For the most part, our sources do not emphasize these figures as having combined their miracles with a specific message.[79] Twelftree summarizes the issue as applying to Paul:

> On the one hand, it is not likely that, as Jews, Paul or his audience would have assumed he would be involved in the miraculous simply on the basis of his being a missionary to the Gentiles. There was no Jewish mission directed to the Gentiles that could have provided a model for their thinking; Paul is the first known Jewish missionary. Nor, on the other hand, were there models in the wider world on which to draw that would have given rise to the expectation that Paul would have been a miracle worker. Despite claims to the contrary . . . we also have no direct evidence from Paul's period of any peripatetic teachers in the wider Hellenistic world including the miraculous in their work.[80]

77. Koskenniemi, "Apollonius of Tyana," 462; cf. pp. 463–64. See also: Twelftree, *Paul and the Miraculous*, 91–105; Eve, *Healer from Nazareth*, 40–44. It is true that miracle stories existed for past figures, such as Pythagoras, but this is different from expectations for a *contemporary* figure.

78. For Vespasian, see Tacitus, *Hist.* 4.81; Suetonius, *Vesp.* 7.2–3; Cassius Dio, *Roman History* 65.8.1–2. For Ḥanina, see m. Ber. 5.5; m. Soṭah 9.15; b. Taʿan. 24b–25a; b. Ber. 33a; 34b; b. Pesaḥ. 112b; b. B. Qam. 50a. For Ḥoni, see m. Taʿan. 3.8. For Eliezar, see Josephus, *Ant.* 8.46–48. For Josephus's sign prophets, see Theudas (*Ant.* 20.97–98), the "Egyptian" (*Ant.* 20.169–70; cf. *J.W.* 2.261–62), a "false prophet" (*J.W.* 6.285), "deceivers" (*J.W.* 2.259; cf. *Ant.* 20.167–68), and Jonathan (*J.W.* 7.437–42). For Apollonius, see, e.g., Philostratus, *Vit. Apoll.* 3.36–41; 4.19–20, 25, 45.

79. Partial exceptions may be Apollonius and Josephus's sign prophets. Yet Apollonius's teachings rarely—if ever—connect with his miracles. Twelftree (*Paul and the Miraculous*, 103) says: "There is nothing to suggest any relationship between the speaking and the miraculous." Yet Reimer (*Miracle and Magic*, 96) argues for an *implicit* support for Apollonius's teaching from his miracles, and this seems a fair assessment. This is contra Petzke (*Die Traditionen über Apollonius*, 181), who sees a connection between teaching and miracles in the vampire incident of *Vit. Apoll.* 4.25. As for the sign prophets that Josephus mentions, it seems the portents they promised were more apocalyptic in nature—not healings or exorcisms like in the case of Jesus—and not connected with a teaching per se—but of course our knowledge of these figures is limited. Origen may be pertinent where he answers Celsus's charge that Jesus was just another sorcerer by arguing that Jesus combined his miracles with a message of moral reformation, which Origen claims sorcerers do not (*Cels.* 1.68). On the Jewish Hasidim, Twelftree (*Jesus the Exorcist*, 210) argues that none of them made a specific connection between their miracles and teachings. Part of the difficulty with these sources, of course, is that surviving evidence is scarce compared to Jesus.

80. Twelftree, *Paul and the Miraculous*, 105. One might appeal to Jonah as an example of a Jewish missionary—though miracles are not part of his actvity.

Notable against this lack is the number of miracle traditions about Jesus, along with the relatively short time elapsed since his life.[81] This, combined with the emphasis on miracles present in the Christian tradition Paul entered, suggests that Paul's focus on miracles came to him from Christian origins.[82] Because Jesus the miracle worker stood as the fountainhead of the Christian movement, it is plausible that this Christian emphasis was modeled on the example of Jesus—a point strengthened for Paul if my arguments be accepted that Paul knew of Jesus's miracles.

So much for the bare fact of a miracle-working ministry, but what about the sign function of gracious inclusion? Here I wish to accept the Hengel-Wedderburn-Simmons-Schoberg argument (discussed earlier in this chapter) about the Hellenists as "the bridge" whereby Jesus's emphasis of grace to outsiders came to Paul and flowered into the law-free gospel to Gentiles. How do miracles play into this as manifestations of God's gracious inclusion? Based on my discussion above of the Hellenists, I can state three premises on which to build. First, we have here a group early and connected enough to know of Jesus as a miracle worker. Second, they plausibly either initiated, or were involved in, the early stages of Gentile inclusion modeled on Jesus's table fellowship. Third, this group was also remembered as charismatic.[83] Putting these three points together, it seems that they could easily convey to Paul the experience and significance of the Spirit's presence as, in some sense, realizing God's gracious inclusion of Gentiles. If the Spirit was working among Gentiles, a prior act of God's cleansing could be assumed (e.g., Gal 3:14; Acts 11:1–18). Philip says this: "What is therefore probable is that it is the Hellenists' understanding of the Spirit, particularly in relation to the Gentiles, which exerted a marked influence on Paul's thought."[84] It is only a short step further to seeing the same implications of gracious inclusion in the Spirit's manifestation in *miracles*, as specific manifestations of the Spirit (e.g., Gal 3:5).

What can we say about Jesus *as the most likely source* of this emphasis in Paul? Here our case essentially depends on (1) seeing Jesus as the most likely source of Paul's emphasis on gracious inclusion of outsiders as mediated by the Hellenists (as argued by Schoberg and others), and (2) Paul likely knowing of the traditions of Jesus as a miracle worker. If one accepts these premises, it is plausible that Paul is dependent on the example of Jesus both for a miracle-working ministry generally

---

81. As highlighted variously by Meier, *A Marginal Jew*, 2:624; Harvey, *Constraints of History*, 103; Eve, *Healer from Nazareth*, 7.

82. As Twelftree (*Paul and the Miraculous*, 149, cf. 106–49) writes, traditions, "which were flush with the miraculous, both in terms of how Jesus was perceived and in the reported activity of his first followers."

83. Paul seems on par with other early Christians in this matter, since he does not seem to receive criticism from any quarter about being *overly* charismatic. As seen in my discussions of 2 Corinthians in chs. 2–3, if anything, the opposite was the case.

84. Philip, *Origins of Pauline Pneumatology*, 223.

and for seeing the Spirit's miraculous activity as a realization of God's gracious inclusion of outsiders.

(Qualified) Signs of Authoritative Power with a Lifestyle of Weakness

In ch. 3, I argued that both Jesus and Paul viewed their miracles as divine authentication in some sense, though they combined this with a refusal to give an authenticating sign on demand. Both also combined the ability to perform miracles with a lifestyle of deprivation, humble service, and suffering—which we have generalized under the category "weakness."

For this point, the criterion of dissimilarity is unhelpful, since none of these aspects is particularly unique against the backgrounds. On the Jewish side especially, we have a rich tradition of prophets offering miracles as authentication.[85] A hesitancy toward giving a sign or the acknowledgment that signs do not authenticate absolutely is also present, in that the possibility of misleading signs is acknowledged.[86] A life of weakness and suffering for a miracle worker also has precedent.[87] In fact, stressing that a numinously gifted individual was poor seems to be a standard way of defending one's intent.[88] Similar is the case of not seeking one's good or submitting to suffering or death.[89]

---

85. E.g., Exod 4; 7:8–12. I discuss this in ch. 3.

86. E.g., Deut 13:1–5; Josephus, *Ant.* 2.284–87; 20.97–98.

87. Betz (*Der Apostel Paulus*, 53–54) claims that Paul's example conforms to the type of a weak oriental sorcerer, pointing to Lucian, *Philops.* 34; *Alex.* 54–56, 59; *Peregr.* 33, 43–44. The evaluation of Dunn (*Jesus and the Spirit*, 330) seems fair: "The parallel between the Lucian passages [Betz] cites and II Cor. 12.9 is hardly close, either in content or in context. Nevertheless the point remains that Paul was neither the first to make the experiential discovery of the paradox, strength in weakness; nor was he the last." Dunn (p. 330 nn. 142–43) adds Philo, *Mos.* 1.69 and Pliny the Younger, *Ep.* 7.26.1 as parallels.

88. Kolenkow ("Paul and Opponents in 2 Cor 10–13," 362) writes: "It should be recognized as a commonplace that Jewish and Hellenistic persons of power must demonstrate their righteousness or the validity of their vocation by being poor." She points to b. Taʿan 25a; Apuleius, *Apol.* 18; Philostratus, *Vit. Apoll.* 8.7; cf. Philo, *Det.* 34; Acts Thom. 107. Reimer (*Miracle and Magic*, 136) calls the theme in Apollonius "overwhelming." Apollonius is presented as having given away the majority of his inheritance, *Vit. Apoll.* 1.13; cf. 1.4 for his rich family background (p. 68). Beyond the giving up of Apollonius's original wealth, Reimer (pp. 136–39) points to: 1.21, 30, 33; 4.41, 45; 6.41; 7.39; although cf. 2.40; 3.41; 8.17. Apollonius is also something of an ascetic, in that he avoided marriage and sex, e.g., *Vit. Apoll.* 1.13 (pp. 68–69). The majority of these references are, of course, late. Yet we have something similar to the theme in Did. 11:6, where a prophet who asks for money is deemed to be false. Remus (*Pagan-Christian Conflict*, 102, 162–63) notes Plato, *Resp.* 3.16m and Pindar, *Pyth.* 3.54–58, which mention Asclepius practicing healing out of avarice, and points to Lucian, *Alex.* 5, 7–8, 32, for accusations of greed meant to discredit a supposed prophet.

89. Kolenkow ("Relationships between Miracle and Prophecy," 1484) calls the theme of not seeking one's good "a common 'miracle defense' motif." Socrates submitted to death to show his sincerity: Plato, *Resp.* 2.5; cf. Origen, *Cels.* 2.17; Peregrinus did the same: Lucian, *Peregr.* 22–27 (Kolenkow, "Paul and Opponents," 362–63). Kolenkow (ibid., 363) says the catalog of 1 Cor 13:1–3 describes a stereotypical person of power, with eloquent speech, prophetic gifts, miracles, poverty, and a surrendering of

What about a bridge whereby these things might have come to Paul? Essentially my answer is the same as the previous section, with the charismatic Hellenists and other early Christian leaders probably conveying these aspects of Jesus's ministry to Paul. Easiest to demonstrate is the aspect of miracles as authentication, since the theme shows up in so many channels of Christian tradition.[90] If Christians often appealed to miracles as authentication, then Paul could easily come into contact with the theme, especially since it is also present in various background materials. The phrase "signs of an apostle" (2 Cor 12:12), whether of Paul's origin or not, also points in this direction—miracles were something that a Christian apostle was expected to demonstrate. As far as the hesitancy toward giving a sign, the verbal similarities between 1 Cor 1:22 and Mark 8:11 (parr.) raise the possibility that Paul is aware of Jesus's refusal to do likewise—though this cannot be finally confirmed.[91]

In arguing for Paul's *dependency* on Jesus for the combination of weakness and suffering with miraculous power, what might outweigh the lack of discontinuity is the way Paul explicitly connects Christ's example of weakness and suffering to how Paul himself and other Christians are to act—as well as how Paul connects his own suffering with Christ's suffering.[92] Christ is marked by "meekness and gentleness," traits which Paul somehow applies to himself (2 Cor 10:1). The Corinthians should be generous in light of Christ's generosity: "For you know the grace of our Lord Jesus Christ, that though he was rich, yet for your sake he became poor, so that you by his poverty might become rich" (2 Cor 8:9).[93] The Philippians are to adopt the same selflessness of Jesus's incarnation (Phil 2:1–11). As Paul sought the betterment of others (1 Cor 10:33), he was able to say immediately: "Be imitators of me, as I am of Christ" (11:1). Not long after discussing his apostolic miracles (2 Cor 12:12), Paul writes: "He is not weak in dealing with you, but is powerful among

---

oneself to flames like Peregrinus: "These are θεῖοι ἄνδρες and they are expected to endure suffering." Yet we may question the usefulness of the term θεῖοι ἄνδρες, and we may note that a burning in 1 Cor 13:3 depends on accepting a debatable variant reading. Reimer (*Miracle and Magic*, 85), dealing with Acts and *Vita Apollonii*, describes the theme as one of "disregarding personal safety and well-being," and notes how followers of the miracle worker urge a less-dangerous path, "a particularly effective way of expressing power and non-ambition simultaneously."

90. E.g., Mark (2:1–12), Q (7:22; 10:13; 11:20), John (6:2; 20:30–31), Acts (2:22; 5:12), Hebrews (2:3–4).

91. On the possible connection, see Fjärstedt, *Synoptic Tradition*, 150–51; Walt, "A Non-Canonical Jesus in Paul?" 62–63; Robinson, "Kerygma and History," 42; Tuckett, "1 Corinthians and Q," 608, 618; Twelftree, *Paul and the Miraculous*, 128; Wenham, *Follower of Jesus*, 353–54.

92. As Weiss (*Paul and Jesus*, 117) puts it: "Now it is a most remarkable fact that Paul invariably appeals to the example of Christ, when he is dealing with commands to unselfishness of life, to renunciation of self-advantage and the like."

93. See Wolff, "Humility and Self-Denial," 149. Knowling (*Testimony of St. Paul*, 506) argues, "Such a statement only receives its full meaning if Jesus belonged, as a man, not to the noble, but to the poor." Cf. Wolfe, "Uses of Jesus Tradition," 171.

you. For he was crucified in weakness, but lives by the power of God. For we also are weak in him, but in dealing with you we will live with him by the power of God" (13:3–4).[94] As noted in ch. 3, Paul describes his suffering as *similar* to Jesus's sufferings (1 Thess 1:6, 2:14–15; 1 Cor 4:12–13; 2 Cor 6:8; cf. Rom 15:3), as well as somehow *connected* to Jesus's suffering (Gal 6:17; 2 Cor 1:5; 4:10; 13:4; Phil 3:10).[95]

Yet there are problems with using this material. Essentially, it embroils us in the debate about whether such references refer only to Jesus's incarnation or death, or if they also refer to knowledge of events in Jesus's life. On the one hand, and most obviously, these statements can refer to the "mere" fact of the incarnation and/or Jesus's death.[96] On the other hand, it is also plausible to see references to aspects of Jesus's life.[97] On 2 Cor 8:9, Wolff writes: "Certainly the poverty of Christ does not *merely* refer to the cross. Even if one finds in 2 Cor 8.9 just as in Phil 2.6–8 the self-emptying of the pre-existent one, his earthly path that led to the cross as the path of the one who was humble, poor and obedient is also in view. The *whole* career of Christ was for Paul characterized by lowliness and renunciation."[98] Similarly, Weiss notes:

> Is it likely that Paul reached this view of life merely by reflecting upon the fact of the Messiah's death? He must have known that this view of suffering was a fundamental principle in the character of Jesus, that He required His followers to undergo suffering in imitation of Himself, and lived in the belief that life was only to be gained by the sacrifice of it. It is impossible that the opinions of Jesus and Paul should have coincided merely by chance.[99]

If Paul knew of these aspects of Jesus's life, it would still be natural for Paul to focus on the crucifixion, since it was the ultimate example of Christ's love and faithfulness.[100] The crucifixion and resurrection of Jesus also formed a more ultimate victory than "mere" physical healings.[101]

---

94. See Stegman, *The Character of Jesus*, 205–11. Sinclair (*Jesus Christ According to Paul*, 132) notes that this statement is in tension with Paul's usual focus on Jesus's power, e.g., Rom 15:18–19.

95. Wolff, "Humility and Self-Denial," 156–57.

96. See, e.g., Walter, "Paul and the Early Christian," 60–61.

97. See Weiss, *Paul and Jesus*, 17–18, 117–18; Fraser, *Jesus and Paul*, 91–92; Thompson, *Clothed with Christ*, 238–39; Stegman, *Character of Jesus*, 112–13.

98. Wolff, "Humility and Self-Denial," 149.

99. Weiss, *Paul and Jesus*, 123.

100. As Thompson (*Clothed with Christ*, 238–39) asks, "Why should Paul adduce as an example Jesus' compassion and humility in touching a leper or eating with sinners, when he was convinced that he *died* for us while we were yet sinners (Rom. 5.8)?"

101. A point seen by Schweitzer (*Mysticism of Paul*, 73): "The miracles and healings with which Jesus in His lifetime combated the powers which opposed the Kingdom of God are for Paul, in comparison with the great final blow which He struck by His death, of so small account that he never refers to them at all." See also Wedderburn, "Story of Jesus," 180–81.

Another way to frame the problem more specifically for our purposes is to say that Paul does not make any reference to Jesus's *power* during the earthly phase of his life, prior to the resurrection. So the contrast between Jesus's power and weakness as presented by Paul is not of a powerful miracle worker who is at the same time physically weak or selfless—rather the contrast is between the weakness of Jesus's entire earthly life prior to the resurrection (e.g., 2 Cor 13:3–4).[102] This means that showing Paul to be dependent on Jesus for the power-in-weakness aspect of miracle working hinges almost entirely on whether Paul knew of Jesus as a miracle worker. If one accepts this likelihood, as argued earlier in this chapter, then my point might still stand, framed as follows. First, Paul probably knows of Jesus's miracles.[103] Second, Paul also clearly views Jesus's life on earth as one of weakness and suffering—exemplified and climaxed of course in crucifixion. Thus, the fact that Paul also performs miracles and focuses on his own weakness and suffering—*with explicit connection to Jesus* (e.g., 2 Cor 12:12; cf. 13:4; 1 Thess 1:6; Phil 3:10)—is striking. It would not then be difficult to understand Paul as viewing his own path of numinous power held with a lifestyle weakness as being done in imitation of Jesus's example. Yet because of the uncertainties, this line of argument must remain tentative.

Signs of the New Age

In ch. 4, I argued that, for both Jesus and Paul, miracles were signs of the eschatological kingdom in an already-but-not-yet arrangement. Can we plausibly argue for dependence on Jesus here? As far as discontinuity, this is a feature of Jesus's miracles that is often identified as distinctive against both Jewish and Greco-Roman backgrounds.[104] To be sure, Josephus's "sign-prophets" promised miracles that are plausibly eschatological and that might have been interpreted as signs of the impending kingdom.[105] Yet as I have mentioned before, Josephus implies they did

---

102. See, e.g., Robinson, "Kerygma and History," 63.

103. Cf. Dodd (*Apostolic Preaching*, 17): "We may presume they did not spend all the time talking about the weather."

104. E.g., Keener (*Miracles*, 1:61) says most scholars hold that Jesus's miracles function as signs of the kingdom: "Such a perspective relates to traditional Jewish expectations while pressing beyond most of them in affirming that the kingdom was already active in Jesus." On the discontinuity of the eschatological tension more generally, see, e.g., Kümmel, *Promise and Fulfillment*, 153; Cullmann, *Salvation in History*, 172. For arguments that Qumran held a partially realized eschatology, see Aune, *The Cultic Setting of Realized Eschatology*, 29–44. Significantly, however, Aune (p. 35) writes: "In contrast with the belief in early Christianity, the Qumran community still looked forward to the miraculous giving of the Spirit in a more complete form at the visitation of Yahweh." For this, he points to 1QS 4.20–22, which anticipates the future bestowal of the Spirit. For arguments against a partially realized eschatological tension in Qumran that would be similar to Jesus and Paul, see Schoberg, *Perspectives of Jesus*, 286–301.

105. See Barnett, "The Jewish Sign Prophets," 679–97. Keener (*Miracles*, 1:61 n. 233) comments: "The sign prophets may have expected to show that the kingdom was present in them."

not perform the promised signs—and their anticipated miracles also seem akin to signs of national deliverance as in the exodus (e.g., the Jordan would divide [*Ant.* 20.97]) and not to exorcisms and healings.[106] Theissen and Merz thus summarize the eschatological nature of Jesus's miracles like this: "The uniqueness of the miracles of the historical Jesus lies in the fact that healings and exorcisms which take place in the present are accorded an eschatological significance.... Nowhere else do we find a charismatic miracle worker whose miraculous deeds are meant to be the end of an old world and the beginning of a new one."[107]

This discontinuity means we are in a stronger position to demonstrate Paul's dependence on Jesus for this sign function than for the one we just considered. As Cullmann writes:

> The tension between "already" and "not yet," which we have said in the chapter on Jesus to be the main characteristic of what is called "eschatology," now stands in the foreground in Paul and forms the most important connecting link in salvation history between him and Jesus. Paul's whole theology is dominated by this tension— his conception of the Holy Spirit, the Church, the sacraments, and his ethics.[108]

What can we say about a bridge whereby this emphasis might have passed from Jesus to Paul? Again, the Hellenists of Acts 6 provide a ready answer, as well as Paul's interaction with other church leaders like Peter.[109] That the Hellenists would have a similar eschatological emphasis is made likely by their charismatic experience of the Spirit, as well as perhaps by their admission of Gentiles into the people of God, an event that in Judaism was associated with eschatological fulfillment.[110] That miracles also implied a present eschatology could be derived not only from the experience of the (eschatological) Spirit but also from the transmission of the Jesus miracle tradition, to which this group probably had access.

What can we say about dependence? Schoberg argues for Paul's dependence on Jesus for the concept of new creation eschatology by showing that Jewish backgrounds would not be sufficient for Paul to come to his already-but-not-yet

---

106. See Eve, *Jewish Context*, 378–81.

107. Theissen and Merz, *Historical Jesus*, 309. Cf. Theissen, *Miracle Stories*, 278–80; so also Eve, *Jewish Context*, 380.

108. Cullmann, *Salvation in History*, 255. Cullmann is speaking generally, instead of about miracles.

109. As Räisänen ("The 'Hellenists,'" 190) notes, "The eschatological consciousness was ... something that united the Hellenists with the Hebrews."

110. On the Hellenists' justification for placing Jesus as a higher authority than Moses or the Jewish law, Hengel (*Acts and the History*, 73) says: "They understood their authority to make this criticism as a gift of the spirit, which they saw as a sign of the dawning of the eschatological age." On the place of Gentile inclusion as an aspect of Jewish eschatological thought, see Donaldson, *Judaism and the Gentiles*, 509–11; cf. 17–75. Cf. Freyne, "The Jesus-Paul Debate Revisited," 154–59; Philip, *Origins of Pauline Pneumatology*, 220. E.g., Isa 2:1–4; 60:2–3; Mic 4:1–4; Tob 13:11–13; 14:5–7.

understanding simply from the experience of the resurrection and the bestowal of the Spirit. Rather, Paul and the other early Christians interpreted these events eschatologically because of the precedent in Jesus's ministry for a partially-realized eschatology.[111] In other words, Jesus must have taught something that prepared his followers to interpret the resurrection and bestowal of the Spirit as elements of present eschatological fulfillment.

But in seeing miracles as signs of the presence of the new age, would Paul be depending on *Jesus's understanding of Jesus's miracles,* or would Paul be seeing present eschatological implications in miracles *only because Paul's miracles were the operation of the eschatological Spirit?* The latter would be easier to argue.[112] But if the view held by Jesus's followers stemmed from Jesus holding a partially realized eschatology consisting in the kingdom's presence demonstrated in miracles (e.g., Luke 11:20 par.), then one can see how Paul's emphasis could also be informed by the miracle tradition of Jesus. Once again, much of the point depends on whether or not Paul knows of the miracle tradition—but, of course, I judge this knowledge to be likely.

As discussed in ch. 4, we do have two passages where Paul seems to treat the kingdom as somehow present (Rom 14:17; 1 Cor 4:20), with one of them coming very close to how Jesus connects miracles with the presence of the kingdom (1 Cor 4:20; cf. Luke 11:20 par.).[113] Again, Paul writes: οὐ γὰρ ἐν λόγῳ ἡ βασιλεία τοῦ θεοῦ ἀλλ' ἐν δυνάμει. Here we have the eschatological kingdom treated as something present and associated with δύναμις, which Paul elsewhere associated with the Spirit and with miracles (1 Cor 12:9–10; Rom 15:18–19). If this does not indicate Paul's knowledge of Jesus's present-eschatological interpretation of his miracles, it is certainly compatible with it.

Conclusion

In this chapter, I first argued for the likelihood that Paul knew of Jesus's miracles. I then suggested that Twelftree's objections to continuity between Jesus and Paul as miracle workers—namely, that Jesus was actively involved in initiating miracles, while Paul (in contradiction to Acts) was more a passive miracle

---

111. Schoberg (*Perspectives of Jesus,* 314, 321) writes: "The point is, that unless Paul (and the early Christians) already had reason to think that the age to come was breaking into the present—for example, from Jesus himself—it is not obvious that his experience of Jesus' resurrection by itself would have given rise to such a view"; "Unless he already had in place a revised eschatological framework that saw a tension between the 'already' and the 'not yet,' it is not clear that his experience of the Spirit likely would have led him to adopt such a framework."

112. Of course, this may be a both/and issue, not either/or.

113. Connections noted, for example, by Thompson, *Clothed with Christ,* 206.

worker—overplayed the evidence. Finally, we explored whether Paul depended on the example of Jesus for his miracle-working ministry and for the sign functions we have adduced—and judged the various aspects either possible or likely.

Due to the uncertainties involved, these results of course fall short of final proof to convince everyone. We are left, nonetheless, with a very suggestive patterns of parallels. Wedderburn's words form a fitting conclusion, and we may even apply to our discussion his initial comments, which were geared toward his treatment of the Hellenists as a bridge between Jesus and Paul:

> The conclusions of the previous section cannot but remain highly hypothetical and controversial. The sort of suggestions made there, however, are nevertheless worth making, even necessary to make, if we are trying to explain historically the rise of the various movements and traditions within earliest Christianity. For parallel phenomena within traditions about Jesus and the various traditions of the early church strongly suggest a causal connection between them; similarities between religious movements that are far removed from one another in time and geographical location, and lack any known historical connection with one another, may be explained as coincidences or products of some factor common to humanity and the human spirit. But it is another matter when the similarities occur shortly after one another, and when, in this case, the one set of similarities occurs within a movement that claims to be a continuation of the other, i.e., within the Christian church that looks back to Jesus as its originator and cause. Then *we are more or less compelled to posit some sort of causal link between the two, even if the link or links remain hidden from our view.*[114]

114. Wedderburn, "Similarity and Continuity," 130; cf. Twelftree, *Paul and the Miraculous*, 146; Simmons, *Theology of Inclusion*, 91 n. 10.

CHAPTER 6

Conclusion

It is time to bring the threads together. I will briefly summarize the entire study before suggesting how the results contribute to the Jesus-Paul debate. I will conclude with a few suggestions for further studies.

Summary

This study set out to investigate the place of miracles within the context of the Jesus-Paul debate. Particularly, I wished to investigate on the one hand the "mere" fact that both figures were miracle workers, along with three specific theological "sign functions" that could plausibly be attributed to the miracles of both Jesus and Paul. Finally, I wished to consider whether Paul might have even consciously imitated this aspect of Jesus's ministry.

In ch. 2, I argued for the historicity of both Jesus and Paul as miracle workers. I then argued that, for both figures, miracles *accompanied* a message of gracious inclusion of outsiders. I then went beyond this and argued that, for both Jesus and Paul, miracles in some sense *initially realized* the gracious inclusion that both proclaimed. For these reasons, it seems fair to see the miracles of Jesus and Paul as *signs of gracious inclusion* in the eschatological kingdom.

Chapter 3 considered the issue of authentication-by-miracles. I argued for three aspects to miracles, held somewhat in tension. First, I argued that both Jesus and Paul in some sense viewed miracles as authenticating their persons and ministries as being legitimately from God. On the other hand, both figures qualified an appeal to miracles as authentication, in that both resisted the demand for signs. Finally, both combined a ministry of numinous power with a lifestyle of deprivation, humble service, and suffering—which I grouped under the term *weakness*. It thus seems reasonable to see miracles for Jesus and Paul as *(qualified) signs of authoritative power with a lifestyle of weakness*.

In ch. 4, I argued that, for both Jesus and Paul, miracles served as signs of the presence of eschatological fulfillment. On the Jesus side, this was supported by explicit statements and on the Pauline side by the connection to the eschatological Spirit, as well as by allusions to the exodus miracles with the language "signs and wonders." In light of this, the miracles of both can plausibly be described as *signs of the new age*.

In ch. 5, we took up three related and important issues. I first argued that—while certainty is impossible—there is every probability that Paul *did* know of Jesus as a miracle worker. We then considered the final arguments for discontinuity between Jesus and Paul as miracle workers in Twelftree's *Paul and the Miraculous*, and I argued that Twelftree was at the same time both under-reading (Acts) and over-reading (Paul's letters) the evidence. Finally, we explored what arguments could be made that Paul was historically dependent on Jesus for the working of miracles and for the three sign functions. I argued that this is plausible, most especially so if one accepts the probability that Paul knows of Jesus as a miracle worker. But I also said the significance of the similarities I have adduced remain notable even if I cannot clearly demonstrate Paul's dependence on Jesus's example.

Contribution

The debate over continuity between Jesus and Paul has raged for a long time, with any explicit connections already having been worked over from many angles. In focusing on miracles, we took up an aspect of similarity that has been largely overlooked. Unfortunately, one reason any potential similarity between Jesus and Paul has been overlooked is probably that there is only minimal evidence available! We have seen on the one hand that this is the case but, on the other hand, that enough evidence exists to note some significant parallels.

How does this study's treatment of miracles advance the Jesus-Paul debate? Essentially, the extent of contribution depends on how one evaluates the arguments for knowledge and dependence in ch. 5. If one accepts that Paul knew about Jesus's miracles and accepts the suggested bridges whereby the significance of our three sign functions might have come to Paul, then one will probably accept the notion of Paul imitating this aspect of Jesus's career. Here then, we would have a significant area of practical and theological similarity between Jesus and Paul. What if one is not impressed with the arguments for knowledge and dependence in ch. 5? In this case—and thus, at minimum—our findings still contribute to the discussion by advancing three lines of argument previously made within the debate.

First, this study builds on Wolff's article to show there is another significant way in which the practical lifestyles of Jesus and Paul are similar—both are miracle workers.[1] Though this study has focused largely on the *sign functions* associated with the miracles of Jesus and Paul, we do not want to overlook the significance of the "mere" fact that both Jesus and Paul incorporated miracles into their ministries.

---

1. Wolff, "Humility and Self-Denial," 145–60.

In terms of the way historical evidence has been preserved for us, Paul is able to join Jesus as one of the best-attested miracle workers of the period.[2]

Second, this study also builds on Schoberg's work, which argues for family resemblance (and dependence) between Jesus and Paul in three important areas.[3] This study bolsters his, because the associations it was able to connect to the miracles of Jesus and of Paul show another way in which Schoberg's family resemblances extend to a practical level. Because inclusion of outsiders, the presence of eschatological fulfilment, and—to a lesser extent—participation in suffering can be connected to miracles, here is another way in which these family resemblances unite the two figures.

Third, this study also contributes to the discussion by, on the one hand, affirming Twelftree's *Paul and the Miraculous* in that Twelftree correctly addresses a much-overlooked issue in Paul—the place of miracles.[4] On the other hand, this study critiques the way Twelftree pits the evidence of Paul's letters against the evidence in Acts, and the way Twelftree over-reads some of the evidence in Paul.[5] In this way, Twelftree's study should really contribute more to continuity between Jesus and Paul than Twelftree allows.

These last three points mean that, even if we cannot clearly demonstrate Paul's historical *dependence* on Jesus for these similarities, these similarities are still significant. They bring both figures closer together both historically and theologically. Even if the connections of *how* Paul adopted these courses of action and views are hidden from us, the end result is much the same—both figures stand very close together in regard to a miracle working ministry.

Directions for Future Study

There are several ways in which this study could be expanded. Most obviously, this would involve bringing Acts more into picture. Having focused intensely on our three sign functions in the Gospels and in Paul, it would be worthwhile to extend the investigation to Acts and see how miracles are treated for both Jesus and Paul there.

Another line of fruitful investigation would be to focus more on the connection between miracles and the Spirit in both Jesus and Paul, something I touched on but did not fully explore. Dunn has argued that Jesus was dependent on the Spirit for his miracles.[6] We see that the same is true of Paul (e.g., 1 Cor 12:8–11;

---

2. In that evidence for Jesus is so early and widespread and that evidence for Paul includes first-person claims in undeniably authentic letters. I discuss this in ch. 2.

3. Schoberg, *Perspectives of Jesus in the Writings of Paul*.

4. Twelftree, *Paul and the Miraculous*.

5. I discuss this in ch 5.

6. E.g., Dunn, *Jesus and the Spirit*, 87–88.

Rom 15:18–19). This deserves more attention as another way in which the miracles of Paul and Jesus are parallel, and it might further inform the contrast of Jesus's numinous power with a lifestyle of personal weakness.

Also promising would be bringing in more exploration of the concept of imitation in Paul and whether this plausibly extends to miracle working. I touched on this at points but because of space constraints did not pursue it fully. Would a follower of a religious leader in the ancient world be expected to imitate the lifestyle of his master? Do we have examples of miracles' being part of this sort of imitation in any background material?

To conclude, we may stitch together a quotation from Wedderburn and a quotation from Eddy and Boyd that—especially if one accepts the arguments of ch. 5—nicely summarize Paul's relation to Jesus in his practical life of ministry, including miracles:

> That Paul was aware that the character of his ministry bore a resemblance to that of Jesus seems to me intrinsically plausible, even probable; is it not, after all, likelier that Paul was convinced that this was the appropriate form for his Christian ministry to take because he saw this form of ministry as following the lines of the pattern of ministry which he detected within the traditions concerning the earthly ministry of Jesus?[7]

> In this light, it cannot be regarded as a coincidence that Paul's own thought, attitude, and conduct paralleled closely what we find in the Jesus of the Gospels. Nor can it be considered a coincidence that Paul's healing ministry, his welcoming of sinners, his life of poverty, and humble service closely paralleled Jesus's life and ministry as recorded in the Gospels. Paul practiced what he preached, and at the foundation of what he preached was a body of knowledge about the ministry and character of the Lord he served.[8]

---

7. Wedderburn, "Paul and the Story of Jesus," 180. Wedderburn is discussing the four similarities adduced by Wolff ("Humility and Self-Denial," 145–60).

8. Eddy and Boyd, *The Jesus Legend*, 209–10.

Bibliography

Achtemeier, Paul J. *Jesus and the Miracle Tradition.* Eugene, OR: Cascade, 2008.

Agosto, Efrain. *Servant Leadership: Jesus and Paul.* St. Louis: Chalice, 2005.

Akenson, Donald Harman. *Saint Saul: A Skeleton Key to the Historical Jesus.* Oxford: Oxford University Press, 2000.

Alkier, Stefan. *Wunder und Wirklichkeit in den Briefen des Apostels Paulus: Ein Beitrag zu einem Wunderverständnis jenseits von Entmythologisierung und Rehistorisierung.* WUNT 134. Tübingen: Mohr Siebeck, 2001.

Allison, Dale C., Jr. *Constructing Jesus: Memory, Imagination, and History.* Grand Rapids: Baker, 2010.

———. "It Don't Come Easy: A History of Disillusionment." Pp. 186–99 in *Jesus, Criteria, and the Demise of Authenticity,* edited by Chris Keith and Anthony Le Donne. London: T&T Clark, 2012.

———. *Jesus of Nazareth: Millenarian Prophet.* Minneapolis: Fortress, 1998.

———. *The Jesus Tradition in Q.* Harrisburg, PA: Trinity Press International, 1997.

———. "Paul and the Missionary Discourse." *ETL* 61 (1985): 369–75.

———. "The Pauline Epistles and the Synoptic Gospels: The Pattern of the Parallels." *NTS* 28 (1982): 1–32.

———. "A Plea for Thoroughgoing Eschatology." *JBL* 113 (1994): 651–68.

Allo, E.-B. *Première Épitre aux Corinthiens.* 2nd ed. Paris: Gabalda, 1934.

Anderson, Paul N., Felix Just, and Tom Thatcher, eds. *John, Jesus, and History.* 3 vols. SymS 44; ECL 2, 18. Atlanta: SBL, 2007–16.

———. *The Fourth Gospel and the Quest for Jesus: Modern Foundations Reconsidered.* Library of Historical Jesus Studies; LNTS 321. London: T&T Clark, 2006.

Aristides, P. Aelius. *The Complete Works 2: Orations 17–53.* Translated by Charles A. Behr. Leiden: Brill, 1981.

Ashton, John. *The Religion of Paul the Apostle.* New Haven: Yale University Press, 2000.

Aune, David E. *The Cultic Setting of Realized Eschatology in Early Christianity.* NovTSup 28. Leiden: Brill, 1972.

———. "Magic in Early Christianity." Pp. 1507–57 in vol. 2.23.2 of *ANRW,* edited by Wolfgang Haase. Berlin: de Gruyter, 1980.

———. *Prophecy in Early Christianity and the Ancient Mediterranean World.* Grand Rapids: Eerdmans, 1983.

Balch, D. L. "Backgrounds of 1 Cor. VII: Sayings of the Lord in Q; Moses as an Ascetic Θειος Ανηρ in II Cor. III." *NTS* 18 (1972): 351–64.

Barclay, John M. G. "Jesus and Paul." pp. 492–503 in *DPL,* edited by Gerald F. Hawthorne, Ralph P. Martin, and Daniel G. Reid. Downers Grove, IL: InterVarsity, 1993.

———. "'Offensive and Uncanny': Jesus and Paul on the Caustic Grace of God." Pp. 1–17 in *Jesus and Paul Reconnected,* edited by Todd D. Still. Grand Rapids: Eerdmans, 2007.

Barker, Margaret. "Atonement: The Rite of Healing." *SJT* 49 (1996): 1–20.

Barnett, Paul W. "Apostle." Pp. 45–51 in *DPL,* edited by Gerald F. Hawthorne and Martin, Ralph P. Downers Grove, IL: InterVarsity, 1993.

———. "The Jewish Sign Prophets—A.D. 40–70: Their Intentions and Origin." *NTS* 27 (1981): 679–97.

———. *Paul: Missionary of Jesus*. Grand Rapids: Eerdmans, 2008.

———. *The Second Epistle to the Corinthians*. NICNT. Grand Rapids: Eerdmans, 1997.

———. "Was Paul's Grace-Based Gospel True to Jesus?" Pp. 99–111 in *Paul as Missionary: Identity, Activity, Theology, and Practice*, edited by Trevor J. Burke and Brian S. Rosner. LNTS 420. London: T&T Clark, 2011.

Barrett, C. K. *A Commentary on the First Epistle to the Corinthians*. HNTC. New York: Harper & Row, 1968.

———. *The Epistle to the Romans*. Rev. ed. BNTC. Peabody, MA: Hendrickson, 1991.

———. *The Second Epistle to the Corinthians*. BNTC. London: Black, 1973. Repr., Peabody, MA: Hendrickson, 1997.

———. *The Signs of an Apostle: The Cato Lecture, 1969*. Philadelphia: Fortress, 1972.

Bartchy, S. Scott. "Who Should Be Called Father? Paul of Tarsus between the Jesus Tradition and Patria Potestas." *BTB* 33 (2003): 135–47.

Bauckham, Richard. *Jesus and the Eyewitnesses: The Gospels as Eyewitness Testimony*. Grand Rapids: Eerdmans, 2006.

———. *Jesus and the God of Israel: God Crucified and Other Studies on the New Testament's Christology of Divine Identity*. Grand Rapids: Eerdmans, 2009.

———. "Kingdom and Church According to Jesus and Paul." *HBT* 18 (1996): 1–26.

Bauer, Walter. *A Greek-English Lexicon of the New Testament and Other Early Christian Literature*. Edited by Frederick William Danker. 3rd ed. Based on Walter Bauer's *Griechisch-Deutsches Wörterbuch zu den Schriften des Neuen Testaments und der frühchristlichen Literatur*, 6th ed., edited by Kurt Aland and Barbara Aland, with Viktor Reichmann, and on previous English editions by William F. Arndt, F. Wilbur Gingrich, and F. W. Danker. Chicago: University of Chicago Press, 2000.

Baum, Armin D. "Die Heilungswunder Jesu als Symbolhandlungen–Ein Versuch." *EuroJTh* 13 (2004): 5–14.

Baur, Ferdinand Christian. *The Church History of the First Three Centuries*. Translated by Allan Menzies. 3rd ed. 2 vols. Theological Translation Fund Library. London: Williams & Norgate, 1878, 1879.

———. "Die Christuspartei in der korinthischen Gemeinde, der Gegensatz des petrinischen und paulinischen Christenthums in der älten Kirche, der Apostel Petrus in Rom." *Tübinger Zeitschrift für Theologie* 4 (1831): 61–206.

———. *Paul, the Apostle of Jesus Christ, His Life and Works, His Epistles and His Doctrine: A Contribution to the Critical History of Primitive Christianity*. Edited by Eduard Zeller. Translated by A. Menzies. 2nd ed. Vol. 2. Theological Translation Fund Library. London: Williams & Norgate, 1875.

Beasley-Murray, G. R. *Jesus and the Kingdom of God*. Grand Rapids: Eerdmans, 1986.

Beker, J. Christiaan. *Paul the Apostle: The Triumph of God in Life and Thought*. Philadelphia: Fortress, 1980.

Bell, Richard H. *Deliver Us from Evil: Interpreting the Redemption from the Power of Satan in New Testament Theology*. WUNT 216. Tübingen: Mohr Siebeck, 2007.

Best, Ernest. "Paul's Apostolic Authority—?" *Journal for the Study of the New Testament* 27 (1986): 3–25.

Best, Thomas F. "St. Paul and the Decline of the Miraculous." *Encounter* 44 (1983): 231–43.

Betz, Hans Dieter. *Der Apostel Paulus und die sokratische Tradition: Eine exegetische Untersuchung zu seiner "Apologie" 2 Korinther 10–13.* BHT 45. Tübingen: Mohr, 1972.

———. *Galatians: A Commentary on Paul's Letter to the Churches in Galatians.* Hermeneia. Philadelphia: Fortress, 1979.

Bird, Michael F., and Joel Willitts, eds. *Paul and the Gospels: Christologies, Conflicts and Convergences.* LNTS 411. London: T&T Clark, 2011.

Black, David Alan. *Paul, Apostle of Weakness: Astheneia and Its Cognates in the Pauline Literature.* American University Studies Series 7: Theology and Religion 3. New York: Peter Lang, 1984.

Black, Matthew. *Romans.* 2nd ed. NCB. Grand Rapids: Eerdmans, 1973.

Blackburn, Barry. "Miracles and Miracle Stories." Pp. 549–60 in *Dictionary of Jesus and the Gospels,* edited by Joel B. Green, Scot McKnight, and I. Howard Marshall. Downers Grove, IL: InterVarsity, 1992.

———. "The Miracles of Jesus." Pp. 113–30 in *The Cambridge Companion to Miracles,* edited by Graham H. Twelftree. Cambridge Companions to Religion. Cambridge: Cambridge University Press, 2011.

———. *Theios Anēr and the Markan Miracle Traditions: A Critique of the Theios Anēr Concept as an Interpretative Background of the Miracle Traditions Used by Mark.* WUNT 2/40. Tübingen: Mohr, 1991.

Blomberg, Craig L. "Healing." Pp. 299–307 in *Dictionary of Jesus and the Gospels,* edited by Joel B. Green, Scot McKnight, and I. Howard Marshall. Downers Grove, IL: InterVarsity, 1992.

———. *Making Sense of the New Testament: Three Crucial Questions.* Grand Rapids: Baker, 2004.

———. "Quotations, Allusions, and Echoes of Jesus in Paul." Pp. 129–43 in *Studies in the Pauline Epistles: Essays in Honor of Douglas J. Moo,* edited by Matthew S. Harmon and Jay E. Smith. Grand Rapids: Zondervan, 2014.

———. "The Authenticity and Significance of Jesus' Table Fellowship with Sinners." Pp. 215–50 in *Key Events in the Life of the Historical Jesus: A Collaborative Exploration of Context and Coherence,* edited by Darrell L. Bock and Robert L. Webb. Grand Rapids: Eerdmans, 2009.

———. *The Historical Reliability of John's Gospel: Issues and Commentary.* Downers Grove, IL: IVP Academic, 2001.

———. "The Miracles as Parables." Pp. 327–59 in *Gospel Perspectives,* vol. 6: *The Miracles of Jesus,* edited by David Wenham and Craig Blomberg. Sheffield: JSOT Press, 1986.

———. "'Your Faith Has Made You Whole': The Evangelical Liberation Theology of Jesus." Pp. 75–93 in *Jesus of Nazareth: Lord and Christ. Essays on the Historical Jesus and New Testament Christology,* edited by Joel B. Green and Max Turner. Grand Rapids: Eerdmans, 1994.

Bock, Darrell L. *Luke.* 2 vols. BECNT 3. Grand Rapids: Baker, 1994, 1996.

Bock, Darrell L., and Benjamin I. Simpson. *Jesus According to Scripture: Restoring the Portrait from the Gospels,* 2nd ed. Grand Rapids: Baker, 2017.

———. *Jesus the God-Man: The Unity and Diversity of the Gospel Portrayals.* Grand Rapids: Baker, 2016.

Bock, Darrell L., and Robert L. Webb, eds. *Key Events in the Life of the Historical Jesus: A Collaborative Exploration of Context and Coherence.* Grand Rapids: Eerdmans, 2009.

Bockmuehl, Markus. *Seeing the Word: Refocusing New Testament Study.* STI. Grand Rapids: Baker, 2006.

————. *This Jesus: Martyr, Lord, Messiah*. Edinburgh: T&T Clark, 1994.

Boer, Martinus C. de. *Galatians: A Commentary*. NTL. Louisville: Westminster John Knox, 2011.

Borg, Marcus J. *Conflict, Holiness, and Politics in the Teachings of Jesus*. London: Continuum, 1998.

————. *Jesus: A New Vision; Spirit, Culture, and the Life of Discipleship*. San Francisco: Harper & Row, 1987.

————. "A Temperate Case for a Non-Eschatological Jesus." Pp. 47–68 in *Jesus in Contemporary Scholarship*. Valley Forge, PA: Trinity Press International, 1994.

Borgen, Peder. "From Paul to Luke: Observations toward Clarification of the Theology of Luke–Acts." *CBQ* 31 (1969): 168–82.

Boring, M. Eugene. "The Unforgivable Sin Logion Mark III 28–29/Matt XII 31–32/Luke XII 10: Formal Analysis and History of the Tradition." *NovT* 18 (1976): 258–79.

Bornkamm, Günther. *Jesus of Nazareth*. Translated by Irene McLuskey and Fraser McLuskey. New York: Harper, 1960.

————. *Paul*. Translated by D. M. G. Stalker. New York: Harper & Row, 1971.

Bovon, François. *Luke*. Translated by Christine M. Thomas, Donald S. Deer, and James Crouch. 3 vols. Hermeneia. Minneapolis: Fortress, 2002, 2012, 2013.

Brown, Colin. *Miracles and the Critical Mind*. Grand Rapids: Eerdmans, 1984.

————. "Quest of the Historical Jesus." Pp. 718–56 in *DJG*, edited by Joel B. Green, Jeannine K. Brown, and Nicholas Perrin. 2nd ed. Downers Grove, IL: InterVarsity, 2013.

Bruce, F. F. *The Epistle to the Galatians: A Commentary on the Greek Text*. NIGTC. Grand Rapids: Eerdmans, 1982.

————. *Paul and Jesus*. Grand Rapids: Baker, 1974.

Bultmann, Rudolf. *The History of the Synoptic Tradition*. Translated by John Marsh. Oxford: Blackwell, 1963.

————. "Jesus and Paul." Pp. 183–201 in *Existence and Faith: Shorter Writings of Rudolf Bultmann*, edited and translated by Schubert M. Ogden. London: Hodder & Stoughton, 1961.

————. *Jesus and the Word*. New York: Scribner's Sons, 1958.

————. "The Problem of Miracle." *Religion in Life* 27 (1957–58): 63–75.

————. *The Second Letter to the Corinthians*. Translated by Roy A. Harrisville. Minneapolis: Augsburg, 1985.

————. "The Significance of the Historical Jesus for the Theology of Paul." Pp. 220–46 in *Faith and Understanding 1*, edited by Robert W. Funk, translated by Louise Pettibone Smith. London: SCM, 1969.

————. *Theology of the New Testament*. Translated by Kendrick Grobel. 2 vols. New York: Scribner's Sons, 1951, 1955.

Burton, Ernest DeWitt. *A Critical and Exegetical Commentary on the Epistle to the Galatians*. ICC. Edinburgh: T&T Clark, 1921.

Caird, G. B. *The Apostolic Age*. Studies in Theology. London: Duckworth, 1955.

————. *The Language and Imagery of the Bible*. Philadelphia: Westminster, 1980.

Caragounis, Chrys C. "Kingdom of God, Son of Man and Jesus' Self-Understanding." *Tyndale Bulletin* 40 (1989): 3–23, 223–38.

Castelli, Elizabeth A. *Imitating Paul: A Discourse of Power*. Literary Currents in Biblical Interpretation. Louisville: Westminster John Knox, 1991.

Cavadini, John C., ed. *Miracles in Jewish and Christian Antiquity*. Notre Dame Studies in Theology 3. Notre Dame, IN: Notre Dame University Press, 1999.

Charlesworth, James H., ed. *The Old Testament Pseudepigrapha*. 2 vols. Peabody, MA: Hendrickson, 1983.

Chilton, Bruce. "An Exorcism of History: Mark 1:21–28." Pp. 215–45 in *Authenticating the Activities of Jesus*, edited by Bruce Chilton and Craig A. Evans. Boston: Brill, 2002.

———. "Ideological Diets in a Feast of Meanings." Pp. 59–89 in *Jesus in Context: Temple, Purity, and Restoration*, edited by Bruce Chilton. AGJU 39. Leiden: Brill, 1997.

———. *The Isaiah Targum: Introduction, Translation, Apparatus and Notes*. ArBib 11. Wilmington, DE: Michael Glazier, 1987.

Cho, Youngmo. *Spirit and Kingdom in the Writings of Luke and Paul*. Paternoster Biblical Monographs. Milton Keynes: Paternoster, 2005.

Ciampa, Roy E., and Brian S. Rosner. *The First Letter to the Corinthians*. Pillar New Testament Commentary. Grand Rapids: Eerdmans, 2010.

Collins, John J. "The Works of the Messiah." *DSD* 1 (1994): 98–112.

Conzelmann, Hans. *1 Corinthians*. Translated by James W. Leitch. Hermeneia. Philadeophia: Fortress, 1975.

Corley, Kathleen E. *Private Women, Public Meals: Social Conflict in the Synoptic Tradition*. Peabody, MA: Hendrickson, 1993.

Cotter, Wendy. *Miracles in Greco-Roman Antiquity: A Sourcebook*. London: Routledge, 1999.

Craffert, Pieter F. *The Life of a Galilean Shaman: Jesus of Nazareth in Anthropological-Historical Perspective*. Matrix: The Bible in Mediterranean Context 3. Eugene, OR: Cascade, 2008.

Crafton, Jeffrey A. *The Agency of the Apostle: A Dramatistic Analysis of Paul's Responses to Conflict in 2 Corinthians*. JSNTSup 51. Sheffield: Sheffield Academic Press, 1991.

Cranfield, C. E. B. *The Epistle to the Romans*. 2 vols. ICC. London: T&T Clark, 1975, 1979. Reprint, London: T&T Clark, 2010.

Crossan, John Dominic. *The Historical Jesus: The Life of a Mediterranean Jewish Peasant*. New York: HarperCollins, 1991.

———. *Jesus: A Revolutionary Biography*. New York: HarperCollins, 1994.

Crossan, John Dominic, and Jonathan L. Reed. *In Search of Paul: How Jesus's Apostle Opposed Rome's Empire with God's Kingdom. A New Vision of Paul's Words and World*. New York: HarperCollins, 2004.

Cullmann, Oscar. *Christ and Time: The Primitive Christian Conception of Time and History*. Translated by Floyd V. Filson. Philadelphia: Westminster, 1950.

———. *Salvation in History*. New York: Harper & Row, 1967.

Daunton-Fear, Andrew. *Healing in the Early Church*. Studies in Christian History and Thought. Milton Keynes: Paternoster, 2009.

Davies, Stevan L. *Jesus the Healer*. New York: Continuum, 1995.

Davies, W. D., and Dale C. Allison Jr. *The Gospel According to Saint Matthew*. 3 vols. ICC. Edinburgh: T&T Clark, 1988, 1991, 1997.

Dawson, Audrey. *Healing, Weakness and Power: Perspectives on Healing in the Writings of Mark, Luke and Paul*. Paternoster Biblical Monographs. Milton Keynes: Paternoster, 2008.

Deines, Roland. Quotation on back cover of *Paul and the Miraculous: A Historical Reconstruction*, by Graham H. Twelftree. Grand Rapids: Baker, 2013.

Derickson, Gary W. "The Cessation of Healing Miracles in Paul's Ministry." *BSac* 155 (1998): 299–315.

DeSilva, David A. *Honor, Patronage, Kinship and Purity: Unlocking New Testament Culture*. Downers Grove, IL: InterVarsity, 2000.

Dibelius, Martin. *From Tradition to Gospel*. Translated by Bertram Lee Woolf. Library of Theological Translations. Cambridge: James Clarke, 1971.

———. *Jesus*. Translated by Charles B. Hedrick and Frederick C. Grant. Philadelphia: Westminster, 1949.

———. *Paul*, edited by Werner Georg Kümmel. Translated by Frank Clarke. Philadelphia: Westminster, 1953.

Dickie, Matthew W. *Magic and Magicians in the Greco-Roman World*. London: Routledge, 2001.

Dodd, C. H. *The Apostolic Preaching and Its Developments*. Chicago: Willett, Clark, 1937.

———. *The Parables of the Kingdom*. Rev. ed. New York: Scribner's Sons, 1961.

Donahue, John R. "Tax Collectors and Sinners: An Attempt at Identification." *CBQ* 33 (1971): 39–61.

Donaldson, Terence L. *Judaism and the Gentiles: Jewish Patterns of Universalism (to 135 CE)*. Waco, TX: Baylor University Press, 2007.

Downing, F. Gerald. *Cynics, Paul and the Pauline Churches: Cynics and Christian Origins II*. London: Routledge, 1998.

Drane, John W. "Patterns of Evangelization in Paul and Jesus." Pp. 281–96 in *Jesus of Nazareth: Lord and Christ; Essays on the Historical Jesus and New Testament Christology*, edited by Joel B. Green and Max Turner. Grand Rapids: Eerdmans, 1994.

Duling, Dennis C. "The Eleazar Miracle and Solomon's Magical Wisdom in Flavius Josephus' *Antiquitates Judaicae* 8.42–49." *HTR* 78/1–2 (1985): 1–25.

Dungan, David L. *The Sayings of Jesus in the Churches of Paul: The Use of the Synoptic Tradition in the Regulation of Early Church Life*. Oxford: Blackwell, 1971.

Dunn, James D. G. *The Epistle to the Galatians*. BNTC. Peabody, MA: Hendrickson, 1993.

———. "From Jesus' Proclamation to Paul's Gospel." Pp. 95–115 in *Jesus, Paul, and the Gospels*. Grand Rapids: Eerdmans, 2011.

———, ed. *The Historical Jesus in Recent Research*. Sources for Biblical and Theological Study 10. Winona Lake, IN: Eisenbrauns, 2005.

———. *Jesus and the Spirit: A Study of the Religious and Charismatic Experience of Jesus and the First Christians as Reflected in the New Testament*. London: SCM, 1975. Reprint, Grand Rapids: Eerdmans, 1997.

———. *Jesus Remembered*. Grand Rapids: Eerdmans, 2003.

———. "Jesus Tradition in Paul." Pp. 169–89 in vol. 1 of *The Christ and the Spirit*. 2 vols. Grand Rapids: Eerdmans, 1998.

———. *Jesus, Paul, and the Law: Studies in Mark and Galatians*. Louisville: Westminster, 1990.

———. "Mark 2.1–3.6: A Bridge between Jesus and Paul on the Question of the Law." *NTS* 30 (1984): 395–415.

———. "Matthew 12:28/Luke 11:20—A Word of Jesus?" Pp. 29–49 in *Eschatology in the New Testament: Essays in Honor of George Raymond Beasley-Murray*, edited by W. Hulitt Gloer. Peabody, MA: Hendrickson, 1988.

———. "The Messianic Secret in Mark." *TynBul* 21 (1970): 92–117.

———. "Paul's Knowledge of the Jesus Tradition: The Evidence of Romans." Pp. 193–207 in *Christus Bezeugen: Festschrift für Wolfgang Trilling zum 65 Geburtstag*, edited by Karl Kertelge, Traugott Holtz, and Claus-Peter März. Leipzig: St. Benno-Verlag, 1989.

———. "Paul's Theology." Pp. 326–48 in *The Face of New Testament Studies: A Survey of Recent Research*, edited by Scot McKnight and Grant R. Osborne. Grand Rapids: Baker, 2004.

———. "The Relationship between Paul and Jerusalem according to Galatians 1 and 2." *NTS* 28 (1982): 461–78.

———. *Romans*. 2 vols. WBC 38. Dallas: Word, 1988.

———. "Spirit and Kingdom." Pp. 133–41 in vol. 2 of *The Christ and the Spirit*, 2 vols. Grand Rapids: Eerdmans, 1998.

———. *The Theology of Paul the Apostle*. Grand Rapids: Eerdmans, 1998.

Eddy, Paul Rhodes, and Gregory A. Boyd. *The Jesus Legend: A Case for the Historical Reliability of the Synoptic Jesus Tradition*. Grand Rapids: Baker, 2007.

Edelstein, Emma J., and Ludwig Edelstein. *Asclepius: Collection and Interpretation of the Testimonies*. 2 vols. Baltimore: Johns Hopkins University Press, 1945. Reprint, Baltimore: John Hopkins University Press, 1998.

Edwards, Richard Alan. *The Sign of Jonah in the Theology of the Evangelists and Q*. Studies in Biblical Theology. Naperville, IL: Allenson, 1971.

Ehrensperger, Kathy. *Paul and the Dynamics of Power: Communication and Interaction in the Early Christ-Movement*. LNTS 325. London: T&T Clark, 2007.

Ehrman, Bart D. *Jesus: Apocalyptic Prophet of the New Millennium*. Oxford: Oxford University Press, 1999.

Epstein, I., ed. *Hebrew-English Edition of the Babylonian Talmud:* Taʻanith. Translated by J. Rabbinowitz. London: Soncino, 1984.

Evans, Craig A. "Exorcisms and the Kingdom: Inaugurating the Kingdom of God and Defeating the Kingdom of Satan." Pp. 151–79 in *Key Events in the Life of the Historical Jesus: A Collaborative Exploration of Context and Coherence*, edited by Darrell L. Bock and Robert L. Webb. Grand Rapids: Eerdmans, 2009.

———. *Fabricating Jesus: How Modern Scholars Distort the Gospels*. Downers Grove, IL: InterVarsity, 2006.

———. *Jesus and His Contemporaries: Comparative Studies*. AGJU 25. Leiden: Brill, 1995.

———. "Life-of-Jesus Research and the Eclipse of Mythology." *TS* 54 (1993): 3–36.

———. *Life of Jesus Research: An Annotated Bibliography*. NTTS 24. Leiden: Brill, 1996.

———. *Mark 8:27–16:20*. WBC 34b. Dallas: Word, 2001.

———. *Matthew*. New Cambridge Bible Commentary. Cambridge: Cambridge University Press, 2012.

———. "Paul the Exorcist and Healer." Pp. 363–79 in *Paul and His Theology*, edited by Stanley E. Porter. Pauline Studies 3. Leiden: Brill, 2006.

———. "'Who Touched Me?' Jesus and the Ritually Impure." Pp. 353–76 in *Jesus in Context: Temple, Purity, and Restoration*, edited by Bruce Chilton. AGJU 39. Leiden: Brill, 1997.

Eve, Eric. *The Healer from Nazareth: Jesus' Miracles in Historical Context*. London: SPCK, 2009.

———. *The Jewish Context of Jesus' Miracles*. JSNTSup 231. London: Sheffield Academic, 2002.

Fee, Gordon D. *The First Epistle to the Corinthians*. Rev. ed. NICNT. Grand Rapids: Eerdmans, 2014.

———. *God's Empowering Presence: The Holy Spirit in the Letters of Paul*. Peabody, MA: Hendrickson, 1994.

———. *Paul's Letter to the Philippians*. NICNT. Grand Rapids: Eerdmans, 1995.

———. *Pauline Christology: An Exegetical-Theological Study*. Peabody, MA: Hendrickson, 2007.

Fisk, Bruce N. "Paul: Life and Letters." Pp. 283–325 in *The Face of New Testament Studies: A Survey of Recent Research*, edited by Scot McKnight and Grant R. Osborne. Grand Rapids: Baker, 2004.

Fitzmyer, Joseph A. *First Corinthians: A New Translation with Introduction and Commentary*. AB 32. New Haven: Yale University Press, 2008.

———. *The Gospel According to Luke*. 2 vols. AB 28. Garden City, NY: Doubleday, 1981, 1985.

Fjärstedt, Biörn. *Synoptic Tradition in 1 Corinthians: Themes and Clusters of Theme Words in 1 Corinthians 1–4 and 9*. Uppsala: Teologiska Institutionen, 1974.

Fletcher-Louis, Crispin. "Jesus and Apocalypticism." Pp. 2877–2909 in vol. 3 of *Handbook for the Study of the Historical Jesus*, edited by Tom Holmén and Stanley E. Porter. 4 vols. Leiden: Brill, 2011.

———. "Jewish Apocalyptic and Apocalypticism." Pp. 1569–1607 in vol. 2 of *Handbook for the Study of the Historical Jesus*, edited by Tom Holmén and Stanley E. Porter, 4 vols. Leiden: Brill, 2011.

Fortna, Robert Tomson. *The Fourth Gospel and Its Predecessor: From Narrative Source to Present Gospel*. London: T&T Clark, 2004.

———. "The Gospel of John and the Signs Gospel." Pp. 149–58 in *What We Have Heard from the Beginning: The Past, Present, and Future of Johannine Studies*, edited by Tom Thatcher. Waco, TX: Baylor University Press, 2007.

———. *The Gospel of Signs: A Reconstruction of the Narrative Source Underlying the Fourth Gospel*. SNTSMS 11. London: Cambridge University Press, 1970.

Foubister, David Ronald. "The Nature and Purpose of Jesus' Miracles in the Gospels." PhD diss., Fuller Theological Seminary, 1981.

Fraser, J. W. *Jesus and Paul: Paul as Interpretor of Jesus from Harnack to Kümmel*. Appleford: Marcham, 1974.

Freyne, Seán. "The Charismatic." Pp. 223–58 in *Ideal Figures in Ancient Judaism: Profiles and Paradigms*, edited by John J. Collins and George W. E. Nicklesburg. Society of Biblical Literature Septuagint and Cognate Studies 12. Chico, CA: Scholars Press, 1980.

———. "The Jesus-Paul Debate Revisited and Re-imaging Christian Origins." Pp. 143–63 in *Christian Origins: Worship, Belief and Society*, edited by Kieran J. O'Mahony. JSNTSup 241. Sheffield: Sheffield Academic Press, 2003.

Funk, Robert W. *Honest to Jesus: Jesus for a New Millennium*. New York: HarperCollins, 1996.

Funk, Robert W., and The Jesus Seminar. *The Acts of Jesus: The Search for the Authentic Deeds of Jesus*. New York: HarperCollins, 1998.

Funk, Robert W., and Roy W. Hoover. *The Five Gospels: The Search for the Authentic Words of Jesus*. San Francisco: HarperSanFrancisco, 1993.

Furnish, Victor Paul. *2 Corinthians*. AB 32A. Garden City, NY: Doubleday, 1984.

———. "The Jesus-Paul Debate: From Bauer to Bultmann." Pp. 17–50 in *Paul and Jesus: Collected Essays*, edited by A. J. M. Wedderburn. JSNTSup 37. Sheffield: Sheffield Academic Press, 1989.

———. *Jesus According to Paul*. Understanding Jesus Today. Cambridge: Cambridge University Press, 1993.

———. *Theology and Ethics in Paul*. Nashville: Abingdon, 1968.

Gaiser, Frederick J. *Healing in the Bible: Theological Insight for Christian Ministry*. Grand Rapids: Baker, 2010.

García Martínez, Florentino. *The Dead Sea Scrolls Translated: The Qumran Texts in English*. Translated by Wilfred G. E. Watson. 2nd ed. Leiden: Brill, 1996.

García Martínez, Florentino, and Eibert J. C. Tigchelaar, eds. *The Dead Sea Scrolls Study Edition*. 2 vols. Leiden: Brill, 1997, 1998.

Garland, David E. *1 Corinthians*. BECNT. Grand Rapids: Baker, 2003.

———. *2 Corinthians*. NAC 29. Nashville: Broadman & Holman, 1999.

Garrett, Susan R. *The Demise of the Devil: Magic and the Demonic in Luke's Writings*. Minneapolis: Fortress, 1989.

Georgi, Dieter. *The Opponents of Paul in Second Corinthians*. Philadelphia: Fortress, 1986.

Gerhardsson, Birger. *The Mighty Acts of Jesus according to Matthew*. Scripta minora Regiae Societatis Humaniorum Litterarum Lundensis 1978–79:5. Lund: CWK Gleerup, 1979.

Gibson, Jeffrey. "Jesus' Refusal to Produce a 'Sign' (Mk 8.11–13)." *JSNT* 38 (1990): 37–66.

Godet, F. *Commentary on St. Paul's Epistle to the Romans*. Translated by A. Cusin. 2 vols. Clark's Foreign Theological Library n.s. 6. Edinburgh: T&T Clark, 1881.

González, Eliezer. "Healing in the Pauline Epistles: Why the Silence?" *JETS* 56 (2013): 557–75.

Goodacre, Mark. "Criticizing the Criterion of Multiple Attestation: The Historical Jesus and the Question of Sources." Pp. 152–69 in *Jesus, Criteria, and the Demise of Authenticity*, edited by Chris Keith and Anthony Le Donne. London: T&T Clark, 2012.

Goppelt, Leonhard. *Theology of the New Testament*. Translated by Jürgen Roloff. 2 vols. Grand Rapids: Eerdmans, 1981–82.

Goulder, Michael. *Paul and the Competing Mission in Corinth*. Library of Pauline Studies. Peabody, MA: Hendrickson, 2001.

———. *St. Paul Versus St. Peter: A Tale of Two Missions*. Louisville: Westminster John Knox, 1994.

Green, Joel B. *The Gospel of Luke*. NICNT. Grand Rapids: Eerdmans, 1997.

Grosheide, F. W. *Commentary on the First Epistle to the Corinthians*. NICNT. Grand Rapids: Eerdmans, 1953.

Guelich, Robert A. *Mark 1–8:26*. WBC 34a. Dallas: Word, 1989.

Gunkel, Hermann. *The Influence of the Holy Spirit: The Popular View of the Apostolic Age and the Teaching of the Apostle Paul*. Translated by Roy A. Harrisville and Philip A. Quanbeck II. Philadelphia: Fortress, 1979.

Haenchen, Ernst. *The Acts of the Apostles: A Commentary*. Translated by Bernard Noble and Gerald Shinn. Philadelphia: Westminster, 1971.

Hägerland, Tobias. *Jesus and the Forgiveness of Sins: An Aspect of His Prophetic Mission*. SNTSMS 150. Cambridge: Cambridge University Press, 2012.

Hagner, Donald A. *Matthew*. 2 vols. WBC 33. Dallas: Word, 1993, 1995.

Hamilton, Neill Q. *The Holy Spirit and Eschatology in Paul*. Scottish Journal of Theology Occasional Papers 6. Edinburgh: Oliver & Boyd, 1957.

Harding, Mark. "Disputed and Undisputed Letters of Paul." Pp. 129–68 in *The Pauline Canon*, edited by Stanley E. Porter. Pauline Studies 1. Leiden: Brill, 2004.

Harnack, Adolf. *What Is Christianity? Lectures Delivered in the University of Berlin During the Winter-Term 1899–1900*. 2nd, Rev. ed. New York: Putnam's Sons, 1908.

Harrington, Wilfrid. *Jesus and Paul: Signs of Contradiction.* Wilmington, DE: Michael Glazier, 1987.

Harris, Murray J. *The Second Epistle to the Corinthians: A Commentary on the Greek Text.* NIGTC. Grand Rapids: Eerdmans, 2005.

Harvey, A. E. *Jesus and the Constraints of History.* Philadelphia: Westminster, 1982.

Häusser, Detlef. *Christusbekenntnis und Jesusüberlieferung bei Paulus.* WUNT 2/210. Tübingen: Mohr Siebeck, 2006.

Hays, Richard B. *First Corinthians.* Interpretation. Louisville: Westminster John Knox, 1997.

Hengel, Martin. *Acts and the History of Earliest Christianity.* Translated by John Bowden. Philadelphia: Fortress, 1979.

———. *Between Jesus and Paul: Studies in the Earliest History of Christianity.* Translated by John Bowden. Minneapolis: Fortress, 1983.

———. *The Charismatic Leader and His Followers.* Edited by John Riches. Translated by James C. G. Greig. Edinburgh: T&T Clark, 1981. Reprint, Edinburgh: T&T Clark, 1996.

———. *The Pre-Christian Paul.* London: SCM, 1991.

Hieke, Thomas. "Q 7,22—A Compendium of Isaian Eschatology." *ETL* 82 (2006): 175–87.

Hildebrandt, Wilf. *An Old Testament Theology of the Spirit of God.* Peabody, MA: Hendrickson, 1995.

Hock, Ronald F. *The Social Context of Paul's Ministry: Tentmaking and Apostleship.* Philadelphia: Fortress, 1980.

Hogan, Larry P. *Healing in the Second Tempel* [*sic*] *Period.* NTOA 21. Freibourg: Universitätsverlag Freibourg, 1992.

Holladay, Carl R. *Theios Aner* in *Hellenistic Judaism: A Critique of the Use of This Category in New Testament Christology.* SBLDS 40. Missoula, MT: Scholars Press, 1977.

Hollander, Harm W. "The Words of Jesus: From Oral Traditions to Written Records in Paul and Q." *NovT* 42 (2000): 340–57.

Holmberg, Bengt. *Paul and Power: The Structure of Authority in the Primitive Church as Reflected in the Pauline Epistles.* Philadelphia: Fortress, 1978.

Holmén, Tom. "An Introduction to the Continuum Approach." Pp. 1–16 in *Jesus from Judaism to Christianity: Continuum Approaches to the Historical Jesus,* edited by Tom Holmén. LNTS 352. London: T&T Clark, 2007.

———, ed. *Jesus from Judaism to Christianity: Continuum Approaches to the Historical Jesus.* LNTS 352. London: T&T Clark, 2007.

———, ed. *Jesus in Continuum.* WUNT 289. Tübingen: Mohr Siebeck, 2012.

Holmes, Michael W., ed. *The Apostolic Fathers: Greek Texts and English Translations.* 3rd ed. Grand Rapids: Baker, 2007.

Holtz, Traugott. "Paul and the Oral Gospel Tradition." Pp. 380–93 in *Jesus and the Oral Gospel Tradition,* edited by Henry Wansbrough. JSNTSup 64. Sheffield: Sheffield Academic Press, 1991.

Holzbrecher, Frank. *Paulus und der historische Jesus: Darstellung und Analyse der bisherigen Forschungsgeschichte.* Texte und Arbeiten zum neutestamentlichen Zeitalter 48. Tübingen: Francke, 2007.

Hooker, Morna D. *The Signs of a Prophet: The Prophetic Actions of Jesus.* London: SCM, 1997.

Horsley, Richard A. *Jesus and Magic: Freeing the Gospel Stories from Modern Misconceptions.* Eugene, OR: Cascade, 2014.

———. *Jesus and the Spiral of Violence: Popular Jewish Resistance in Roman Palestine.* New York: Harper & Row, 1987.

Hultgren, Arland J. *Paul's Letter to the Romans: A Commentary.* Grand Rapids: Eerdmans, 2011.

Hunter, Archibald M. *Paul and His Predecessors.* Rev. ed. Philadelphia: Westminster, 1961.

Hurtado, Larry W. "Jesus as Lordly Example in Philippians 2:5–11." Pp. 113–26 in *From Jesus to Paul: Studies in Honour of Francis Wright Beare,* edited by Peter Richardson and John C. Hurd. Waterloo, ON: Wilfrid Laurier University Press, 1984.

———. *Lord Jesus Christ: Devotion to Jesus in Earliest Christianity.* Grand Rapids: Eerdmans, 2003.

Iamblichus. *On the Pythagorean Way of Life: Text, Translation, and Notes,* edited by John Dillon and Jackson Hershbell. SBLTT 29; Graeco-Roman Religion Series 11. Atlanta: Scholars Press, 1991.

Inwood, Brad. *The Poem of Empedocles: A Text and Translation with an Introduction.* Rev. ed. Phoenix Supplementary 39. Toronto: Toronto University Press, 2001.

Isaacs, Marie E. *The Concept of Spirit: A Study of Pneuma in Hellenistic Judaism and Its Bearing on the New Testament.* Heythrop Monographs 1. London: Heythrop, 1976.

Jackson, T. Ryan. *New Creation in Paul's Letters: A Study of the Historical and Social Setting of a Pauline Concept.* WUNT 2/272. Tübingen: Mohr Siebeck, 2010.

Janowitz, Naomi. *Magic in the Roman World: Pagans, Jews and Christians.* Religion in the First Christian Centuries. London: Routledge, 2001.

Jeremias, Joachim. *The Parables of Jesus.* Translated by S. H. Hooke. 3rd rev. ed. London: SCM, 1972.

Jervell, Jacob. "Der schwache Charismatiker." Pp. 185–98 in *Rechtfertigung: Festschrift für Ernst Käsemann zum 70. Geburtstag,* edited by Johannes Friedrich, Wolfgang Pöhlmann, and Peter Stuhlmacher. Tübingen: Mohr, 1976.

———. "The Signs of an Apostle." Pp. 77–95 in *The Unknown Paul: Essays on Luke–Acts and Early Christian History.* Minneapolis: Augsburg, 1984.

———. "The Unknown Paul." Pp. 52–67 in *The Unknown Paul: Essays on Luke–Acts and Early Christian History.* Minneapolis: Augsburg, 1984.

Jewett, Robert. *Romans: A Commentary.* Hermeneia. Minneapolis: Fortress, 2007.

Johnson, William Hallock. "Was Paul the Founder of Christianity?" *The Princeton Theological Review* 5 (1907): 398–422.

Johnston, George. "'Kingdom of God' Sayings in Paul's Letters." Pp. 143–56 in *From Jesus to Paul: Studies in Honour of Francis Wright Beare,* edited by Peter Richardson and John C. Hurd. Waterloo, ON: Wilfrid Laurier University Press, 1984.

Jones, Christopher P. Introduction to *Philostratus: The Life of Apollonius of Tyana; Books 1–4.* LCL. Cambridge, MA: Harvard University Press, 2005.

Kahl, Werner. *New Testament Miracle Stories in Their Religious-Historical Setting: A Religionsgeschichtliche Comparison from a Structural Perspective.* Göttingen: Vandenhoeck & Ruprecht, 1994.

Käsemann, Ernst. *Commentary on Romans.* Translated by Geoffrey W. Bromiley. Grand Rapids: Eerdmans, 1980.

———. "Die Legitimität des Apostels: Eine Untersuchung zu II Korinther 10–13." Pp. 475–521 in *Das Paulusbild in der neueren deutschen Forschung,* edited by Karl Heinrich Rengstorf. Wege der Forschung 24. Darmstadt: Wissenschaftliche Buchgesellschaft, 1982.

———. "Ministry and Community in the New Testament." Pp. 63–94 in *Essays on New Testament Themes*, translated by W. J. Montague. SBT. Naperville, IL: Allenson, 1964.

Kazen, Thomas. *Jesus and Purity* Halakhah: *Was Jesus Indifferent to Impurity?* Rev. ed. Coniectanea Biblica New Testament Series 38. Winona Lake, IN: Eisenbrauns, 2010.

Kee, Howard Clark. *Medicine, Miracle and Magic in New Testament Times*. SNTSMS 55. Cambridge: Cambridge University Press, 1986.

———. *Miracle in the Early Christian World: A Study in Sociohistorical Method*. New Haven: Yale University Press, 1983.

Keener, Craig S. *Acts: An Exegetical Commentary*. 4 vols. Grand Rapids: Baker, 2012–15.

———. *A Commentary on the Gospel of Matthew*. Grand Rapids: Eerdmans, 1999.

———. *The Historical Jesus of the Gospels*. Grand Rapids: Eerdmans, 2009.

———. *Miracles: The Credibility of the New Testament Accounts*. 2 vols. Grand Rapids: Baker, 2011.

Keith, Chris, and Anthony Le Donne, eds. *Jesus, Criteria, and the Demise of Authenticity*. London: T&T Clark, 2012.

Kelhoffer, James A. "The Apostle Paul and Justin Martyr on the Miraculous: A Comparison of Appeals to Authority." *GRBS* 42 (2002): 163–84.

———. "Ordinary Christians as Miracle Workers in the New Testament and the Second and Third Century Christian Apologists." *Biblical Research* 44 (1999): 23–34.

Keller, Ernst, and Marie-Luise Keller. *Miracles in Dispute: A Continuing Debate*. Translated by Margaret Kohl. London: SCM, 1969.

Kim, Seyoon. "Jesus, Sayings of." Pp. 474–92 in *Dictionary of Paul and His Letters*, edited by Gerald F. Hawthorne, Ralph P. Martin, and Daniel G. Reid. Downers Grove, IL: InterVarsity, 1993.

———. *The Origin of Paul's Gospel*. WUNT 2/4. Tübingen: Mohr, 1984.

Kirk, J. R. Daniel. *Jesus Have I Loved, but Paul? A Narrative Approach to the Problem of Pauline Christianity*. Grand Rapids: Baker, 2001.

Kittel, Gerhard, and Gerhard Friedrich, eds. *TDNT*. Translated by Geoffrey W. Bromiley. 10 vols. Grand Rapids: Eerdmans, 1964–76.

Klausner, Joseph. *From Jesus to Paul*. Translated by William F. Stinespring. Boston: Beacon, 1943.

Klawans, Jonathan. *Impurity and Sin in Ancient Judaism*. Oxford: Oxford University Press, 2000.

Klutz, Tod. *The Exorcism Stories in Luke–Acts: A Sociostylistic Reading*. SNTSMS 129. Cambridge: Cambridge University Press, 2004.

Knowling, Richard John. *The Testimony of St. Paul to Christ, Viewed in Some of Its Aspects*. London: Hodder & Stoughton, 1905.

Koch, Dietrich-Alex. *Die Bedeutung der Wundererzählungen für die Christologie des Markusevangeliums*. Beiheft zur Zeitschrift für die neutestamentliche Wissenschaft und die Kunde der älteren Kirche 42. Berlin: de Gruyter, 1975.

Koester, Helmut. "*GNOMAI DIAPHOROI*: The Origin and Nature of Diversification in the History of Early Christianity." Pp. 114–57 in *Trajectories through Early Christianity*, edited by James M. Robinson and Helmut Koester. Philadelphia: Fortress, 1971.

———. "One Jesus and Four Primitive Gospels." Pp. 158–204 in *Trajectories through Early Christianity*, edited by James M. Robinson and Helmut Koester. Philadelphia: Fortress, 1971.

Kolenkow, Anitra Bingham. "Paul and Opponents in 2 Cor 10–13: *Theioi Andres* and Spiritual Guides." Pp. 351–74 in *Religious Propaganda and Missionary Competition in the New Testament World,* edited by Lukas Bormann, Kelly Del Tredici, and Angela Standhartinger. NovTSup 74. Leiden: Brill, 1994.

———. "Relationships between Miracle and Prophecy in the Greco-Roman World and Early Christianity." Pp. 1470–1506 in vol. 2.23.2 of *ANRW,* edited by Wolfgang Haase. Berlin: de Gruyter, 1980.

Kollmann, Bernd. *Jesus und die Christen als Wundertäter: Studien zu Magie, Medizin und Schamanismus in Antike und Christentum.* Forschungen zur Religion und Literatur des Alten und Neuen Testaments 170. Göttingen: Vandenhoeck & Ruprecht, 1996.

———. "Paulus als Wundertäter." Pp. 76–96 in *Paulinische Christologie: Exegetische Beiträge,* edited by Udo Schnelle and Thomas Söding. Göttingen: Vandenhoeck & Ruprecht, 2000.

Koskenniemi, Erkki. "Apollonius of Tyana: A Typical ΘΕΙΟΣ ΑΝΗΡ?" *JBL* 117 (1998): 455–67.

———. *The Old Testament Miracle-Workers in Early Judaism.* WUNT 2/206. Tübingen: Mohr Siebeck, 2005.

Köstenberger, Andreas J. *A Theology of John's Gospel and Letters.* Biblical Theology of the New Testament. Grand Rapids: Zondervan, 2009.

Kuhn, Heinz-Wolfgang. "Der irdische Jesus bei Paulus als traditionsgeschichtliches und theologisches Problem." *ZTK* 67 (1970): 295–320.

Kümmel, Werner Georg. "Jesus und Paulus." *NTS* 10 (1964): 163–81.

———. *Promise and Fulfillment: The Eschatological Message of Jesus.* Translated by Dorothea M. Barton. Studies in Biblical Theology 23. Naperville, IL: Allenson, 1957.

———. *The Theology of the New Testament According to Its Major Witnesses. Jesus— Paul—John.* Translated by John E. Steely. Nashville: Abingdon, 1973.

Kvalbein, Hans. "The Wonders of the End-Time: Metaphoric Language in 4Q521 and the Interpretation of Matthew 11.5 Par." *JSP* 18 (1998): 87–110.

Kysar, Robert. *John, the Maverick Gospel.* Rev. ed. Louisville: Westminster John Knox, 1993.

Labahn, Michael. "The Non-Synoptic Jesus: An Introduction to John, Paul, Thomas, and Other Outsiders of the Jesus Quest." Pp. 1933–96 in vol. 3 of *Handbook for the Study of the Historical Jesus,* edited by Tom Holmén and Stanley E. Porter, 4 vols. Leiden: Brill, 2011.

Labahn, Michael, and Bert Jan Lietaert Peerbolte, eds. *Wonders Never Cease: The Purpose of Narrating Miracle Stories in the New Testament and Its Religious Environment.* LNTS 288. London: T&T Clark, 2006.

Ladd, George Eldon. *Jesus and the Kingdom: The Eschatology of Biblical Realism.* 2nd ed. Waco, TX: Word, 1964.

———. *A Theology of the New Testament,* edited by Donald A. Hagner. Rev. ed. Grand Rapids: Eerdmans, 1993.

Laertius, Diogenes. *Lives of Eminent Philosophers.* Translated by R. D. Hicks. 2 vols. LCL. London: Heinemann, 1959.

Lagrange, M.-J. *Saint Paul, Épitre aux Romains.* Paris: Librairie Lecoffre, 1950.

Latourelle, René. *The Miracles of Jesus and the Theology of Miracles.* New York: Paulist, 1988.

Lee, Yongbom. *Paul, Scribe of Old and New: Intertextural Insights for the Jesus-Paul Debate.* LNTS 512. London: Bloomsbury T&T Clark, 2015.

Leenhardt, Franz J. *The Epistle to the Romans: A Commentary.* London: Lutterworth, 1961.

Lemmer, H. R. "Mnemonic Reference to the Spirit as a Persuasive Tool (Galatians 3:1–6 within the Argument, 3:1–4:11)." *Neot* 26 (1992): 359–88.

LiDonnici, Lynn R. *The Epidaurian Miracle Inscriptions: Text, Translation and Commentary.* SBLTT 36. Graeco-Roman Religion Series 11. Atlanta: Scholars Press, 1995.

Lightfoot, J. B. *Notes on the Epistles of St. Paul (I and II Thessalonians, I Corinthians 1–7, Romans 1–7, Ephesians 1:1–14): Based on the Greek Text from Previously Unpublished Commentaries.* Classic Commentary Library. Grand Rapids: Zondervan, 1957.

Lim, Timothy H. "'Not in Persuasive Words of Wisdom, but in the Demonstration of the Spirit and Power.'" *NovT* 29 (1987): 137–49.

Lincoln, A. T. "'Paul the Visionary': The Setting and Significance of the Rapture to Paradise in 2 Corinthians 12:1–10." *NTS* 25 (1979): 204–20.

Linton, Olof. "The Demand for a Sign from Heaven." *ST* 19 (1965): 112–29.

Litwak, Kenneth D. Review of *Paul and the Miraculous: A Historical Reconstruction*, by Graham H. Twelftree. *JETS* 57 (2014): 632–35.

Lloyd, Rhys Rees. "The Historic Christ in the Letters of Paul." *BSac* 58 (1901): 270–93.

Lockwood, Gregory J. *1 Corinthians.* ConcC. Saint Louis: Concordia, 2000.

Longenecker, Bruce W. "Good News to the Poor: Jesus, Paul, and Jerusalem." Pp. 37–65 in *Jesus and Paul Reconnected*, edited by Todd D. Still. Grand Rapids: Eerdmans, 2007.

Longenecker, Richard N. *Galatians.* WBC 41. Dallas: Word, 1990.

Loos, H. van der *The Miracles of Jesus.* NovTSup 9. Leiden: Brill, 1965.

Lucas, Bernard. *The Fifth Gospel: Being the Pauline Interpretation of the Christ.* London: Macmillian, 1907.

Lüdemann, Gerd. *Opposition to Paul in Jewish Christianity.* Translated by M. Eugene Boring. Minneapolis: Fortress, 1989.

———. *Paul: The Founder of Christianity.* Amherst, NY: Prometheus, 2002.

Lull, David John. *The Spirit in Galatia: Paul's Interpretation of* Pneuma *as Divine Power.* SBLDS 49. Chico, CA: Scholars Press, 1978.

Luz, Ulrich. *Matthew.* Translated by James E. Crouch. 3 vols. Hermeneia. Minneapolis: Fortress, 2001, 2005, 2007.

———. "The Secrecy Motif and the Marcan Christology." Pp. 75–96 in *The Messianic Secret*, edited by Christopher Tuckett. IRT 1. Philadelphia: Fortress, 1983.

Ma, Wonsuk. *Until the Spirit Comes: The Spirit of God in the Book of Isaiah.* JSOTSup 271. Sheffield: Sheffield Academic Press, 1999.

Maccoby, Hyam. *The Mythmaker: Paul and the Invention of Christianity.* New York: Harper & Row, 1986.

Machen, John Gresham. "Jesus and Paul." Pp. 545–78 in *Biblical and Theological Studies by The Members of the Faculty of Princeton Theological Seminary.* New York: Scribner's Sons, 1912.

Mack, Burton L. *A Myth of Innocence.* Philadelphia: Fortress, 1988.

MacMullen, Ramsay. *Christianizing the Roman Empire (A.D. 100–400).* New Haven: Yale University Press, 1984.

———. *Paganism in the Roman Empire.* New Haven: Yale University Press, 1981.

Marcus, Joel. "Jesus' Baptismal Vision." *NTS* 41 (1995): 512–21.

Marshall, I. Howard. *The Gospel of Luke: A Commentary on the Greek Text.* NIGTC 3. Grand Rapids: Eerdmans, 1978.

———. "The Hope of a New Age: The Kingdom of God in the New Testament." Pp. 213–38 in *Jesus the Saviour: Studies in New Testament Theology*, edited by I. Howard Marshall. Downers Grove, IL: InterVarsity, 1990.

Martin, Ralph P. *2 Corinthians*. WBC 40. Dallas: Word, 1986.

———. "The Opponents of Paul in 2 Corinthians: An Old Issue Revisited." Pp. 279–89 in *Tradition and Interpretation in the New Testament: Essays in Honor of E. Earle Ellis*, edited by Gerald F. Hawthorne and Otto Betz. Grand Rapids: Eerdmans, 1987.

Martyn, J. Louis. *Galatians: A New Translation with Introduction and Commentary*. AB 33a. New York: Doubleday, 1997.

Matera, Frank J. *2 Corinthians: A Commentary*. NTL. Louisville: Westminster John Knox, 2003.

Matheson, George. "The Historical Christ of St. Paul." *The Expositor* 2/1–2 (1881): 1:43–62, 125–38, 193–208, 264–75, 352–71, 431–43; 2:27–47, 137–54, 287–301, 357–71.

McCartney, Dan G. "No Grace Without Weakness." *WTJ* 61 (1999): 1–13.

McCasland, S. Vernon. "Signs and Wonders." *JBL* 76 (1957): 149–52.

McGiffert, Arthur Cushman. "Was Jesus or Paul the Founder of Christianity?" *American Journal of Theology* 33 (1909): 1–20.

McKnight, Scot. *A Light Among the Gentiles: Jewish Missionary Activity in the Second Temple Period*. Minneapolis: Fortress, 1991.

———. "Why the Authentic Jesus Is of No Use for the Church." Pp. 173–85 in *Jesus, Criteria, and the Demise of Authenticity*, edited by Chris Keith and Anthony Le Donne. London: T&T Clark, 2012.

Meeks, Wayne A. Introduction to the Westminster John Knox Press edition of *Paul and the Anatomy of Apostolic Authority*, by John Howard Schütz. NTL. Cambridge: Cambridge University Press, 2007.

Meggitt, Justin. "The Historical Jesus and Healing: Jesus' Miracles in Psychosocial Context." Pp. 17–43 in *Spiritual Healing: Scientific and Religious Perspectives*, edited by Fraser Watts. Cambridge: Cambridge University Press, 2011.

Meier, John P. "Jesus in Josephus: A Modest Proposal." *CBQ* 52 (1990): 76–103.

———. *Mentor, Message, and Miracles*, vol. 2 of *A Marginal Jew: Rethinking the Historical Jesus*. ABRL. New York: Doubleday, 1994.

———. *The Roots of the Problem and the Person*, vol. 1 of *A Marginal Jew: Rethinking the Historical Jesus*. ABRL. New York: Doubleday, 1991.

Menzies, Robert P. *Empowered for Witness: The Spirit in Luke–Acts*. Journal of Pentecostal Theology Supplement Series 6. Sheffield: Sheffield Academic Press, 1994.

Merrill, Eugene H. "The Sign of Jonah." *JETS* 23 (1980): 23–30.

Meyer, Arnold. *Jesus or Paul?* Translated by J. R. Wilkinson. Harper's Library of Living Thought. London: Harper, 1909.

Meyer, Ben F. *The Aims of Jesus*. Princeton Theological Monograph Series 48. Eugene, OR: Pickwick, 2002.

Moffatt, James. "Paul and Jesus." *The Biblical World* 32 (1908): 168–73.

Moles, John. "Jesus the Healer in the Gospels, the *Acts of the Apostles*, and Early Christianity." *Histos* 5 (2011): 117–82.

Montague, George T. *Holy Spirit: Growth of a Biblical Tradition*. Peabody, MA: Hendrickson, 1976.

Moo, Douglas J. *The Epistle to the Romans*. NICNT. Grand Rapids: Eerdmans, 1996.

———. *Galatians*. BECNT. Grand Rapids: Baker, 2013.

Morgan, W. "The Jesus-Paul Controversy." *Expository Times* 20 (1908): 9–12, 55–58.

Moule, G. C. G. *Studies in Philippians*. Cambridge: Cambridge University Press, 1893. Reprint, Grand Rapids: Kregel, 1977.

Murphy-O'Connor, Jerome. *Paul: A Critical Life*. Oxford: Clarendon, 1996.

———. *The Theology of the Second Letter to the Corinthians.* New Testament Theology. Cambridge: Cambridge University Press, 1991.

Mussner, Franz. *The Miracles of Jesus: An Introduction.* Translated by Albert Wimmer. Contemporary Catechetics. Notre Dame, IN: University of Notre Dame Press, 1968.

Neale, David A. *None but the Sinners: Religious Categories in the Gospel of Luke.* JSNTSup 58. Sheffield: Sheffield Academic Press, 1991.

Neirynck, Frans. "Paul and the Sayings of Jesus." Pp. 265–321 in *L'Apôtre Paul: Personnalité, style et conception du ministère,* edited by A. Vanhoye. Leuven: Leuven University Press, 1986.

Neve, Lloyd. *The Spirit of God in the Old Testament.* Tokyo: Seibunsha, 1972.

Nielsen, Helge Kjaer. *Heilung und Verkündigung: Das Verständnis der Heilung und ihres Verhältnisses zur Verkündigung bei Jesus und in der ältesten Kirche.* Acta Theologica Danica 22. Leiden: Brill, 1987.

Noack, Bent. "Teste Paulo: Paul as the Principal Witness to Jesus and Primitive Christianity." Pp. 9–28 in *Die Paulinische Literatur und Theologie,* edited by Sigfred Pedersen. Teologiske Studier 7. Århus: Vandenhoeck & Ruprecht, 1979.

Nolland, John. *Luke.* 3 vols. WBC 35. Dallas: Word, 1989, 1993.

Osborne, Grant R. *Romans.* IVP New Testament Commentary Series 6. Downers Grove, IL: InterVarsity, 2004.

Paget, James C. "Miracles in Early Christianity." Pp. 131–48 in *The Cambridge Companion to Miracles,* edited by Graham H. Twelftree. Cambridge Companions to Religion. Cambridge: Cambridge University Press, 2011.

———. "Some Observations on Josephus and Christianity." *JTS* 52 (2001): 539–624.

Pao, David W., and Eckhard J. Schnabel. "Luke." Pp. 251–414 in *Commentary on the New Testament Use of the Old Testament,* edited by G. K. Beale and D. A. Carson. Grand Rapids: Baker, 2007.

Patterson, Stephen J. "Paul and the Jesus Tradition: It Is Time for Another Look." *HTR* 84 (1991): 23–41.

Peerbolte, Bert Jan Lietaert. "Paul the Miracle Worker." Pp. 180–99 in *Wonders Never Cease: The Purpose of Narrating Miracle Stories in the New Testament and Its Religious Environment,* edited by Michael Labahn and Bert Jan Lietaert Peerbolte. LNTS 288. London: T&T Clark, 2006.

Penella, Robert J. *The Letters of Apollonius of Tyana: A Critical Text with Prolegomena, Translation, and Commentary.* Leiden: Brill, 1979.

Perrin, Norman. *The Kingdom of God in the Teaching of Jesus.* NTL. Philadelphia: Westminster, 1963.

———. *Rediscovering the Teaching of Jesus.* New York: Harper & Row, 1967.

Petzke, G. *Die Traditionen über Apollonius von Tyana und das Neue Testament.* SCHNT 1. Leiden: Brill, 1970.

Philip, Finny. *The Origins of Pauline Pneumatology: The Eschatological Bestowal of the Spirit upon Gentiles in Judaism and in the Early Development of Paul's Theology.* WUNT: 2/194. Tübingen: Mohr Siebeck, 2005.

Philostratus. *The Life of Apollonius of Tyana: Books 1–4.* Translated by Christopher P. Jones. LCL. Cambridge, MA: Harvard University Press, 2005.

Pilch, John J. *Healing in the New Testament: Insights from Medical and Mediterranean Anthropology.* Minneapolis: Fortress, 2000.

Pokorný, Petr. "Words of Jesus in Paul: On the Theology and Praxis of the Jesus Tradition." Pp. 3437–67 in vol. 4 of *Handbook for the Study of the Historical Jesus,* edited by Tom Holmén and Stanley E. Porter, 4 vols. Leiden: Brill, 2011.

Polaski, Sandra Hack. *Paul and the Discourse of Power*. Gender, Culture, Theory 8; Bib-Sem 62. Sheffield: Sheffield Academic Press, 1999.

Porter, Stanley E. *The Criteria for Authenticity in Historical-Jesus Research: Previous Discussion and New Proposals*. JSNTSup 191. Sheffield: Sheffield Academic Press, 2000.

———. *The Paul of Acts: Essays in Literary Criticism, Rhetoric, and Theology*. WUNT 115. Tübingen: Mohr Siebeck, 1999.

———. *When Paul Met Jesus: How an Idea Got Lost in History*. Cambridge: Cambridge University Press, 2016.

Porterfield, Amanda. *Healing in the History of Christianity*. Oxford: Oxford University Press, 2005.

Powell, Mark A. *Jesus as a Figure in History*. 2nd ed. Louisville, KY: Westminster John Knox, 2013.

———. "Table Fellowship." Pp. 925–31 in *Dictionary of Jesus and the Gospels*, edited by Joel B. Green, Jeannine K. Brown, and Nicholas Perrin, 2nd ed. Downers Grove, IL: InterVarsity, 2013.

Praeder, Susan Marie. "Miracle Worker and Missionary: Paul in the Acts of the Apostles." Pp. 107–29 in *Society of Biblical Literature 1983 Seminar Papers*, edited by Kent Harold Richards. Society of Biblical Literature Seminar Papers 22. Chico, CA: Scholars Press, 1983.

Puig i Tàrrech, Armand. "The Use of the Story and the Words of Jesus in the Letters of Paul." Pp. 1–14 in *Paul, John, and Apocalyptic Eschatology: Studies in Honour of Martinus C. de Boer*, edited by Jan Krans et al. Leiden: Brill, 2013.

Räisänen, Heikki. "The 'Hellenists': A Bridge between Jesus and Paul?" Pp. 149–202 in *Jesus, Paul and Torah: Collected Essays*, translated by David E. Orton. JSNTSup 43. Sheffield: Sheffield Academic Press, 1992.

———. "The 'Messianic Secret' in Mark's Gospel." Pp. 132–39 in *The Messianic Secret*, edited by Christopher Tuckett. Philadelphia: Fortress, 1983.

Reimarus, H. S. *Reimarus: Fragments*. Edited by Charles H. Talbert. Translated by Ralph S. Fraser. Lives of Jesus Series. Philadelphia: Fortress, 1970.

Reimer, Andy M. *Miracle and Magic: A Study of the Acts of the Apostles and the Life of Apollonius of Tyana*. JSNTSup 235. London: Sheffield Academic Press, 2002.

Remus, Harold. *Jesus as Healer*. Understanding Jesus Today. Cambridge: Cambridge University Press, 1997.

———. *Pagan-Christian Conflict over Miracle in the Second Century*. Patristic Monograph Series 10. Cambridge, MA: Philadelphia Patristic Foundation, 1983.

Resch, Alfred. *Der Paulinismus und die Logia Jesu in ihrem gegenseitigen Verhältnis*. TUGAL 2/12. Leipzig: Hinrichs, 1904.

Rescio, Mara, and Luigi Walt. "'There Is Nothing Unclean': Jesus and Paul Against the Politics of Purity?" *Annali di Storia dell'Esegesi* 29 (2012): 53–82.

Richardson, Alan. *The Miracle-Stories of the Gospels*. New York: Harper, 1941.

Richardson, Peter, and John C. Hurd, eds. *From Jesus to Paul: Studies in Honour of Francis Wright Beare*. Waterloo, ON: Wilfrid Laurier University Press, 1984.

Robinson, James M. "Kerygma and History in the New Testament." Pp. 20–70 in *Trajectories through Early Christianity*, edited by James M. Robinson and Helmut Koester. Philadelphia: Fortress, 1971.

Robinson, James M., Paul Hoffmann, and John S. Kloppenborg, eds. *The Critical Edition of Q*. Hermeneia. Minneapolis: Fortress, 2000.

Rodríguez, Rafael. "Re-framing End-Time Wonders: A Response to Hans Kvalbein." *JSP* 20 (2011): 219–40.

Roetzel, Calvin J. *The Letters of Paul: Conversations in Context.* 5th ed. Louisville: Westminster John Knox, 2009.

Roskovec, Jan. "Jesus as Miracle Worker: Historiography and Credibility." Pp. 874–96 in *Jesus Research: New Methodologies and Perceptions. The Second Princeton-Prague Symposium on Jesus Research, Princeton 2007*, edited by James H. Charlesworth. Princeton-Prague Symposia Series on the Historical Jesus 2. Grand Rapids: Eerdmans, 2014.

Salier, Willis Hedley. *The Rhetorical Impact of the* Sēmeia *in the Gospel of John.* WUNT 2/186. Tübingen: Mohr Siebeck, 2004.

Sanday, W. "Paul." Pp. 886–92 in vol. 2 of *A Dictionary of Christ and the Gospels*, edited by James Hastings. New York: Scribner's Sons, 1908.

Sanders, E. P. *The Historical Figure of Jesus.* London: Lane, 1993.

———. *Jesus and Judaism.* Philadelphia: Fortress, 1985.

———. "Jesus and the Sinners." *JSNT* 19 (1983): 5–36.

———. *Paul.* Past Masters. Oxford: Oxford University Press, 1991.

———. *Paul, the Law, and the Jewish People.* Philadelphia: Fortress, 1983.

Sanders, Jack T. *Charisma, Converts, Competitors: Societal and Sociological Factors in the Success of Early Christianity.* London: SCM, 2000.

Savage, Timothy B. *Power through Weakness: Paul's Understanding of the Christian Ministry in 2 Corinthians.* SNTSMS 86. Cambridge: Cambridge University Press, 1996.

Schlatter, Adolf. *The Theology of the Apostles: The Development of New Testament Theology.* Translated by Andreas J. Köstenberger. Grand Rapids: Baker, 1999.

Schmithals, Walter. *Der Römerbrief: Ein Kommentar.* Gütersloher: Mohn, 1988.

———. *Gnosticism in Corinth: An Investigation of the Letters to the Corinthians.* Translated by John E. Steely. Nashville: Abingdon, 1971.

———. *The Office of Apostle in the Early Chruch.* Translated by John E. Steely. Nashville: Abingdon, 1969.

Schnelle, Udo. "The Signs in the Gospel of John." Pp. 231–43 in *Jesus, John and History,* vol. 3: *Glimpses of Jesus through the Johannine Lens*, edited by Paul N. Anderson, Felix Just, and Tom Thatcher. SymS 44; ECL 18. Atlanta: SBL, 2016.

Schoberg, Gerry. *Perspectives of Jesus in the Writings of Paul: A Historical Examination of Shared Core Commitments with a View to Determining the Extent of Paul's Dependence on Jesus.* Princeton Theological Monograph 190. Eugene, OR: Pickwick, 2013.

Schoeps, H. J. *Paul: The Theology of the Apostle in the Light of Jewish Religious History.* Translated by Harold Knight. Philadelphia: Westminster, 1961.

Schreiber, Stefan. *Paulus als Wundertäter: Redaktionsgeschichtliche Untersuchungen zur Apostelgeschichte und den authentischen Paulusbriefen.* BZNW 79. Berlin: de Gruyter, 1996.

Schreiner, Thomas R. *Galatians.* Zondervan Exegetical Commentary on the New Testament. Grand Rapids: Zondervan, 2010.

———. *Paul: Apostle of God's Glory in Christ. A Pauline Theology.* Downers Grove, IL: IVP Academic, 2001.

———. *Romans.* BECNT 6. Grand Rapids: Baker, 1998.

Schüssler Fiorenza, Elisabeth. "Miracles, Mission, and Apologetics: An Introduction." Pp. 1–25 in *Aspects of Religious Propaganda in Judaism and Early Christianity*, edited by Elisabeth Schüssler Fiorenza. University of Notre Dame Center for the Study of Judaism and Christianity in Antiquity 2. Notre Dame, IN: University of Notre Dame Press, 1976.

Schütz, John Howard. *Paul and the Anatomy of Apostolic Authority.* Cambridge: Cambridge University Press, 1975. Reprint, Louisville: Westminster John Knox, 2007.

Schweitzer, Albert. *The Mysticism of Paul the Apostle.* Translated by William Montgomery. New York: Macmillan, 1956.

———. *Paul and His Interpreters: A Critical History.* Translated by W. Montgomery. New York: Macmillan, 1956.

———. *The Quest for the Historical Jesus: First Complete Edition.* Edited by John Bowden. Translated by W. Montgomery et al. London: SCM, 2000.

Scott, Charles Archibald Anderson. "Jesus and Paul." Pp. 329–77 in *Essays on Some Biblical Questions of the Day by Members of the University of Cambridge,* edited by Henry Barclay Swete. London: Macmillan, 1909.

Seccombe, David. *The King of God's Kingdom: A Solution to the Puzzle of Jesus.* Milton Keynes: Paternoster, 2002.

Shaw, Graham. *The Cost of Authority: Manipulation and Freedom in the New Testament.* Philadelphia: Fortress, 1983.

Shillington, V. George. *Jesus and Paul before Christianity: Their World and Work in Retrospect.* Eugene, OR: Cascade, 2011.

Simmons, William A. *A Theology of Inclusion in Jesus and Paul: The God of Outcasts and Sinners.* Mellen Biblical Press Series 39. Lewiston, NY: Edwin Mellen Biblical Press, 1996.

Sinclair, Scott Gambrill. *Jesus Christ according to Paul: The Christologies of Paul's Undisputed Epistles and the Christology of Paul.* Bibal Monograph Series 1. Berkeley, CA: Bibal, 1988.

Smith, Dennis E. *From Symposium to Eucharist: The Banquet in the Early Christian World.* Minneapolis: Fortress, 2003.

Smith, Morton. *Jesus the Magician.* San Francisco: Harper & Row, 1978.

Snyder, Graydon F. *First Corinthians: A Faith Community Commentary.* Macon, GA: Mercer University Press, 1992.

Spencer, William David. "The Power in Paul's Teaching (1 Cor 4:9–20)." *JETS* 32 (1989): 51–61.

Staalduine-Sulman, Eveline van. *The Targum of Samuel.* Studies in the Aramaic Interpretation of Scripture 1. Leiden: Brill, 2002.

Stegman, Thomas. *The Character of Jesus: The Linchpin to Paul's Argument in 2 Corinthians.* Analecta Biblica 158. Rome: Pontifical Biblical Institute, 2005.

Steinleitner, Franz. *Die Beicht im Zusammenhange mit der sakralen Rechtspflege in der Antike.* Leipzig: Kommissionsverlag der Dieterich'schen Verlagsbuchhandlung, Theodor Weicher, 1913.

Stettler, Christian. "The 'Command of the Lord' in 1 Cor 14,37—A Saying of Jesus?" *Bib* 87 (2006): 42–51.

Still, Todd D., ed. *Jesus and Paul Reconnected: Fresh Pathways into an Old Debate.* Grand Rapids: Eerdmans, 2007.

Stone, Michael E. *The Testament of Abraham: The Greek Recensions.* SBLTT 2. Missoula, MT: Society of Biblical Literature, 1972.

Strauss, David Friedrich. *The Life of Jesus Critically Examined.* Translated by George Eliot. Lives of Jesus Series. Philadelphia: Fortress, 1972.

Stuhlmacher, Peter. "Jesus of Nazareth: The Christ of our Faith." Pp. 271–309 in *Crisis in Christology: Essays in Quest of Resolution,* edited by William R. Farmer. Livonia, MI: Dove, 1995.

———. *Paul's Letter to the Romans: A Commentary.* Translated by Scott J. Hafemann. Louisville: Westminster John Knox, 1994.

Sumney, Jerry L. *Identifying Paul's Opponents: The Question of Method in 2 Corinthians.* JSNTSup 40. Sheffield: Sheffield Academic Press, 1990.

———. *'Servants of Satan,' 'False Brothers' and Other Opponents of Paul.* JSNTSup 188. Sheffield: Sheffield Academic Press, 1999.

———. "Studying Paul's Opponents: Advances and Challenges." Pp. 7–58 in *Paul and His Opponents*, edited by Stanley E. Porter. Pauline Studies 2. Leiden: Brill, 2005.

Swinburne, Richard. *The Concept of Miracle.* New Studies in the Philosophy of Religion. London: Macmillan, 1970.

Tabor, James D. *Paul and Jesus: How the Apostle Transformed Christianity.* New York: Simon & Schuster, 2012.

Talbert, Charles H. *Reading John: A Literary and Theological Commentary on the Fourth Gospel and the Johannine Epistles.* Reading the New Testament. New York: Crossroad, 1992.

Talbott, Rick F. *Jesus, Paul, and Power: Rhetoric, Ritual, and Metaphor in Ancient Mediterranean Christianity.* Eugene, OR: Cascade, 2010.

Taylor, Nicholas. *Paul, Antioch and Jerusalem.* JSNTSup 66. Sheffield: Sheffield Academic Press, 1992.

Theissen, Gerd. *The Miracle Stories of the Early Christian Tradition.* Edited by John Riches. Translated by Francis McDonagh. Philadelphia: Fortress, 1983.

Theissen, Gerd, and Annette Merz. *The Historical Jesus: A Comprehensive Guide.* Translated by John Bowden. Minneapolis: Fortress, 1998.

Theissen, Gerd, and Dagmar Winter, *The Quest for the Plausible Jesus: The Question of Criteria.* Translated by M. Eugene Boring. Louisville: Westminster John Knox, 2002.

Thiselton, Anthony C. *The First Epistle to the Corinthians: A Commentary on the Greek Text.* NIGTC. Grand Rapids: Eerdmans, 2000.

Thomas, John Christopher. *The Devil, Disease and Deliverance: Origins of Illness in New Testament Thought.* Journal of Pentecostal Theology Supplement 13. Sheffield: Sheffield Academic Press, 1998.

Thompson, Marianne Meye. "Signs and Faith in the Fourth Gospel." *Bulletin for Biblical Research* 1 (1991): 89–108.

Thompson, Michael B. *Clothed with Christ: The Example and Teaching of Jesus in Romans 12.1–15.13.* JSNTSup 59. Sheffield: JSOT, 1991.

———. "Paul in the Book of Acts: Differences and Distance." *Expository Times* 122 (2011): 425–36.

Thrall, Margaret E. *A Critical and Exegetical Commentary on the Second Epistle to the Corinthians.* 2 vols. ICC. Edinburgh: T&T Clark, 1994, 2000.

Tibbs, Clint. *Religious Experience of the Pneuma: Communication with the Spirit World in 1 Corinthians 12 and 14.* WUNT 2/230. Tübingen: Mohr Siebeck, 2007.

Trebilco, Paul. *Jewish Communities in Asia Minor.* SNTSMS 69. Cambridge: Cambridge University Press, 1991.

Tuckett, Christopher M. "1 Corinthians and Q." *JBL* 102 (1983): 607–19.

———. "Paul and the Synoptic Mission Discourse?" *ETL* 60 (1984): 376–81.

———. "Paul, Tradition and Freedom." *TZ* 47 (1991): 307–25.

Turner, Max. *The Holy Spirit and Spiritual Gifts: Then and Now.* Carlisle: Paternoster, 1996.

———. *Power from on High: The Spirit in Israel's Restoration and Witness in Luke–Acts.* Journal of Pentecostal Theology Supplement 9. Sheffield: Sheffield Academic Press, 1996.

Twelftree, Graham H., ed. *The Cambridge Companion to Miracles*. Cambridge Companions to Religion. Cambridge: Cambridge University Press, 2011.

———. "Demon, Devil, Satan." Pp. 163–72 in *Dictionary of Jesus and the Gospels*, edited by Joel B. Green, Scot McKnight, and I. Howard Marshall. Downers Grove, IL: InterVarsity, 1992.

———. "The History of Miracles in the History of Jesus." Pp. 191–208 in *The Face of New Testament Studies: A Survey of Recent Research*, edited by Scot McKnight and Grant R. Osborne. Grand Rapids: Baker, 2004.

———. *In the Name of Jesus: Exorcism among Early Christians*. Grand Rapids: Baker, 2007.

———. "Jesus and Magic in LukeActs." Pp. 46–58 in *Jesus and Paul: Global Perspectives in Honor of James D. G. Dunn. A Festschrift for His 70th Birthday*, edited by B. J. Oropeza, C. K. Robertson, and Douglas C. Mohrmann. LNTS 414. London: T&T Clark, 2009.

———. *Jesus the Exorcist: A Contribution to the Study of the Historical Jesus*. WUNT 2/54. Tübingen: Mohr, 1993.

———. *Jesus the Miracle Worker: A Historical and Theological Study*. Downers Grove, IL: InterVarsity, 1999.

———. "Miracles and Miracle Stories." Pp. 594–604 in *DJG*, edited by Joel B. Green, Jeannine K. Brown, and Nicholas Perrin. 2nd ed. Downers Grove, IL: InterVarsity, 2013.

———. "The Miracles of Jesus: Marginal or Mainstream?" *Journal for the Study of the Historical Jesus* 1 (2003): 104–24.

———. *Paul and the Miraculous: A Historical Reconstruction*. Grand Rapids: Baker, 2013.

———. "Signs, Wonders, Miracles." Pp. 875–77 in *DPL*, edited by Gerald F. Hawthorne and Ralph P. Martin. Downers Grove, IL: InterVarsity, 1993.

Vermes, Geza. "The Jesus Notice of Josephus Re-Examined." *JJS* 38 (1987): 1–10.

———. *Jesus the Jew: A Historian's Reading of the Gospels*. New York: Macmillan, 1973.

———. *The Religion of Jesus the Jew*. Minneapolis: Fortress, 1993.

Walker, William. O., Jr. "Jesus and the Tax Collectors." *JBL* 97 (1978): 221–38.

Wallace, Daniel B. *Greek Grammar Beyond the Basics: An Exegetical Syntax of the New Testament*. Grand Rapids: Zondervan, 1996.

Walt, Luigi. "A Non-Canonical Jesus in Paul? *I Corinthians* 1–4 as a Test Case." *Annali di Storia dell'Esegesi* 25 (2008): 55–74.

Walter, Nikolaus. "Paul and the Early Christian Jesus-Tradition." Pp. 51–80 in *Paul and Jesus: Collected Essays*, edited by A. J. M. Wedderburn. JSNTSup 37. Sheffield: Sheffield Academic Press, 1989.

Webb, Robert L. "Jesus' Baptism by John: Its Historicity and Significance." Pp. 95–150 in *Key Events in the Life of the Historical Jesus: A Collaborative Exploration of Context and Coherence*, edited by Darrell L. Bock and Robert L. Webb. Grand Rapids: Eerdmans, 2009.

———. "The Historical Jesus Enterprise and Historical Jesus Research." Pp. 9–93 in *Key Events in the Life of the Historical Jesus: A Collaborative Exploration of Context and Coherence*, edited by Darrell L. Bock and Robert L. Webb. Grand Rapids: Eerdmans, 2009.

Wedderburn, A. J. M., ed. *Paul and Jesus: Collected Essays*. JSNTSup 37. Sheffield: Sheffield Academic Press, 1989.

———. "Paul and Jesus: Similarity and Continuity." Pp. 117–43 in *Paul and Jesus: Collected Essays*, edited by A. J. M. Wedderburn. JSNTSup 37. Sheffield: Sheffield Academic Press, 1989.

———. "Paul and the Story of Jesus." Pp. 161–89 in *Paul and Jesus: Collected Essays*, edited by A. J. M. Wedderburn. JSNTSup 37. Sheffield: Sheffield Academic Press, 1989.

Weder, Hans. "*Deus Incarnatus*: On the Hermeneutics of Christology in the Johannine Writings." Pp. 327–45 in *Exploring the Gospel of John: In Honor of D. Moody Smith*, edited by R. Alan Culpepper and C. Clifton Black. Louisville, KY: Westminster John Knox, 1996.

Weeden, Theodore J. *Mark—Traditions in Conflict*. Philadelphia: Fortress, 1971.

Weiss, Johannes. *Paul and Jesus*. Translated by H. J. Chaytor. Harper's Library of Living Thought. London: Harper & Brothers, 1909.

Weiß, Wolfgang. *Zeichen und Wunder: Eine Studie zu der Sprachtradition und ihrer Verwendung im Neuen Testament*. WMANT 67. Neukirchen-Vluyn: Neukirchener Verlag, 1995.

Weizsäcker, Carl Heinrich von. *The Apostolic Age of the Christian Church*. Translated by James Millar. 2nd ed. 2 vols. Theological Translation Library. London: Williams & Norgate, 1897.

Wenham, David. *Did St. Paul Get Jesus Right?* Oxford: Lion Hudson, 2010.

———. "Jesus Tradition in the Letters of the New Testament." Pp. 2041–57 in vol. 3 of *Handbook for the Study of the Historical Jesus*, edited by Tom Holmén and Stanley E. Porter. 4 vols. Leiden: Brill, 2011.

———. *Paul and Jesus: The True Story*. Grand Rapids: Eerdmans, 2002.

———. *Paul: Follower of Jesus or Founder of Christianity?* Grand Rapids: Eerdmans, 1995.

———. "The Story of Jesus Known to Paul." Pp. 297–311 in *Jesus of Nazareth: Lord and Christ. Essays on the Historical Jesus and New Testament Christology*, edited by Joel B. Green and Max Turner. Grand Rapids: Eerdmans, 1994.

Wenk, Matthias. *Community-Forming Power: The Socio-Ethical Role of the Spirit in Luke–Acts*. Journal of Pentecostal Theology Supplement 19. Sheffield: Sheffield Academic Press, 2000.

———. "Holy Spirit." Pp. 387–94 in *DJG*, edited by Joel B. Green, Jeannine K. Brown, and Nicholas Perrin. 2nd ed. Downers Grove, IL: IVP Academic, 2013.

Whealey, Alice. *Josephus on Jesus: The* Testimonium Flavianum *Controversy from Late Antiquity to Modern Times*. Studies in Biblical Literature 36. New York: Peter Lang, 2003.

———. "The *Testimonium Flavianum* in Syriac and Arabic." *NTS* 54 (2008): 573–90.

White, L. Michael. "Rhetoric and Reality in Galatians: Framing the Social Demands of Friendship." Pp. 307–49 in *Early Christianity and Classical Culture: Comparative Studies in Honor of Abraham J. Malherbe*, edited by John T. Fitzgerald, Thomas H. Olbricht, and L. Michael White. NovTSup 110. Leiden: Brill, 2003.

Wilkinson, John. *The Bible and Healing: A Medical and Theological Commentary*. Edinburgh: Handsel, 1998.

Wilson, A. N. *Paul: The Mind of the Apostle*. New York: Norton, 1997.

Wilson, S. G. "From Jesus to Paul: The Contours and Consequences of a Debate." Pp. 1–21 in *From Jesus to Paul: Studies in Honour of Francis Wright Beare*, edited by Peter Richardson and John C. Hurd. Waterloo, ON: Wilfrid Laurier University Press, 1983.

Winter, Bruce W. *Philo and Paul Among the Sophists: Alexandrian and Corinthian Responses to a Julio-Claudian Movement*. 2nd ed. Grand Rapids: Eerdmans, 2002.

Witherington, Ben, III. *Jesus, Paul and the End of the World: A Comparative Study in New Testament Eschatology*. Downers Grove, IL: InterVarsity, 1992.

———. *Paul's Narrative Thought World: The Tapestry of Tragedy and Triumph*. Louisville, KY: Westminster John Knox, 1994.

Witmer, Amanda. *Jesus, the Galilean Exorcist*. LNTS 459. London: T&T Clark, 2012.

Wittgenstein, Ludwig. *Philosophische Untersuchungen = Philosophical Investigations*. Translated by G. E. M. Anscombe. 3rd ed. New York: Macmillan, 1958.

Wolfe, Robert Fredrick. "The Uses of Jesus Tradition in Pauline Correspondence, with Special Reference to the Letter to the Romans." PhD diss., Southwestern Baptist Theological Seminary, 1996.

Wolff, Christian. "Humility and Self-Denial in Jesus' Life and Message and in the Apostolic Existence of Paul." Pp. 145–60 in *Paul and Jesus: Collected Essays*, edited by A. J. M. Wedderburn. JSNTSup 37. Sheffield: Sheffield Academic Press, 1989.

Wong, Eric K. C. "The De-Radicalization of Jesus' Ethical Sayings in Romans." *NovT* 43 (2001): 245–63.

———. "The Deradicalization of Jesus' Ethical Sayings in 1 Corinthians." *NTS* 48 (2002): 181–94.

Woods, Edward J. *The 'Finger of God' and Pneumatology in Luke–Acts*. JSNTSup 205. Sheffield: Sheffield Academic Press, 2001.

Wrede, William. *Paul*. Translated by Edward Lummis. Boston: American Unitarian Association, 1908. Reprint, Lexington, KY: American Theological Library Association, 1962.

Wright, N. T. *Jesus and the Victory of God*. Minneapolis: Fortress, 1996.

———. "The Letter to the Romans: Introduction, Commentary, and Reflections." Pp. 395–770 in *Acts, Introduction to Epistolary Literature, Romans, 1 Corinthians*, vol. 10 of *NIB*, edited by Leander E. Keck. Nashville: Abingdon, 2002.

———. *The New Testament and the People of God*. Minneapolis: Fortress, 1992.

———. *Paul and the Faithfulness of God*. Minneapolis: Fortress, 2013.

———. *The Resurrection of the Son of God*. Minneapolis: Fortress, 2003.

———. *What Saint Paul Really Said: Was Paul of Tarsus the Real Founder of Christianity?* Grand Rapids: Eerdmans, 1997.

Yamauchi, Edwin. "Magic or Miracle? Diseases, Demons and Exorcisms." Pp. 89–183 in *Gospel Perspectives*, vol. 6: *The Miracles of Jesus*, edited by David Wenham and Craig Blomberg. Sheffield: JSOT, 1986.

Yeboah, Charles. "Demon Possession and Exorcism in the Context of Divine Providence in Luke–Acts." PhD diss., Loyola University, 1999.

Yeung, Maureen W. *Faith in Jesus and Paul: A Comparison with Special Reference to "Faith That Can Remove Mountains" and "Your Faith Has Healed/Saved You."* WUNT 2/147. Tübingen: Mohr Siebeck, 2002.

Zahl, Paul F. M. *The First Christian: Universal Truth in the Teachings of Jesus*. Grand Rapids: Eerdmans, 2003.

New Testament

Ephesians

1:21   101

Philippians

1:8   117
1:23   101
2:1   50
2:1–11   131
2:4–8   85
2:6–8   132
2:25–30   57
2:27   44, 57
3:3   50
3:6   47, 115
3:8–10   85
3:9   48, 102
3:10   85, 132–33

Philippians (cont.)

3:16   94

1 Thessalonians

1:4   50
1:5   2, 16, 38, 41, 44, 49, 50,
      55, 77, 80, 110
1:6   50, 85, 132–33
1:9   50
1:10   101
2:5   84
2:9   84
2:12   102, 109
2:14–15   85, 132
2:19–20   38
4:8   50, 52, 118
5:14   117

2 Thessalonians

2:9   45, 53, 106

Hebrews

1:8   109
2:3–4   131
2:4   45, 106
11:33   109
12:28   109

James

2:5   109

2 Peter

1:11   109

Deuterocanonical Literature

Baruch

2:11   45, 106–8

2 Esdras

7:50   101
7:112–13   101
8:1–2   101

2 Maccabees

3:24–40   35
3:25–29   35

Sirach

36:5   106
36:6–9   108
36:1–17   108

Sirach (cont.)

38:9–15   35
44:23–45:5   62

Tobit

1:3   35
4:17   28
11:14–15   35
13:11–13   134
14:5–7   134

Wisdom of Solomon

5:17–23   107
5:21–23   107
8:8   106–7
10:16   45, 106–7
11–19   107

Wisdom of Solomon (cont.)

16:5–14   35
19:22   107

4 Ezra

3:20   98
4:2   101
4:52–5:13   71
6:9   101
6:12–27   71
6:26–28   98
7:47   101
7:53[123]   91
7:112–13   101
8:1   101
9:19   101
13:43   108

Bulletin for Biblical Research Supplements